ILLEGAL BEINGS

Many people think human reproductive cloning should be a crime. Some states already have outlawed cloning, and Congress is working to enact a national ban. Meanwhile, scientific research continues here and abroad. Soon reproductive cloning may become possible. If that happens, cloning cannot be stopped. Infertile couples and others will choose to have babies through cloning even if they have to break the law. This book explains that the most common objections to cloning are false or exaggerated. The objections reflect and inspire unjustified stereotypes about human clones. Anticloning laws reinforce these stereotypes and stigmatize human clones as subhuman and unworthy of existence. This injures not only human clones but also the egalitarianism upon which our society is based. Applying the same reasoning used to invalidate racial segregation, this book argues that anticloning laws violate the equal protection guarantee and are unconstitutional.

Kerry Lynn Macintosh is a member of the law and technology faculty at Santa Clara University School of Law. She received her B.A. from Pomona College and her J.D. from Stanford Law School, where she was elected to the Order of the Coif. She has published papers and articles in the field of law and technology in journals such as the *Harvard Journal of Law & Technology, Boston University Journal of Science & Technology Law*, and *Berkeley Technology Law Journal*.

Illegal Beings

Human Clones and the Law

Kerry Lynn Macintosh
Santa Clara University School of Law

CAMBRIDGE
UNIVERSITY PRESS

CAMBRIDGE UNIVERSITY PRESS
Cambridge, New York, Melbourne, Madrid, Cape Town, Singapore, São Paulo

Cambridge University Press
40 West 20th Street, New York, NY 10011-4211, USA

www.cambridge.org
Information on this title: www.cambridge.org/9780521853286

First published 2005

Printed in the United States of America

A catalog record for this publication is available from the British Library.

Library of Congress Cataloging in Publication Data
Macintosh, Kerry Lynn.
Human cloning and legal rights / Kerry Lynn Macintosh.
   p.   cm.
Includes bibliographical references and index.
ISBN 0-521-85328-1 (hardback)
1. Human cloning – Law and legislation – United States.   2. Human reproductive
technology – Law and legislation – United States.   3. Human cloning – Research –
Law and legislation.   4. Human cloning – Moral and ethical aspects.   I. Title.
KF3831.M33   2005
344.7304'196 – dc22   2005011732

ISBN-13   978-0-521-85328-6 hardback
ISBN-10   0-521-85328-1 hardback

To Mark Donald Eibert

Contents

Acknowledgments

Many individuals have helped me research, write, edit, and publish this book. I am deeply grateful to them all.

Two experts on the science, ethics, and law of human reproductive cloning were generous enough to read drafts of this book and offer constructive advice: Mark D. Eibert and Dr. Lee M. Silver. I thank them for reading my work and providing me with the benefit of their expertise.

Colleagues, too, provided me with helpful input on drafts of this book. Thanks are due to Professors Brad Joondeph and Gary Spitko of Santa Clara University School of Law and Professor Hiroshi Motomura of the University of North Carolina School of Law.

Law students from Santa Clara University School of Law played a role in bringing this project to fruition. In particular, I wish to acknowledge the consistently energetic and insightful advice and support I have received from my research assistant, Rich Seifert, J.D. 2006. His critique has improved my work immeasurably.

I also want to thank Matthew Brown, J.D. 2005; Susan Hunt McArthur, J.D. 2004; Shaham Parvin, J.D. 2004; David Creeggan, J.D. 2004; and Brian Solon, J.D. 2001, all of whom provided me with helpful research assistance.

Last but not least, I wish to thank my editor, John Berger, my project manager, Susan Detwiler, and the staffs of Cambridge University Press and TechBooks. The success of this book is due in large part to their diligence and patience.

Introduction

In 1997, Drs. Ian Wilmut and Keith Campbell shocked the world by announcing the birth of Dolly.[1] Dolly was just an ordinary lamb, but the way in which the two scientists had conceived her was extraordinary.

Drs. Wilmut and Campbell removed the nucleus from a sheep egg, leaving the egg without chromosomes and thus without any nuclear DNA. Then the scientists used electricity to fuse the egg together with a cell taken from the udder of an adult sheep. The effect was to substitute the nuclear DNA of the adult sheep for that which had been taken out of the egg. After the fused product subdivided into an embryo, the scientists implanted that embryo into a surrogate mother sheep. Several months later, Dolly was born.[2] In effect, she was the later-born identical twin of the adult sheep that donated the nuclear DNA for the procedure.

Dolly's birth was scientific heresy. For years, biologists believed it to be impossible to clone mammals.[3] Later, when it was discovered that mammals can be cloned from cells taken from embryos,[4] biologists adjusted their beliefs slightly, asserting it to be impossible to clone mammals from adult cells that had taken on specialized functions such as skin, muscle, organs, and so on. Skeptics refused to believe that Dolly could have been cloned from an adult cell. They asserted that Drs. Wilmut and Campbell must have unwittingly cloned her from a stray stem or fetal cell circulating in the body of the pregnant sheep that had donated the nuclear DNA for the procedure.[5]

But, Dolly was not a fluke. Since that fateful announcement in 1997, scientists have cloned cows,[6] pigs,[7] goats,[8] cats,[9] rabbits,[10] mice,[11] rats,[12] horses,[13] deer,[14] and other mammals from adult cells.[15] Even the mule, a sterile cross of horse and donkey, has reproduced through cloning.[16]

Meanwhile, mainstream scientists have become interested in human cloning for research purposes (research cloning). They believe that cloned human embryos could help them learn about genetic diseases, develop pharmaceutical treatments, produce tissues for transplant, and assist in gene therapy.[17]

In 2004, South Korean scientists reported that they had cloned dozens of human embryos. The embryos grew to the blastocyst stage, meaning that each one contained hundreds of cells.[18] From the South Koreans' point of view, their research was important because they derived a line of embryonic stem cells from one of the blastocysts.[19]

From a reproductive point of view, however, the South Korean research was important because it proved that scientists have the capability of cloning human embryos to the same stage of advanced development that immediately precedes implantation in the lining of the uterus.[20] Such research, published in readily available scientific journals, increases the odds that a scientist working outside the mainstream will develop the knowledge and expertise required to clone a human baby (human reproductive cloning).[21]

Indeed, attempts to clone human babies may be under way. In 2003, Dr. Panayiotis Zavos published a report in an online scientific journal claiming that he had created a cloned human embryo of eight to ten cells. Dr. Zavos created the embryo for reproductive purposes, that is, so that his infertile male patient could have a child. Dr. Zavos froze that embryo pending molecular analysis.[22] In January 2004, he shocked the world by announcing that he had transferred another fresh cloned embryo into the womb of his patient's wife.[23] However, this effort did not produce a pregnancy.[24]

As Dr. Zavos's activities suggest, if human reproductive cloning can be perfected, there will be a market for it. Infertile men and women who lack functional sperm or eggs may turn to cloning to conceive children to whom they are genetically related.[25] Fertile men and women who are healthy themselves but are carriers of one or more genetic diseases may also be interested in the technology. Today, when such individuals reproduce sexually, they run the risk of creating new genomes in which the diseases are active. Soon, cloning may allow them to pass down to their children their own genomes in which the diseases have been proven to be inactive.[26] Lastly, gay and lesbian couples[27] may find that cloning can give them children of their own without introducing the unwanted genes of a third-party sperm or egg donor.[28]

In an effort to squelch this market, lawmakers have made human reproductive cloning a crime in many states, and more laws are pending.[29] However, if human reproductive cloning can be done safely and effectively, it cannot be stopped – even if it is illegal. The biological drive to reproduce is a powerful one. That is why infertile men and women are willing to endure painful and expensive medical treatments that might give them children.[30] Carriers of genetic diseases, gays, and lesbians also have the same fundamental drive. Faced with the painful alternative of childlessness, many of these individuals will choose instead to flout the anticloning laws. Some may travel to countries that permit cloning and come home pregnant or with babies in their arms. Others may ask doctors to create cloned embryos for them, ostensibly for therapeutic purposes, and then transfer the embryos to their wombs. Those with scientific backgrounds may even be able to clone in the privacy of their own laboratories without enlisting the assistance of outsiders.[31]

Thus, we face a realistic possibility that humans conceived with the aid of cloning technology will be born in our maternity wards, attend our public schools, become our friends, marry into our families, and work alongside us. But if cloning is a crime, these individuals will endure a society that has attempted through its democratic institutions to prevent their very existence.

Although many have emphasized the dangers of human reproductive cloning, few have discussed the dangers of laws against cloning. One exception is Professor Laurence Tribe. In 1998, he published an essay that questioned the wisdom of a ban on cloning:

> When the technology at issue is *a method for making human babies* – whether that method differs from a society's conventional and traditionally approved mode because of some socially constructed "fact" such as the marital status or kinship relation or racial identity of a participant, or differs in a more intrinsic way as in the case of in vitro fertilization, or surrogate gestation, or cloning so as to achieve asexual reproduction with but a single parent – applying the counter-technology of criminalization has at least one additional, and qualitatively distinct, social cost. That cost, to the degree any ban on using a given mode of baby making is bound to be evaded, is the very considerable one of creating a class of potential outcasts – persons whose very *existence* the society has chosen, through its legal system, to label as a misfortune and, in essence, to condemn.
>
> Even the simple example of what the "politically correct" call nonmarital children and what others call illegitimates (or more bluntly, bastards) powerfully illustrates the high price many individuals and their families are forced to pay for a society's decision to reinforce, through outlawing nonmarital reproduction and discriminating against nonmarital offspring, particular norms about how children ought to be brought into the world. How much higher would that price be when the basis on which the law decides to condemn a given baby-making method (like cloning) is ... the far more personalized and stigmatizing judgment that *the baby itself* – the child that will result from the condemned method – is morally incomplete or existentially flawed by virtue of its unnaturally manmade and deliberately determined (as opposed to "open") origin and character? ... [T]he human clone – in a world where cloning is forbidden as unnatural – is likely in the end to become the object of a form of contempt: the contempt that the (supposedly) spontaneous, natural, and unplanned would tend to feel toward the (supposedly) manufactured and allegedly artificial.[32]

Thus, Professor Tribe argued, laws against human reproductive cloning could create a "particularly pernicious form of caste system, in which an entire category of persons, while perhaps not labeled untouchable, is marginalized as not fully human."[33]

I share Professor Tribe's concerns and expand upon them in this book. Part 1 describes five common objections to human reproductive cloning and critiques them, exposing weaknesses in their underlying reasoning. Also explained is how the objections reflect, reinforce, and inspire unjustified stereotypes about human clones.[34]

Part 2 describes various laws against human reproductive cloning and traces their roots to the five objections. Reasoning by analogy to antimiscegenation laws, which once sought to prevent the birth of mixed-race children, I explain that anticloning laws are designed to prevent the existence of human clones. A description of the costs that the anticloning laws will impose on human clones, their families, and society at large is then offered. Because the laws provide few compensating benefits, I conclude that they are bad public policy.

Part 3 shifts from public policy analysis to constitutional challenge and explains why the courts should recognize human clones as a suspect class and subject laws against human reproductive cloning to strict scrutiny. I conclude that such laws are not narrowly tailored to achieve a compelling governmental interest; therefore, they violate the equal protection guarantee and are unconstitutional.

PART ONE

FIVE COMMON OBJECTIONS TO HUMAN REPRODUCTIVE CLONING REFLECT, REINFORCE, AND INSPIRE STEREOTYPES ABOUT HUMAN CLONES

In the years since Dolly was born, society has fiercely debated the advantages and disadvantages of human reproductive cloning. Certain objections to cloning, and human clones, tend to crop up again and again. In Part 1 of this book, I critique these objections and explain how they reflect, reinforce, and inspire unfair stereotypes about human clones.

Chapter 1 presents the objection that cloning offends God and nature. Chapter 2 details the argument that cloning reduces humans to the level of manmade objects. Chapter 3 examines the objection that human clones lack individuality. Chapter 4 discusses arguments that human clones threaten the survival of humanity. Chapter 5 addresses what I call the safety objection. This includes not only the argument that the technology of cloning is unsafe for participants but also the argument that human clones inevitably must have serious birth defects.

In the analysis that follows, I emphasize four reports that have recommended a ban on human reproductive cloning. These reports are
useful because they state the five objections clearly and concisely. Each
of these reports, moreover, was designed to influence, and has influenced, public opinion and lawmakers. Thus, the reports set the stage
for Part 2 of this book in which I document the influence that the five
objections have had on public opinion and lawmakers. In chronological
order, the reports are as follows:

National Bioethics Advisory Commission, *Cloning Human Beings,
Report and Recommendations of the National Bioethics Advisory Commission* (1997) (NBAC report). President Bill Clinton established the
National Bioethics Advisory Commission (NBAC) to provide advice to
the National Science and Technology Council and other governmental
entities on bioethical issues arising from research on human biology and
behavior.[1] After Dolly's birth was announced in 1997, President Clinton
asked NBAC to issue a report on human reproductive cloning within
90 days.[2] The NBAC report assayed the scientific, religious, ethical, legal, and policy implications of cloning and recommended that Congress
enact a 3- to 5-year ban on human reproductive cloning.[3]

California Advisory Committee on Human Cloning, *Cloning Californians? Report of the California Advisory Committee on Human
Cloning* (2002) (California report). In 1997, the California State Legislature enacted a 5-year ban on human reproductive cloning.[4] At the
same time, it passed a resolution urging the California Department of
Health Services to appoint an advisory committee to evaluate the medical, social, legal, and ethical implications of human reproductive cloning
and advise the legislature and governor.[5] In 2002, the California Advisory Committee on Human Cloning issued its report recommending
that the legislature replace the temporary ban on human reproductive
cloning with a permanent one.[6]

The National Academies,[7] *Scientific and Medical Aspects of Human
Reproductive Cloning* (2002) (NAS report). Unlike the other reports,
which span the full range of public policy issues associated with human
reproductive cloning, the NAS report covers only the scientific and medical aspects of cloning. The NAS report recommends that lawmakers

enact a ban on human reproductive cloning that could be reevaluated after 5 years.[8]

The President's Council on Bioethics, *Human Cloning and Human Dignity: An Ethical Inquiry* (2002) (Council report). President George W. Bush established the President's Council on Bioethics to advise the president on bioethical issues related to advances in biomedical science and technology.[9] The council reviewed the science and ethics of cloning and issued its report recommending that human reproductive cloning be outlawed.[10]

CHAPTER ONE

Does Human Reproductive Cloning Offend God and Nature?

The first charge against human reproductive cloning is that it is an expression of hubris. This idea can be expressed in one of two ways: first, that cloning is an offense against God; or second, that cloning is an offense against nature. I will examine each of these variations in turn.

1. God

The idea that cloning offends God is one of the most commonly asserted arguments in the cloning debate. The California Advisory Committee on Human Cloning summarized the argument as follows:

> Reproduction, according to this argument, is solely God's domain. When we take it upon ourselves to create humans through reproductive cloning,

we are infringing on the divine domain, "playing God," as it were. On this view, finite and fallible beings should not make decisions properly limited to the infinite and infallible. Many religious accounts give humans the responsibility for being caretakers of the rest of creation. The cloning of human beings oversteps the limits of this responsibility and runs counter to the responsibility itself.[1]

The media reflect and propagate this common objection. In a fascinating study of American news stories on cloning, Patrick Hopkins documented how the media portray human reproductive cloning as an immoral and dangerous intrusion into the Creator's domain.[2] Frequent references to the novels *Brave New World*[3] and *Frankenstein*[4] hammer home the message that arrogant scientists are crossing the line.[5]

Ironically, scientists have helped the media frame the cloning debate in these terms. A recent study of print news media in Australia found that scientists often distinguish research cloning, which they represent as useful and legitimate science, from reproductive cloning, which they depict as dangerous and illegitimate science.[6] This is a strategy designed to protect research cloning against public hysteria and legislative action. By casting the debate in terms of "good" versus "bad" science, mainstream scientists have reinforced the notion that some knowledge should be off-limits for mankind.

It is impossible to know whether human reproductive cloning does, in fact, offend God. For one thing, there is no scientific proof that God exists. Furthermore, even if God does exist, there is no objective way to show what God thinks about cloning.

Even while proclaiming the evils of hubris, fallible humans have dared to speculate about what God *might* think. Even these speculations are in conflict, however. For example, when Dolly was born, the National Bioethics Advisory Commission took testimony from representatives of many different religions. Roman Catholic witnesses condemned cloning outright, but Jewish witnesses argued that cloning humans could be justified in some circumstances, including infertility.[7] Moreover, people who believe in God, but do not claim membership in any organized religion, are the fastest growing religious group in the United States.[8] Many of these individuals are likely to have their own personal views about whether cloning offends God.

The only thing one can say with confidence is that many people *believe* that human reproductive cloning offends God. Unfortunately, this religious belief comes at a heavy price, for it holds the potential to harm the humans who will be born through that technology.

If human reproductive cloning infringes on the divine domain, the implication is that scientists and doctors who use the technology are committing the deadly sin of pride. Although the resulting babies should be blameless, their perceived origin in sin could taint them by association. Thus, even though the warning against playing God is not, in and of itself, based on any stereotypes about human clones, there is a strong risk that it could encourage the formation of such stereotypes. In particular, people who regard cloning as a sin may leap to the unfortunate conclusion that human clones are a form of evil incarnate.

2. Nature

Not everyone believes in God. However, the moral argument that cloning is an act of hubris can be cast in other terms. As prominent scientist Dr. Lee Silver has noted, "The political right and the political left are both against reproductive cloning. The political right says man has no right to do God's work. . . . Man should not be creating life. God creates life. What does the political left say? The political left says people should not interfere with nature. . . . Both sides think cloning is an example of scientific hubris."[9]

From the leftist point of view, human reproductive cloning is morally wrong because it is a kind of technological rape of Mother Nature. That which is "natural" is good; that which is "unnatural" is bad.

One immediate problem with this argument concerns the concepts of "natural" and "unnatural." Although these terms may seem simple to apply, they are not. Biology does not determine what is "natural" – cultural and moral values, which change over time, do.

For example, one might wonder why some people oppose human reproductive cloning on the grounds that it is unnatural when they calmly accept in vitro fertilization (IVF) and related assisted reproductive technologies. For the uninitiated, here is a brief description of an IVF cycle: an infertile woman takes powerful drugs to stimulate the production of multiple eggs; a doctor punches a large needle through her vaginal wall to siphon the eggs out of her ovaries; the eggs are then mixed with ejaculated sperm in a dish; if any eggs are fertilized, the embryos are grown in the laboratory until they are developed enough to be transferred back into her uterus through a catheter.[10] If sperm quality is poor, fertilization may be accomplished through a process known as intracytoplasmic sperm injection (ICSI) in which a technician forcibly injects individual sperm into individual eggs.[11]

When IVF was new, back in 1978, the world was horrified by it. According to polls, 85 percent of the public thought it should be banned.[12] Scientists, doctors, and philosophers decried the practice, asserting that "test-tube babies" would be physically deformed and psychologically impaired.[13] Political activists complained that scientists were meddling with nature.[14] But after healthy babies were born, the firestorm died down.[15] Today, 25 years later, IVF has led to the birth of over one million babies worldwide.[16] IVF has become commonplace and has enriched the lives of many individuals and families. Certain religions still hold that assisted reproductive technologies are contrary to the will of God,[17] but one seldom hears complaints about how unnatural it is.

From this history, it appears that what we consider to be natural depends on how experienced and comfortable we are with a reproductive method rather than on how similar that method is to sexual intercourse. Human reproductive cloning seems strange now because it is new; however, if society stood aside and allowed cloning to develop without legal interference, it could seem entirely natural within a few decades.

Nevertheless, opponents insist that human reproductive cloning is much stranger than IVF and other assisted reproductive technologies. This is because cloning makes *asexual* reproduction possible for mammals. The California Advisory Committee on Human Cloning duly noted this fact:

> Certainly, cloning could be considered 'unnatural' as it relies on human intervention in a 'natural process.' It clearly runs counter to a normally functioning natural environment, *at least for mammals*. It does not provide for the random combination of genetic material from eggs and sperm that is the essence of sexual reproduction. In addition, it could theoretically render males reproductively obsolete.[18]

Asexual reproduction, however, is not as contrary to nature as opponents assert. Scientists believe that *all* life on Earth evolved from simple
one-celled organisms that reproduced asexually by cell division.[19] Many
organisms, ranging from bacteria[20] to worms[21] to the trees in an aspen
forest (which are clones propagated from a single seedling)[22] continue
to reproduce asexually today. Thus, asexual reproduction is entirely natural for much of Earth life; it simply is not the way that humans have
reproduced up until now. The truly stunning thing about the science of
cloning is its unexpected revelation of a basic truth: even humans and
other mammals retain, in every cell of their bodies, the ability to reproduce asexually just as their distant evolutionary ancestors once did.
Human reproductive cloning may require a greater level of technological intervention than does IVF, but this is a difference of degree rather
than one of fundamental character.

What it boils down to is this: Different people have different ideas
about how far humanity should go in using technology to expand our
inborn capabilities. Novel reproductive technologies, like cloning, tend
to draw the most disapproval. If a person believes that cloning goes
too far, he or she might use the word "unnatural" as a concise way of
expressing that moral judgment.

Unfortunately, the use of this particular shorthand to express a complex moral judgment has strong implications for human clones. If the
technology of human reproductive cloning is unnatural, it follows that
human clones must also be unnatural. This is a damaging stereotype.

Moreover, the dictionary defines the word "unnatural" as including
the following concepts: "abnormal," "strange," "artificial," and "evil."[23]
These related meanings encourage the public to view human clones as
abnormal, strange, artificial, and evil.

Nor do the stereotypes stop there. Simple organisms reproduce
asexually; traditionally, humans and other mammals have not. Thus,
some people may infer that sexual reproduction goes along with a higher
level of evolution.[24] The argument that cloning is unnatural because
it is asexual reproduction implies a hierarchy of reproductive origin in
which human clones rank alongside bacteria and worms in quality and
importance.

It might be argued that, once cloned babies are born and everyone
sees how cute they are, such stereotypes will wither away. After all, that

is what happened when the public saw photographs of adorable "test-tube babies" and forgot about its fears.[25] The unfortunate difference is that IVF was never outlawed, but cloning already has been. As a result, fewer cute babies will be born; those that are born are likely to go underground along with their frightened parents. The anticloning laws themselves will make it harder for society to develop experience with human reproductive cloning and thus harder for society to accept cloning as a natural process.[26]

3. Cloning and *Frankenstein*

Before moving on to the next objection, I would like to make one final point. When discussing human reproductive cloning, the media and policymakers frequently invoke the novel *Frankenstein* as a shorthand warning against the dangers of scientific hubris.[27] The media also have been known to refer to babies born through cloning as Franken-babies.[28] To expose the stereotypes that could arise out of such casual references, I must briefly remind the reader of the plot and theme of the novel.

Dr. Frankenstein discovers the cause of life and learns how to animate lifeless matter.[29] Then he cobbles together a gigantic man from body parts raided from graves, charnel houses, dissecting rooms, and slaughterhouses.[30] He animates this patchwork corpse only to find that his "creature" is physically grotesque.[31]

The creature's appearance is so hideous that Dr. Frankenstein and others reject him. Enraged, the creature declares war against the human species – especially the scientist who created him.[32] He murders Dr. Frankenstein's young brother[33] and dupes the authorities into executing an innocent servant for the crime.[34] Then the creature demands that Dr. Frankenstein create a mate of his own kind. Dr. Frankenstein is moved by the creature's loneliness and consents.[35] Later, however, Dr. Frankenstein reflects on the consequences if the creature were given the chance to reproduce and destroys the half-completed mate.[36] The creature responds by murdering Dr. Frankenstein's friend.[37] He even murders Dr. Frankenstein's bride on their wedding night.[38] Dr. Frankenstein pursues the creature to the Arctic but dies of exhaustion before he can destroy him.[39] The creature, having discovered and mourned his dead creator, vows to travel to the North Pole and erect his own funeral pyre.[40]

Although there is more than one way to read this series of fictional events, one of the most common interpretations holds that, if humans meddle in the secrets of life, which are the proper domain only of God and nature, they may unleash unimaginable horrors. From this point of view, the creature's physical and moral flaws result from his origin in scientific hubris.

Human reproductive cloning does not involve the reanimation of dead matter;[41] like in vitro fertilization, it produces embryos that grow into normal babies and adults who are indistinguishable from other adults. Humans born through cloning will not, by any stretch of the imagination, be gigantic monsters intent on wreaking havoc.

Unfortunately, the analogies that the media and policymakers have drawn between *Frankenstein* and cloning encourage the public to experience a strong aversion toward cloning and human clones. Subconsciously, we are being primed to feel (rather than reason) that human clones are physically flawed (even if the flaws cannot be detected by casual observation),[42] immoral, and dangerous.

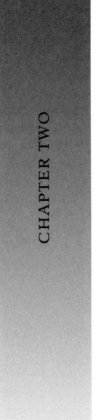

CHAPTER TWO

Should Children Be Begotten and Not Made?

In its 2002 report on human cloning, the President's Council on Bioethics emphasized a second objection to human reproductive cloning. This objection holds that children who are "begotten" (i.e., conceived through sexual reproduction) are gifts from God; as such, they stand as the equal of their parents in dignity and humanity. By contrast, cloning is a human project that treats children as manmade products designed to genetic order. This project violates human dignity.[1]

Like the argument that cloning offends God, this second objection also finds its roots in religious values. The National Bioethics Advisory Commission noted that "[a]ppeals to human dignity are prominent in Roman Catholic analyses and assessments of the prospects of human cloning, which base 'human dignity' on the creation story and on the Christian account of God's redemption of human beings. The Catholic moral tradition views the cloning of a human being as 'a violation of human dignity.'"[2]

A trendier secular version of this same objection asserts that parents would, in effect, have to buy their cloned children by paying money to egg donors, doctors, and laboratories. Society could come to regard children as products traded on the market. Ultimately, cloning would result in the "commodification" not only of children born through the technology, but all children.[3] As Professor Ashutosh Bhaghwat has pointed out, this objection can be interpreted as a moral argument against applying the norms of the marketplace in the context of family relationships.[4]

Whether rooted in religion or secular values, moral arguments are hard to prove. There is no scientific proof that God exists, let alone that God views cloning as an offense to human dignity. Nor is it possible to prove that aversion to the application of marketplace norms in family matters reflects a superior morality. (For some, marketplace norms may be the most honorable and dependable norms of all.) Again, what we can say with certainty is that some people *believe* that cloning violates human dignity or are offended by what they consider to be the improper extension of marketplace norms.

Although moral judgments are hard to prove, there is another way to interpret the argument that cloning offends human dignity. If parents would view their cloned children as products, or if cloning would inexorably lead to the (misplaced) view that all humans are products, then one might worry that cloning could lead to an increase in human suffering. Two premises are essential to the validity of these concerns. Let us examine each in turn.

1. Lessons from Assisted Reproductive Technologies

The first premise is this: When parents purchase medical services in order to reproduce, the involvement of technology and money will cause them to view their children as products and commodities. The evidence is very much to the contrary.

Although cloning is new, medical intervention in human reproduction is not. In vitro fertilization (IVF), which involves both technology and money, is legal and popular. Donor sperm and eggs are available in exchange for fees intended to reflect the time and effort of the donor rather than the value of the gametes themselves.[5] Recipients select donors for their physical characteristics, education, and IQs.[6] Surrogate motherhood is an available service for pay in some states.[7]

Critics have complained that assisted reproductive technologies violate human dignity[8] and commodify children.[9] After many years of experience with these technologies, however, there is no evidence that infertile men and women who use IVF, donor gametes, or surrogacy view their children as if they were manufactured products or commodities.[10] Indeed, recent psychological studies of children conceived through sperm donation or IVF provide contrary evidence. Families built through these assisted reproductive technologies are stable and loving. The children function well and are not different psychologically from children who were adopted or conceived through sexual intercourse.[11] Nor is there any evidence that the use of assisted reproductive technologies has led to a more general degradation of the preciousness or humanity of children within our society.[12]

The second premise is that human reproductive cloning involves a greater element of manufacture than do assisted reproductive technologies. For example, opponents of cloning argue that infertile couples who utilize assisted reproductive technologies do not entirely control the character of the children who are born through the technologies. By contrast, cloning poses a greater threat to human dignity because it promises to produce a specific end product. In the words of the President's Council on Bioethics, "[e]ven were cloning to be used solely to remedy infertility, the decision to clone the (sterile) father would be a decision, willy-nilly, that the child-to-be should be the near-twin of his 'father.'"[13]

This hypothetical is unpersuasive; if a sterile man resorted to cloning, his motive undoubtedly would be reproduction (by the only means possible for him) and not the deliberate design of a specific child.

More importantly, the premise that human reproductive cloning involves a greater degree of manufacture is fundamentally flawed because it is impossible for cloning to deliver a specific end product. As explained at length in Chapter 3, genes are not destiny. Even if one selects a particular genome for cloning, the environment (which begins with the womb) will have a powerful effect on the body and psychology of the resulting baby, child, and adult. Human clones simply cannot be duplicates of the persons who donate nuclear DNA for the procedure; any prospective parent who expects to receive a made-to-order product is doomed to disappointment.[14] Given these basic medical facts, even if cloning becomes possible, a market for tailor-made children will never get off the ground. Early attempts will fizzle; as information accumulates, prospective parents who investigate the prospect of creating a made-to-order child will quickly learn that their project is impossible.

2. Stereotypes

In sum, there is no evidence that the involvement of medical services or money in reproduction has caused parents or society to view children as manufactured products. Nor is it possible for human reproductive cloning to produce made-to-order children; it can produce only ordinary babies. Thus, there is no evidence that cloning, in and of itself, threatens to increase human suffering.

Unfortunately, the same cannot be said of the *objection* that cloning treats humans as if they were manufactured products. The Catholic Church has asserted that, although human cloning violates human dignity, the dignity of a human being born through cloning is not diminished.[15] Unfortunately, this important point may prove too nice for many to grasp. The public could interpret the objection that cloning *treats* humans as manufactured products as a statement that cloning produces humans who *are* manufactured products.

This risk is heightened by the fact that many people already believe that genes are destiny and that "clones" are identical copies.[16] As explained in Chapter 3, this belief is flatly wrong; however, people who lack personal involvement with cloning might not realize this. Trapped by the illusion of genetic determinacy, they could more readily jump to the false conclusion that human clones are, indeed, made to order.

The cure for all of this is to demonstrate to the public through scientific fact and education that human clones are not, and can never be, manufactured products. A ban on cloning based on concerns about manufacture would have the opposite effect; the public could infer that cloning *does* carry with it the potential to turn humans into designer products and must be stopped for that reason.

Even if there was a ban on human reproductive cloning, some humans would be born through that technology anyway. Thus, the last step in this analysis is to ask what stereotypes might emerge if the public was encouraged by policy arguments and anticloning laws to believe that human clones are manufactured products. To answer this question, it is useful to consider how most people view store-bought goods. Does a chair have a soul? Is a table human? Does a washing machine have any feelings? Which has more human dignity – a lunch box, or your best friend? The argument that cloning treats children as manufactured products could lead to the mistaken belief that human clones are soulless, inert, unfeeling, and inferior to other humans.

CHAPTER THREE

Do Human Clones Lack Individuality?

There is a third objection to human reproductive cloning (or, more accurately, to human clones). This objection is founded on a basic scientific error: the idea that a human clone is the same person as, or a copy of, the person who donated the nuclear DNA for the procedure (DNA donor). For convenience, I will refer to this error as the "identity fallacy."

Unlike the first two objections discussed in the preceding chapters, the identity fallacy is unique to cloning. It has been particularly popular with the media, which has used it to great provocative effect. Magazines and television shows repeatedly have used the word "copy" to refer to human clones and have churned out demeaning images to illustrate their stories such as identical babies in laboratory beakers, gumball machines dispensing identical men, and ink stamps making identical copies of babies.[1]

1. Why Is the Identity Fallacy Wrong?

Most readers and viewers probably never get beyond these inflammatory and misleading images. However, those who read far enough, or listen long enough, may find buried within some stories the acknowledgment that human clones would *not* be copies after all.[2]

This is no surprise, for, as many scientists,[3] philosophers,[4] and lawyers[5] have taken great care to explain, the identity fallacy is flatly wrong.

To understand why, let us begin by considering the characteristics of naturally occurring human clones: identical twins. Identical twins occur when a single fertilized egg splits in two early in the course of embryonic development. As a result of the split, the twins share the same DNA.

Dr. Nancy L. Segal, a developmental psychologist and twins researcher, has noted that identical twins are more alike behaviorally and physically than other human pairs.[6] Nevertheless, her findings also show that the heritability of such characteristics as intelligence, cognitive skills, and personality traits ranges only around 50 percent.[7] In short, identical twins are far from identical. This is consistent with personal experience; anyone who has ever known identical twins realizes that each member of a twin pair is a unique individual.

The bizarre case of Chang and Eng Bunker offers a striking example of the individuality of twins. Born in Thailand in the nineteenth century, Chang and Eng were joined at the chest and shared a liver. Billed as "Siamese Twins" by P. T. Barnum, the two traveled America as a sideshow. Despite their common DNA and conjoined bodies, Chang and Eng had very different personalities. Eng was an optimist and teetotaler who enjoyed the company of other people. By contrast, Chang was a moody, introverted, antisocial alcoholic.[8]

Such differences between identical twins should reassure us. If two people who are conceived at the same moment, gestated in the same womb, and raised together in the same environment can be unique individuals, it stands to reason that human clones can be unique individuals also. Further, human clones are likely to differ from DNA donors more than identical twins differ from each other[9] for four reasons.

First, the cytoplasm of every human egg contains mitochondria, that is, tiny structures that produce energy within human cells.[10] When an egg is fertilized, it contains the newly formed nuclear DNA of the embryo and the mitochondrial DNA of the egg. Because identical twins are conceived when a single fertilized egg splits, they share the same nuclear DNA and mitochondrial DNA.[11] As a result, their cells may generate energy in a similar way. By contrast, human clones will be conceived by inserting the nuclear DNA of one person into donor eggs harvested from another person (in most cases).[12] Because human clones will inherit mitochondrial DNA from their egg donors, scientists believe that differences may show up in parts of the body that need high levels of energy such as the muscle, heart, eye, and brain or in body systems that use mitochondria to moderate cell numbers.[13]

Second, identical twins are gestated together in the womb of one mother at the same time. This accident of birth means that the two experience a uterine environment that is similar though not necessarily identical.[14] By contrast, human clones will be conceived after their DNA donors have been born. Therefore, they will be gestated at a different time in a different womb. This is an important distinction. Most people simply do not realize the key role that gestation plays in developing the individual. The uterine environment influences how the embryo develops; what the mother does can affect its development for better (e.g., proper nutrition and exercise) or worse (e.g., exposure to stress, pollution, or alcohol). The uterine environment also affects gene expression.[15] Even if a human clone shares a gene with the DNA donor, the developmental process may suppress or exaggerate the degree to which that gene functions. Thus, the physical and psychological traits of human clones could diverge significantly from those of their DNA donors despite their common genetic heritage.

Third, every female mammal inherits two copies of the X chromosome – one from the mother and one from the father. Nature manages this redundancy through a simple biological process known as random inactivation of the X chromosome. As the embryo grows and produces new cells, each cell randomly switches off one of the two X chromosomes. This early developmental process creates an embryo that is a genetic mosaic as far as the X chromosomes are concerned.[16] Consistent with this, researchers have found that female identical twins can differ significantly in traits found on the X chromosome.[17] When an embryo splits after X inactivation, the resulting cell patterns in twins are more alike than when an embryo splits at a very early point in development before X inactivation.[18]

We know from animal research that cloned embryos undergo random inactivation of the X chromosome.[19] Thus, we can expect that cloned women will differ from their DNA donors in X-linked traits. Moreover, these differences are likely to be more significant than the differences between most identical twins. As noted in the previous paragraph, embryos can split after X inactivation, leading to similar cell patterns in the resulting twins. By contrast, reproductive cloning occurs when a scientist or doctor uses nuclear transfer to create a new embryo. This embryo will experience X inactivation and develop a cell pattern without being influenced by whatever happened to the DNA donor when she was a developing embryo.

Fourth, because identical twins are born at the same time, they necessarily grow up in the same era. Unless they are separated at birth, they also experience the same family environment and national culture. These common influences and experiences may lead to shared personality traits, habits, tastes, and values. The same cannot be said for DNA donors and their cloned offspring. Human clones will be raised in a different era, family, and culture than were their DNA donors. These divergent influences and experiences will contribute to differences in personality traits, habits, tastes, and values.[20]

Do experimental data support these predictions? As yet, there are no human clones; therefore, there has been no opportunity to study and compare them with DNA donors. Experiments have demonstrated, however, that cloned animals are far from the carbon copies that the public imagines them to be.

In 1999, the Roslin Institute reported that four cloned rams that shared the same genome had marked differences in their size, appearance, and temperament.[21]

More recently, researchers at Texas A & M University set out to determine whether the technology is a reliable means of replicating animals with desirable behavioral characteristics.[22] The researchers cloned two litters of pigs from the same fetal cell line and compared their food preferences, temperaments, and time budgets[23] with two control litters of naturally bred pigs of the same age, breed, and gender. In 2003, the researchers reported that the cloned pigs varied from each other in food preferences, temperaments, and time budgets as much or more as the control pigs varied from each other.[24] The researchers concluded that nuclear transfer cannot be used to replicate animals with certain behavioral characteristics.[25]

Similarly, the cloning of the first household pet, a cat named "Rainbow," led to significant physical and personality differences between the DNA donor and the clone. Rainbow is a fat, quiet calico with brown, tan, and gold fur on white. Her clone, "Cc," however, has grown up to be a sleek, energetic animal with a striped gray coat over white.[26] Fur color in cats is determined by the X chromosome; thus, Cc's divergent coat is the result of random inactivation of the X chromosome.[27]

Despite these scientific facts, many otherwise intelligent people continue to argue against cloning on the basis of the identity fallacy. Such arguments are not limited to the lay public; they often are voiced even by scientists and scholars who should know better. Most disappointingly, the political commissions that have studied cloning grudgingly admit that human clones are not carbon copies[28] but insist that human clones face many problems based on their supposed lack of individuality.

Identity-based arguments against cloning take many forms. In the pages that follow, I criticize and debunk these arguments.

2. Can Hitler Be Reborn?

The public fears that cloning could be used to generate multiple copies of evil people.[29] Some of the blame for this ridiculous fear belongs to the writers and producers of science fiction.[30]

For example, in *The Boys from Brazil*, Dr. Josef Mengele flees to South America, where he clones Adolf Hitler 94 times. Then he places the resulting babies in suitably unhappy home environments, all in a devilish (but impossible) plot to recreate Hitler and revive the Third Reich.[31] Similarly, in *Star Wars, Episode II, Attack of the Clones*, we learn that the Imperial storm troopers are the multitudinous clones of one bad man (Jango Fett). Lest we miss the point, the movie concludes with a scene of thousands of the armor-clad troopers standing ready for battle in massive formations.[32]

These nightmare scenarios have no basis in fact whatsoever. Even the National Bioethics Advisory Commission (NBAC), which was not friendly to reproductive cloning, pointed out that visions of clone armies and revived dictators were based on "gross misunderstandings of human biology and psychology."[33]

Similarly, some people seem to believe that cloning could be used to duplicate popular and talented public figures. The NBAC attempted to debunk this belief also, pointing out that it would be impossible to create an entire physics department of Albert Einsteins or a basketball team of Michael Jordans.[34]

One final, crude version of the identity fallacy asserts that cloning is a way to conquer death and achieve immortality.[35] Of course, this is impossible, for a human clone would never be the same person as the DNA donor. If the DNA donor were dead, he or she would stay dead.

That basic scientific fact somehow eluded the producers of *The Sixth Day*.[36] In that movie, a rich and arrogant businessman runs a company that can clone an identical, adult body within 2 hours of a person's death. The company then makes a recording of the memories of the person who died and uploads them into the new body. The business-man uses this technology to overcome his own death and maintain his financial empire. However, he makes a big mistake: he clones a heli-copter pilot named Adam Gibson (played by Arnold Schwarzenegger) without his consent.

The movie hammers home the notion that cloning is an illicit means of achieving immortality. Adam battles the same cloned assassins over and over again, leading him to complain that no one stays dead anymore. The rich businessman urges Adam to embrace cloning on the ground that the technology is a means of conquering death.

Needless to say, before the movie ends, Adam kills the businessman, reassuring the audience that, although evil people may attempt to play God, God always wins. Thus, the identity fallacy is parlayed back into the objection that cloning is a form of hubris, for only God should de-cide who lives and who dies.

3. Individuality and Autonomy

These, of course, are the most lurid manifestations of the identity fallacy. Some opponents have voiced objections that are more subtle but still derive from the same wrong idea.

For example, the NBAC, the President's Council on Bioethics, and the California Advisory Committee on Human Cloning all raised this concern: even if a human clone is not a copy per se, his or her individuality will be significantly diminished because he or she shares a genome with another person. As a result, the clone must suffer from identity issues and psychological damage.[37]

As it happens, we already have research data proving this argument to be incorrect. Identical twins are born into every human society on the planet. They are naturally occurring human clones.[38] Even though the members of each twin pair share a genome, identical twins are not overrepresented among psychiatric patients.[39] Rather, most twins are happy to be twins. They may share a particularly close social bond, but this does not imply loss of individuality.[40]

Similarly, consider the objection that a human clone lacks an open future because he or she and others already know how the "original" turned out.[41] The President's Council on Bioethics expressed the idea this way:

> Everything about the predecessor – from physical height and facial appearance, balding patterns and inherited diseases, to temperament and native talents to shape of life and length of days, and even cause of death – will appear before the expectant eyes of the cloned person, always with at least the nagging concern that there, notwithstanding the grace of God, go I. The crucial matter, again, is not simply the truth regarding the extent to which genetic identity actually shapes us – though it surely does shape us to some extent. What matters is the cloned individual's *perception* of the significance of the "precedent life" and the way that perception cramps and limits a sense of self and independence.[42]

Such concerns are unfounded. Contrary to *The Sixth Day*, cloning does not produce a life that can be played back again and again with the same results. Rather, every person, from gestation to death, is the unique product of physical and psychological events and influences that interact with and upon his or her genes to generate a unique individual. There is no reason why a human clone should have the perception of being cramped or limited in independence unless society raises him or her with that false expectation.

Millennia of experience with identical twins shows that humans who share the same genome can shape their own futures and lead distinct lives. The President's Council on Bioethics attempted to distinguish identical twins on the grounds that they are born and raised at the same time and thus do not know how their joint genome is destined to turn out.[43] From the moment of their birth (and probably long before that), however, identical twins observe each other's preferences, choices, talents, efforts, and outcomes in every aspect of life. It would be impossible not to react to such a wealth of information regarding one's closest genetic relative. But everyone understands that the lives of identical twins are not secondhand or inherently constrained.

Some opponents might admit that human clones are not copies lacking in individuality or autonomy. Because *other* people will think of them that way, however, human clones will suffer psychological damage. Thus, cloning must be banned lest a bigoted public inflict psychological pain and suffering upon children who would be better off nonexistent.

The problem with this argument is that anything that can be done will be done. Some human clones will be born whether the technology is legal or not. Once cloning has become a reality, the only way to protect the individuality and autonomy of each and every person will be to debunk the identity fallacy. Surrendering to stereotypes and prejudice is not ethical.[44] Laws against cloning cannot eliminate stereotypes; they can only elevate stereotypes to the level of public policy, as explained in Part 2 of this book.

4. Family Relationships

The identity fallacy has also inspired several objections to cloning that focus on the way that rearing parents would relate to cloned children.

First, opponents of cloning sometimes voice the concern that parents would have unrealistic expectations about the characteristics of their cloned children. This is far from unusual of course; many parents make the mistake of pressuring their children to be something that they are not (or do not wish to be). However, the President's Council on Bioethics suggested that cloned children would face a far greater burden: "The shadow of the cloned child's 'original' might be hard for the child to escape, as would parental attitudes that sought in the child's very existence to replicate, imitate, or replace the 'original.'"[45]

This problem may turn out to be real, but cloning itself is not to blame. As we have seen, cloning produces unique individuals who are not copies in any sense of that word. We do not face a future in which parents clone Stephen Hawking and end up with babies that are destined to be scientific geniuses. Parents will never be able to clone Michael Phelps and end up with babies who will one day win Olympic gold medals in swimming. These fantasies are just fantasies.

Because cloning cannot create duplicates, why would any parents hold such false expectations? The identity fallacy is to blame. The fallacy could mislead some people into believing that cloned children would have the same characteristics as their DNA donors. Thus, the objection that parents might hold false expectations is an objection not to cloning but to ignorance. This problem can be corrected through education.

Second, opponents complain that cloning confuses the traditional family structure and blurs generational boundaries. For example, if a woman gives birth to a child who shares her genome, how should family, friends, society, and the law treat the child? Is the woman the mother of the child, or is she the sister of the child?[46]

This concern seems overblown. Families, friends, society, and the law are resilient and recently have proven their ability to adjust to other nontraditional structures (e.g., families formed through adoption or with the aid of sperm donors, egg donors, or surrogates).[47]

Nevertheless, the President's Council on Bioethics, suggested that cloning is more problematic:

> What the exact effects of cloning-to-produce-children might be for families is highly speculative, to be sure, but it is still worth flagging certain troubling possibilities and risks. The fact that the cloned child bears a special tie to only one parent may complicate family dynamics. As the child developed, it could not help but be regarded as specially akin to only one of his or her parents. The sins or failings of the father (or mother), if reappearing in the cloned child, might be blamed on the progenitor, adding to the chances of domestic turmoil.[48]

This observation overstates the similarity of the child and the rearing parent who donated the genes for the procedure. Genes would not account for every trait in the child or for every action the child might take. The other parent, who lacks the genetic tie but who also rears the child, could just as easily be the one to inculcate values and take the blame for "sins or failings."

Concerns about confused family structures and blurred generational boundaries have shaded into a third objection. The President's Council on Bioethics speculated that a father could be attracted to his daughter because she was the twin of his wife: "The problems of being and rearing an adolescent could become complicated should the teenage clone of the mother 'reappear' as the double of the woman the father once fell in love with."[49] In other words, cloning could lead to improper sexual attraction and even child abuse.[50]

There is no evidence to support this argument. Indeed, the evidence we have cuts the other way. Although science has not yet created human clones, nature has produced thousands in the form of identical twins. These identical twins fall in love and get married all the time. This has not led to any surge in infidelity or family discord. Why not? A person who marries one twin is not necessarily attracted to the other because each twin is a unique individual.[51]

Moreover, many children strongly resemble one parent or the other. In thousands of homes across America, fathers are raising daughters who resemble their mothers, and mothers are raising sons who resemble their fathers. These resemblances do not trigger child abuse. Instead, most parents find their children sexually unattractive. Similarly, most brothers and sisters find each other sexually unattractive.[52]

These taboos on parent–child and sibling–sibling sexual relationships serve an evolutionary purpose: they reduce the chance that offspring will inherit damaging recessive genes.[53] However, the taboos attach to membership in the family group rather than genetic relation per se. Our species has learned to use rearing and growing up together, which we can sense, as a reasonably good proxy for genes, which we cannot sense.[54]

No taboo is perfect, and child abuse does occur within families.[55] There is no reason to believe, however, that the taboo would be less effective simply because a child was conceived through cloning. So long as such a child is reared from a young age within the family group, the same taboo should attach.

In sum, there is no good reason to believe that the father of a cloned daughter would find her particularly attractive or mistake her for her mother, *for she is not her mother.* The argument that cloning could lead to child abuse is rooted in the identity fallacy.

5. Identity Theft

Some opponents theorize that cloning would harm not only human clones but others as well.

For example, the California Advisory Committee on Human Cloning speculated that a person who donates the nuclear DNA for cloning could experience a loss of individuality and self-worth upon learning that his or her clone has been born and that he or she is no longer unique.[56] This reasoning suggests that cloning can compromise our very identities, when, in fact, that is not scientifically possible. As I explained at the outset of this chapter, environmental factors before and after birth influence how genes express themselves and how an organism grows and develops. Cloning cannot create duplicates.

Science fiction writers are fond of a related scenario in which a rogue scientist steals nuclear DNA from a victim and clones him or her without consent. Such misconduct would violate the victim's reproductive freedom in the same way rape does in some cases.[57] However, it could not compromise the victim's individuality. "Identity theft" may be a growing problem in the world of credit cards and personal information, but it can never be accomplished through reproductive cloning.

The California Advisory Committee on Human Cloning included one last concern based on the identity fallacy. Supposedly, once we see that "predictable" human clones exist, we will cease to believe that humans are autonomous individuals who have free will. This, in turn, will undermine our political and social institutions, which are founded on the need to protect the rights of autonomous individuals.[58] In other words, cloning inexorably erodes the very foundations of our democratic society.

This slippery slope argument lacks a basis in scientific fact. Granted, the Dolly experiment revealed a surprising and unwelcome truth about mammals: *we can reproduce both sexually and asexually.* That means that each and every one of us is not necessarily *genetically* unique. The problem arises when we generalize from the new premise. If we recognize that we are not genetically unique (true) but also swallow the notion that genes imply destiny (untrue), we may conclude falsely that cloning threatens not only our self-image as unique and autonomous individuals but also the democratic institutions we have founded on that self-image. We may react by outlawing cloning in an attempt to suppress the terrible "truth" about ourselves and our institutions.

Denial may be a common and comforting psychological defense mechanism for some people. Nevertheless, when denial poses unreasonable risks to the welfare of other humans, we have a moral obligation to face reality. If we do not confront and rethink the false message that we have incorrectly derived from the science of cloning, we are likely to express fear and hostility toward those persons who, by virtue of their very existence, will take on the role of unwelcome messengers regarding our own putative lack of individuality and autonomy. Arguably, we have already done so through our frantic drive to pass anticloning laws far in advance of any human births.

6. Stereotypes

Thus far, I have explained how the identity fallacy has inspired many erroneous arguments. I am now ready to explain how the fallacy reflects and inspires stereotypes about human clones.

As we have seen, the identity fallacy teaches that human clones are equivalents or copies of their DNA donors. This is a damaging stereotype in and of itself. From this poisonous root, other, related stereotypes grow like the distorted branches of a pest-ridden tree.

First, if the public persists in believing that cloning is a way of recreating dictators or armies of soldiers, it may associate human clones with violence and evil.

Second, even if the public takes a more positive view and imagines that "good" people like Albert Einstein can be copied, the identity fallacy spawns negative stereotypes. Copies of patented, trademarked, or copyrighted products (such as artwork, music, clothing, electronics, and jewelry) are often unlicensed, fraudulent, and inferior in quality. This experience has embedded in our culture the idea that "original" products have more authenticity and value than copies. Thus, to the extent the identity fallacy presents human clones as copies, it prejudges them as fraudulent or inferior.[59]

Third, the link between cloning and immortality, though entirely false, suggests that human clones are a sickening abomination in the eyes of God akin to vampires or zombies.

Fourth, the argument that sharing a genome with another would diminish individuality, impair autonomy, and result in psychological damage paints human clones as duplicative, constrained, pathetic, and disturbed.

Fifth, arguments that depict families formed through cloning as dysfunctional imply additional psychological damage to human clones. The father–daughter hypothetical adds a particularly nasty twist. As explained in Section 4, humans have placed an evolutionary taboo on sex within the family group. The suggestion that a father might be attracted to his cloned daughter holds the power to inspire feelings of intense disgust toward cloning and, by extension, to anyone associated with the technology, including human clones.[60]

Sixth, the idea that cloning can be used to steal our identities portrays human clones as identity thieves and destroyers. Worse, their alleged lack of individuality and autonomy makes them a threat to democratic institutions.

Finally, individuality is an essential element of human nature. Therefore, any argument based on the identity fallacy necessarily implies that a person born through cloning is less than human.

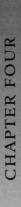

CHAPTER FOUR

Could Human Clones Destroy Humanity?

In the novel *Frankenstein*, the scientist begins to make a mate for his creature. However, he destroys the mate before she is completed. He is afraid that if the hideous pair reproduced, their offspring would terrorize the human race.[1]

The fourth objection is similarly melodramatic: human clones could destroy the human species. This could occur in three alarming ways: (1) human clones could overpopulate the planet, leading to the depletion of natural resources, pollution, and environmental disaster;[2] (2) human clones could reduce genetic diversity, leaving humanity vulnerable to disease;[3] and (3) programs of eugenics and genetic engineering could produce cloned and "designer" humans who would make the current strain of humanity obsolete.[4]

In this chapter, I address these doomsday scenarios and explain why they are speculative and improbable. The stereotypes arising from the scenarios, however, are not.

1. Overpopulation

Let us begin with the idea that human clones could overpopulate the planet. Fear of overpopulation has haunted the world at least since 1798, when Thomas Robert Malthus first predicted that humans would breed until the demand for natural resources exceeded supply, resulting in famine, disease, and death.[5] Today, with the benefit of twenty-twenty hindsight, we know that Malthus's gloomy predictions were overstated. He did not foresee the many agricultural, medical, technological, and political advances that have multiplied resources (e.g., the Green Revolution) while decreasing the inevitability or desirability of high birth rates (e.g., birth control, better medical care for infants and children, and improved social and political status for women). However, the fear of what could happen when too many people chase too few resources remains potent in our society. Modern expressions of the Malthusian theory include the concern that rampant population growth will lead to pollution and serious environmental damage to Earth, the only realistic home our species has at present.

I do not propose to debate whether overpopulation is a true menace or a modern-day bogeyman. My inquiry here is more limited. If we assume that overpopulation is a realistic threat to the survival of our species, does human reproductive cloning significantly increase the risk of overpopulation?

Functional gametes (eggs and sperm) are required to reproduce sexually. This hard truth leaves women who lack functional eggs, and men who lack functional sperm, out of the sexual reproductive loop. With the aid of cloning, however, even the most hopelessly infertile men and women could have their own genetic offspring.

However, one cannot prove that making cloning available to this relatively small demographic group would result in the birth of more children. Even without cloning, these infertile men and women might have employed egg or sperm donors to have just as many children through sexual reproduction.

Gay couples and lesbian couples could also be attracted to asexual reproduction, which would grant them the chance to have biologically related offspring without involving a third party. Again, however, one cannot prove that making cloning available to gays and lesbians would result in an increase in population. In the absence of cloning, gays and lesbians might have employed egg or sperm donors and surrogates to reproduce sexually.

Men and women who carry but do not express heritable diseases in their genomes are a third group that might be attracted to cloning as a means of reproducing without risk. However, even in the absence of cloning, such individuals might have chosen to reproduce sexually, relying on their right to screen embryos prior to implantation or to abort fetuses that would express the diseases. Once again, one cannot be confident that more babies would be born to men and women who carry heritable diseases as a result of cloning.

The three aforementioned demographic groups are a minority of the population. What of the majority? The argument that cloning would lead to overpopulation implicitly assumes that asexual reproduction would be appealing to that majority – so appealing that the average man or woman, who could have reproduced sexually without risk, would not only elect to reproduce asexually *but also would have many more children than he or she otherwise would have had through sexual reproduction.* Just the opposite is true! Sexual reproduction is cheaper, easier, and more fun than asexual reproduction, which is going to require as much or more expense, effort, and stress as IVF and other assisted reproductive technologies.[6]

But, would the additional expense, effort, and stress be worth it? Could the average man or woman use cloning to bear another Einstein, recreate a beloved relative, revive a dead child, or copy his or her narcissistic self? By asking this question, I reveal that the root of the overpopulation objection is the identity fallacy. Because cloning cannot be used to make copies, not one of these goals is realistic, meaning that the average man or woman has no incentive to pursue asexual reproduction. The invention of the copy machine may have inundated society with excessive numbers of paper copies, but cloning will not inundate society with excessive numbers of human copies.

What, then, does the overpopulation objection add to the identity fallacy? It associates human clones with rabbits, rats, mice, insects, and other pests that breed quickly, steal food belonging to others, generate waste, and carry disease. But that is not all. The popular Malthusian view links overpopulation with dire consequences ranging from famine and disease to death. Thus, the overpopulation objection implicitly portrays human clones as dangerous, destructive, and even murderous as their imaginary multitudes drive the entire human species to the brink of extinction.

2. Genetic Diversity

The next doomsday argument is that human clones will reduce genetic diversity.

Sexual reproduction is a game of chance. Every combination of genes from mother and father results in a new genome. Generally, a species that reproduces sexually is more diverse, in a genetic sense, than is a species that reproduces asexually (although there are exceptions).[7] Genetic diversity protects a species against predators, parasites (bacteria, viruses, and fungi), and other environmental stressors. The greater the variety of genomes a species includes, the less likely it is that a particular disease or hardship could exploit its genetic vulnerabilities and lead to a catastrophic number of injuries or deaths.[8]

The benefits of sexual reproduction do not stop there. Parasites (bacteria, viruses, and fungi) have short life spans. As they reproduce, they evolve rapidly in an effort to defeat the natural defenses to infection and disease of their hosts. To stop these enemies, a host species must also reproduce and evolve. By creating new genomes, sexual reproduction constantly changes the biological "locks" that parasites must open.[9]

From this, it follows that sexual reproduction and genetic diversity are valuable strategies for our species. I do not question that proposition. The error lies in the assumption that cloning is a threat to sexual reproduction and genetic diversity.

This bears repeating: Sexual reproduction is easy, cheap, and fun. The average man or woman is not likely to give it up in favor of asexual reproduction, which requires expense, effort, and stressful medical intervention.[10] This is particularly true, given that the purported goals to be achieved (e.g., replicating geniuses, raising the dead, and achieving immortality) are nothing more than fantastic ships that must founder upon the hard and unforgiving rock of scientific fact.

If some infertile men and women, gays and lesbians, and carriers of heritable diseases choose to clone themselves, their collective offspring will be a drop in the genetic bucket. Over six billion different human genomes are already in existence, and men and women are busily creating many more new genomes via sexual reproduction every minute of every day.[11] When it comes to the genetic diversity of the species, this is quite a safety margin. Indeed, cloning may *encourage* genetic diversity to the extent it results in the descent of genes that otherwise would be lost owing to infertility or other causes.[12]

The genetic diversity argument is so questionable that it raises the question of why otherwise rational people would believe in it. Again, I believe that the root of the argument is the identity fallacy. If cloning could be used to make copies, someone somewhere might find an advantage in churning out multitudinous copies of the same genome over and over again. This raises the false specter of a reduction in genetic diversity. However, as we have seen, cloning cannot be used to make copies.

What does the genetic diversity argument add to the core stereotype that human clones are copies? It inspires new stereotypes by associating duplicative "clones" with disease and death on a catastrophic scale.

3. Eugenics and Genetic Engineering

The third doomsday argument begins with the notion that cloning could facilitate eugenics programs designed to improve the human species.

Eugenics programs have a bad reputation for two reasons. First, such programs have an ugly history of state-sponsored coercion. Early in the twentieth century, many American states enacted laws that mandated the sterilization of individuals who had been convicted of certain crimes, the insane, and others with specified physical and mental disabilities.[13] California was the workhorse of the American eugenics movement, performing more sterilizations than any other state.[14] Nazi

Germany used the California experience as the inspiration for its own Law on Preventing Hereditarily Ill Progeny, which mandated the sterilization of persons who suffered from what were believed at the time to be heritable disabilities, including feeblemindedness, schizophrenia, epilepsy, blindness, alcohol addiction, and physical deformities.[15] The Nazi enthusiasm for eugenics progressed from sterilization to euthanasia and extermination camps.[16]

Given this deplorable history, it is understandable that many people associate eugenics programs with coercion, sterilization, and even death. However, there is nothing inherently coercive about the technology of human reproductive cloning. Only the *government* has the power to coerce its citizens to reproduce – or not reproduce – according to its dictates.[17]

Second, eugenics programs have a bad reputation because they are antiegalitarian. Any concerted effort to improve the human species offensively suggests that some humans are more desirable than others.[18]

Given these two concerns, the question is whether cloning is dangerous because the government could use it to produce superior human beings through coercive and antiegalitarian eugenics programs.

The answer is no. Even if one assumes that society could identify certain individuals who exhibited physical and mental superiority, there would be no way to manufacture hundreds or thousands of copies of those individuals. As the National Bioethics Advisory Commission recognized, human traits and characteristics "result from complicated interactions among a number of genes and the environment."[19] *A genome that contributed toward the development of a person with particular traits and characteristics could never produce the same individual again.*

In other words, the root of the eugenics argument is, once again, the identity fallacy. Federal and state governments will have no incentive to implement cloning programs because cloning cannot achieve eugenic goals.

Moreover, even if federal or state governments were deluded by the identity fallacy into thinking that eugenic cloning could succeed, they would soon confront another problem: for every "superior" human born through asexual reproduction, there would be many thousands more "ordinary" people born through sexual reproduction. As philosopher

Gregory Pence has noted: "A primary law of population genetics is re-gression to the mean.... Even the most vast attempts to improve the human genome will not get around the inherent tendency of the human population to revert to the normal range."[20]

Thus, the only way that eugenic cloning could succeed would be if the government mandated asexual reproduction and banned or severely restricted sexual reproduction. This is not likely in our democratic soci-ety. Unpopular minorities sometimes have been the targets of eugenics laws, but majorities have the power to fight back through the vote.[21]

In sum, cloning will not lead to government-sponsored eugenics pro-grams. However, the *argument* that cloning leads to eugenics could in-spire damaging stereotypes about human clones.

The eugenics argument associates human clones with the steriliza-tion programs of twentieth-century America and the atrocities of Nazi Germany. (This is particularly ironic, given that human clones are them-selves the victims of coercive laws, as explained in Parts 2 and 3 of this book.[22]) In this way, human clones are forced to bear an undeserved taint of coercion, pain, mutilation, and death.

The argument further associates human clones with genetic superior-ity. At the very least, this association will inspire envy and resentment. Human clones will be viewed as arrogant (how dare they imagine their genomes to be superior?) or, perhaps, as cheaters who were given an unfair head start in the footrace of life. At worst, "normal" people may view superior "clones" as a threat to their own existence, the vanguard of a new species that must be crushed at its inception.

Reasoning such as this leads logically to the next fear about cloning, namely, that it could be used in combination with genetic engineering. By "genetic engineering," I mean the genetic alteration of embryos be-fore implantation in the womb, or, more radically, the genetic alteration of sperm or ova before conception. In theory, scientists could add genes that produce desirable traits (such as health, beauty, and intelligence) or subtract genes that produce undesirable traits (such as disease).[23]

Thus, for example, the California Advisory Committee on Human Cloning raised the possibility that embryos cloned from desirable geno-types could be further enhanced through genetic engineering.[24] Alter-natively, as the President's Council on Bioethics suggested, once babies with genetically enhanced traits were born, cloning might be used to perpetuate their traits.[25] Either way, genetic engineering, in combination with cloning, could change the nature of humanity.

The prospect of genetic engineering has been a popular book and lecture topic in recent years. Some, like Gregory Stock, have argued that genetic engineering is a desirable technology that can improve our bodies and minds.[26] Others, like Francis Fukuyama and Bill McKibben, have argued strenuously against the morality of genetic engineering and our looming "posthuman" future.[27] Still others, like Steven Pinker, have argued that the debate is premature because genetic engineering is riskier and harder to accomplish than people think. This is because it is not possible to match physical or mental traits to individual genes. Rather, traits manifest themselves when many genes work together in the context of environmental factors. Also, most genes have multiple effects, some good and some bad. Removing a "bad" gene could undermine positive traits; adding a "good" gene could cause unexpected medical problems. Prospective parents are unlikely to want to take medical risks in pursuit of uncertain benefits.[28]

Interestingly, in its 2004 report on assisted reproductive technologies, the President's Council on Bioethics acknowledged that "designer babies" and "super babies" are not likely in the foreseeable future[29] for the same scientific reasons that Pinker noted:

> There are today no safe and effective means of genetic modification of early embryos. For reasons described above, the effects of direct gene-transfer into an embryo are unpredictable – there is no reliable way to control the insertion, function, and heritability of the new genetic information. There is no reliable way to guarantee that the gene will express itself in the intended way or to prevent the gene from expressing itself (or triggering other genetic expressions) in an adverse manner. Prospective genetic modification of offspring by germ-line gene-transfer to the gonads of the parents (or to isolated ovum and sperm) is equally, if not more, problematic, given that the effects of the gene insertion are even more attenuated (by the vagaries of sexual recombination) and thus less controllable.[30]

Thus, genetic engineering is not imminent, and concerns about its potential to alter the nature of humanity are speculative at best. Moreover, even if the threat to humanity were real, it would come from widespread

genetic engineering and not cloning, which, for the reasons that Greg
Pence has advanced, cannot "improve" humankind.

It is very interesting, however, that opponents of cloning associate it
with genetic engineering. The association links cloning to yet another
doomsday scenario in which humanity is not literally destroyed but is
so altered as to be unrecognizable. By this account, human clones are
the harbingers of genetic doom, the merciless destroyers of what was
once their own kind.

In sum, what do concerns about cloning and overpopulation, genetic diversity, and eugenics or genetic engineering all have in common?
These three concerns are rooted in the identity fallacy. Thus, they are
founded on the stereotype that human clones are copies. In addition, the concerns inspire further stereotypes by associating menacing
"clones" with the destruction or irrevocable alteration of humanity. The
scenarios command much attention, not because they are accurate predictions of the future but because they are predictions of doomsday.
The stakes are high. It is human nature to fear that which is dangerous and to hate that which we fear. Unfortunately, that includes human
clones.

CHAPTER FIVE

Does Human Reproductive Cloning
Harm Participants and Produce
Children with Birth Defects?

The last objection focuses both on the technology of human reproductive cloning and the nature and characteristics of human clones. This "safety objection" holds that reproductive cloning is unsafe for participants and produces children with serious birth defects.

I do not believe that safety concerns are the primary force motivating public and political opposition to cloning and human clones. If safety were the main concern, legislators and regulators would not frequently cite the first four objections to justify a complete ban on reproductive cloning.[1] Nor would advisory committees and councils have devoted countless hours and hundreds of pages to the analysis of the first four objections.[2]

Moreover, if safety were the main concern, federal and state governments would have treated reproductive cloning (a potential treatment for infertility) very differently. Typically, promising but unperfected medical treatments, devices, and drugs are regulated but are not prohibited. Through medical licensing and tort law, state governments prevent unqualified and careless practitioners from applying new treatments to patients too quickly. Through funding and related regulations, the federal government seeks to promote the safety of clinical trials. Through the Food and Drug Administration (FDA), the federal government controls but does not block the entry of new drugs and medical devices into the marketplace. Instead of taking this moderate approach, state legislatures have criminalized reproductive cloning, presidents have blocked federal funding for cloning experiments,[3] and the FDA has asserted that it will not allow cloning experiments.

Nevertheless, safety has achieved prominence as a secularized objection to a technology that is unpopular for religious and other reasons. For example, the National Bioethics Advisory Commission recommended a 3–5 year legislative moratorium on human reproductive cloning – in part on safety grounds.[4] Similarly, the National Academies advocated that human reproductive cloning be outlawed on safety grounds but also recommended that scientific and medical concerns be reviewed within 5 years; if by then the technology had become safe and effective and the national dialogue on social, religious, and ethical issues supported it, the ban could be reconsidered.[5]

In 1997, the California State Legislature banned reproductive cloning for a limited, 5-year term. In 2002, the California Advisory Committee on Human Cloning advised the legislature to adopt a flat ban on human reproductive cloning with no expiration date.[6] The committee recognized that the science and ethics of cloning could change in future years; thus, it could have recommended another ban for a limited period of years that would have given the law room to evolve along with the scientific and ethical discussion. Instead, the committee justified its recommendation of a flat ban by reasoning in part that cloning was not yet safe enough for human use.[7]

Lastly, the President's Council on Bioethics also recommended a flat ban – in part on safety grounds. Its reasoning was the most extreme: cloning could never be made safe because the necessary research would itself be unethical experimentation upon the children to be born.[8]

Is there any *scientific* basis for these recommendations?

At present, there are no data on the safety of human reproductive cloning as such. Some limited conclusions can be drawn from recent experiments in human research cloning.

In 2004, South Korean scientists reported success in cloning human blastocysts, that is, advanced embryos containing hundreds of cells.[9] They started with very fresh human eggs. Rather than using needles to aspirate the original nuclei, as other scientists had done, the South Koreans squeezed the eggs gently until their nuclei popped out.[10] They injected each egg with a cumulus cell taken from the same woman who had donated the egg. By experimenting with reprogramming time, egg activation method, and in vitro culture conditions, the South Koreans developed protocols that produced blastocysts from eggs at rates of up to 29 percent.[11] They also succeeded in harvesting and culturing a line of embryonic stem cells from 1 of 30 blastocysts.[12] The stem cell line had a normal karyotype (i.e., complete diploid set of chromosomes).

This experiment indicates that human embryos can be cloned for research purposes. Moreover, because human embryos ordinarily implant in the lining of the uterus only a day or so after they grow into blastocysts,[13] the experiment also implies that human reproductive cloning is possible.

In the absence of more extensive human data, many scientists have assumed that other primates (our closest evolutionary relatives) provide the next best research model. So far, however, researchers have been unable to clone monkeys from adult cells.[14]

In 2003, Dr. Calvin Simerly and some of his colleagues in primate research reported that cloned monkey embryos did not divide properly, leading to chromosomal abnormalities.[15] The primate researchers theorized that, while removing the original nucleus from the monkey egg, they inadvertently removed proteins clustered around the nucleus that were necessary for cell division to take place properly. (In other species that have been cloned successfully, the proteins necessary to promote cell division are dispersed more widely throughout the egg and are not entirely removed during the cloning process.[16]) Predictably, this bad news received considerable media attention with many people taking it as a sign that human reproductive cloning will be impossible.

That failed monkey experiment, however, was published *before* the South Koreans reported their success in growing cloned human embryos to the blastocyst stage. Their startling feat could not have been accomplished unless the cells of the embryos were dividing in an orderly fashion.[17] Moreover, the stem cell line that they derived from one of the blastocysts had a normal karyotype.

Indeed, after the South Korean experiment was published, Dr. Simerly and his colleagues decided to see what would happen if they applied some of the South Korean methods. To their delight, the researchers succeeded in growing cloned monkey embryos to the blastocyst stage for the first time.[18] Although transfers of the monkey embryos produced no pregnancies, this recent experiment shows how quickly failure can turn to success as cloning technology advances.

Because human and primate cloning are still in their infancy, the debate over the safety of human cloning has focused on data drawn from experiments involving cattle, sheep, pigs, mice, and other nonprimates. Opponents of human reproductive cloning, and human clones, have used these data to support four safety-related arguments.

First, opponents argue that cloning is an inherently inefficient technology that requires many failed attempts for every live birth. Because some animal mothers and babies have died, opponents reason that human mothers and babies will die if cloning is permitted. Second, opponents assert that cloning leads to the birth of oversized and deformed animals and (presumably) oversized and deformed humans. Third, opponents claim that there are no normal cloned animals; they all are flawed at the epigenetic level. Therefore, there can be no normal human clones. Fourth, opponents insist that clones, whether animal or human, are prematurely aged.

This chapter critiques these four arguments and explains how they misstate, misapply, and overstate the results of animal experiments. In the course of this critique an explanation is also provided of how the arguments have been influenced by other objections that have nothing to do with safety such as the false notion that human clones are copies.

Following this critique, a discussion of how the safety arguments incorporate and promote unfair stereotypes is presented.

Finally, the chapter concludes by explaining that the safety arguments do more than advocate reasonable prudence when applying a new technology to humans. Rather, they portray human reproductive cloning as inherently unsafe and human clones as irremediably flawed. This exaggerated portrayal poses its own dangers to society, including the risk that legislatures will prohibit the very research necessary to make cloning safe.

1. The Efficiency of Cloning

The first safety argument is that cloning is an inefficient and dangerous technology. According to this argument, animal experiments show that many eggs, embryos, fetuses, newborns, and mothers must die to generate a handful of live clones. Reasoning by analogy, opponents argue that human reproductive cloning is also likely to be inefficient and dangerous to embryos, fetuses, babies, egg donors and gestational mothers.[19]

This charge amounts to a half-truth. Yes, mammalian cloning is a new science, it has not been perfected yet, and success rates are low at present. Opponents, however, have painted a picture that is darker and more disturbing than the reality by presenting data in manner that is one-sided and often erroneous.

a) Dolly and the 277 "Attempts"

Because the Dolly experiment is often cited as proof of just how inefficient and dangerous cloning can be, I begin by providing the basic data on that experiment. In 1996, Dr. Ian Wilmut and his associates at the Roslin Institute injected the nuclei of cells taken from a 6-year-old sheep into 277 unfertilized eggs. The experiment produced 29 embryos that were inserted into 13 ewes. One ewe became pregnant and gave birth to a healthy lamb (Dolly).[20]

Unfortunately, reporters and lawmakers often misstate the facts of this adult-cell experiment, describing the 277 eggs as 277 "attempts" involving miscarriages, deformities, and deaths. Consider the following example from a Congressional report that recommended a complete ban on human cloning: "Cloning experiments produced 277 stillborn, miscarried or dead sheep before Dolly was successfully cloned. That failure rate, which has remained steady since 1997, is not acceptable for human beings."[21] In fact, there were no miscarriages, no deformed lambs, and no deaths resulting from the transfer of the *adult* cell nuclei in the Dolly experiment.[22]

There are two possible reasons for this confusion. First, the Dolly experiment had three distinct parts. The best known part is the one relevant to this chapter: the cloning of Dolly from an adult cell. In the two other parts of the experiment, Dr. Wilmut tried to clone sheep from embryonic and fetal cells. Some of those pregnancies did end in miscarriages.[23] Thus, perhaps some errors in Dolly reporting occur because the media and policymakers have a tendency to merge three very different sets of experimental data.

When it comes to cloning, it is important to distinguish adult cell experiments from fetal and embryonic cell experiments whenever possible. Many embryos and fetuses do not implant, or they miscarry; often, this is because the gamble of sexual reproduction has produced an inadequate genome. For example, in human reproduction, up to 75 percent of embryos conceived through sexual intercourse never make it to birth; most do not implant in the uterus and are spontaneously aborted.[24] Thus, when cloning from nuclear DNA harvested from embryos and fetuses, one might expect a fairly significant number of failures to occur simply because the selected genomes are inadequate. By contrast, nuclear DNA taken from an adult animal already has proven its ability to generate a healthy term birth (of that adult). What this means is that one must be cautious in extrapolating from experiments that involve cloning from embryonic and fetal cells. Dr. Wilmut's efforts to clone sheep from embryonic and fetal cells may not predict success in adult cell cloning, but they do not necessarily predict failure either.

A second possible reason for the misreporting of the Dolly experiment has to do with expectations. If a person views cloning as a Frankenstein horror, a spit in the face of God, or a rape of nature, then he or she might logically expect disastrous results such as miscarriages and deaths. This expectation has led not only to mistakes in the original reporting of the scientific data but also to the endless reiteration of those mistakes. Reporters and policymakers have not corrected the errors because the errors do not look like errors to them. Instead, they have repeated the errors over and over. This constant repetition has cloaked the myth of the 277 "attempts" with the mantle of an irrefutable truth.

b) Current Success Rates

Too often, reporters and lawmakers rely on the Dolly experiment (undertaken back in 1996) as if it were the only one. Cloning is a science, and science constantly changes. Recent publications more accurately state the current success rates for animal cloning.

In November 2001, scientists at Advanced Cell Technology (ACT) summarized their work with cows cloned from fetal cells.[25] In this work, the scientists transferred a total of 496 blastocysts into 247 surrogate cows.[26] Of these, 110 became pregnant, but 80 had miscarriages. (This was a miscarriage rate of 73 percent compared with a 7–24-percent miscarriage rate for cow pregnancies derived from in vitro fertilization.)[27] Thirty fetuses developed to term, but six calves died shortly after birth. The remaining 24 cloned calves grew into a vigorous and healthy adulthood.[28] In terms of the percentage of healthy births to embryos transferred, this represented a success rate of about 5 percent; or, to put it negatively, a failure rate of about 95 percent. Most failures (386 out of 496) involved embryos that were transferred but did not implant in the womb.

Similarly, in January 2002, a team of Japanese researchers working with mice reported that about 2.8 percent of blastocysts cloned from adult and fetal cells developed to term after transfer into surrogate mice. Of the newborn pups, 92.9 percent were healthy.[29] In terms of the percentage of healthy births to embryos transferred, this was a success rate of 2–3 percent or, to put it negatively, a failure rate of about 97–98 percent.

In 2002, the National Academies published a report on cloning, which included a table summarizing success and failure rates in other animal cloning experiments, most of which were conducted before 2001. In reviewing those experiments that involved cloning from adult cells, one finds the same basic pattern. The percentage of live births to embryos transferred ranged from 0.32 to 11 percent.[30] The vast majority of cloning failures (from about 83 to 99 percent) involved embryos that never developed to the point of transfer or never produced a pregnancy.[31] Once a pregnancy was established, the miscarriage rate ranged widely from zero (the Dolly experiment) to a high of 94 percent.[32] Although the vast majority of newborns survived, some died of causes that might or might not have been related to cloning.[33]

c) Efficiency in the Future
The low success rates in animal cloning raise several questions. Why do more embryos not implant? Why do some pregnancies miscarry? Why do some newborn animals die shortly after birth?

Today, it is not possible to answer these questions definitively. Cloning involves many steps as follows:

- Eggs must be removed from the bodies of females and matured in the laboratory,
- Technicians must take the original maternal chromosomes out of the eggs,
- Donor cells must be selected (by type and individually) and removed from the adult to be cloned,
- The donor cells must be brought to a state of rest,
- The chromosomes must be extracted from the quiescent donor cells,
- Those chromosomes must be introduced into the eggs,
- The reconstituted eggs must be induced through electricity or chemicals to start dividing,
- The resulting embryos must be cultured, and
- The embryos must be transferred into the uteri of surrogate mothers.[34]

Errors or suboptimal procedures in any of these steps could lead to failures. Cloning, however, is a new science that will continue to advance so long as experimentation is allowed to continue. Most experiments that have been published so far report the experiences of scientists who are cloning for the first or second time.[35] Comparing the results of their own early experiments with those of others, scientists have the chance to generate hypotheses about which methodologies and protocols work and which do not. Scientists can test those hypotheses through more research, which ultimately can lead to the development of an effective and safe technology.

Given that cloning technology is a work in progress, any assessment of its efficiency is likely to become dated within a short time. This fact weighs against the enactment of laws that impose flat bans on the ground that human reproductive cloning is inefficient.

2. The Role of Large Offspring Syndrome

Although the precise causes of failures in animal cloning remain unknown, some animal researchers believe that many of those failures can be attributed to general laboratory conditions and practices as opposed to factors specific to cloning (such as nuclear transfer).

Animal researchers have known for years that cows and sheep conceived through standard IVF sometimes suffer from large offspring syndrome (LOS).[36] Fetuses and newborns affected by LOS can grow to an abnormally large size, jeopardizing their own health and the health of the mothers who carry and give birth to them.[37] LOS also can include abnormal placentas, fluid accumulation associated with maternal and fetal distress, and cardiovascular abnormalities.[38] Although the causes of LOS are not fully understood, some scientists believe that the syndrome results when embryos are exposed to suboptimal culture conditions in the laboratory, leading to changes in normal gene expression patterns.[39]

LOS has also been observed in animals conceived through cloning.[40] Extrapolating from these animal data, the President's Council on Bioethics and others have asserted that human reproductive cloning could be dangerous for mothers and children.[41] When it comes to LOS, at least, that seems quite unlikely. Even though IVF produces LOS in cows and sheep, it does not result in the same syndrome in humans.[42]

There is a possible explanation for this species difference, but before this chapter progresses any further, I offer the reader a modest outline of the relevant biology. DNA holds two types of information: genetic information in its basic nucleotide sequence, and epigenetic information in its structure.[43] Epigenetic information influences how genes are expressed and thus contributes to the phenotype of an organism.[44] (A "phenotype" is a type distinguished by visible characters rather than by genetic traits.)[45]

One type of epigenetic information is parental imprinting. When an organism reproduces sexually, a sperm carrying one set of chromosomes joins with an egg carrying another set of chromosomes to create an embryo with a set of chromosome pairs.[46] Most genes are expressed on both maternal and paternal chromosomes; however, genes subject to parental imprinting are expressed only on *either* the maternal *or* paternal chromosome.[47] The parental "imprint" consists of chemical markings that are established when an egg or sperm is formed.[48] By convention, a gene is said to be imprinted if it is repressed,[49] that is, "switched off" and not functioning.

In 2001, a team of scientists published findings on how genetic evolution has diverged in different species in an article entitled "Divergent

Evolution in M6P/IGF2R Imprinting from the Jurassic to the Quaternary." They noted that M6P/IGF2R both protects against cancer and regulates fetal growth. Cows, sheep, pigs, and mice receive two copies of M6P/IGF2R from their two parents, but one copy is imprinted. Humans and other primates also receive two copies, but both copies function. The imprinting disappeared from our evolutionary lineage over 75 million years ago.[50]

Noting that livestock conceived through IVF and cloning often suffer from LOS, the scientists reasoned that this could be the result of reduced M6P/IGF2R expression.[51] Laboratory manipulation of embryos could alter epigenetic imprint programming, thereby causing fetal overgrowth.

However, because M6P/IGF2R is not imprinted in humans, laboratory manipulation might not harm the development of human embryos to the same extent. On the basis of this distinction, the scientists reasoned that human clones would be less likely to suffer from LOS than animal clones. In support of this conclusion, they noted that human babies conceived through IVF do not suffer from LOS.[52]

Unfortunately, when the media and policymakers have reported on the hazards of LOS, they have ignored or downplayed such distinctions between humans and animals.

For example, the National Academies admitted that IVF has not caused LOS in humans but refused to rule out the possibility that cloning would cause LOS in humans.[53] The Academies rejected the optimistic conclusions drawn in the article "Divergent Evolution in M6P/IGF2R Imprinting from the Jurassic to the Quaternary." Instead, the Academies reasoned that, even if M6P/IGF2R was not imprinted in humans, there are many other imprinted genes that could cause problems in human clones.[54]

Some of this pessimism could be due to risk aversion; if there is any chance of a major birth defect in a human baby, policymakers may think it is sensible to err on the side of caution.

However, this pessimism could also be the result of predetermined expectations. The mental image of oversized and deformed young ripping themselves out of the ruptured wombs of dying mothers is extraordinarily gruesome. It is also consistent with a view of cloning as technological hubris. Consider the following premise: a scientist has no business meddling in reproduction; that is the domain of God. If one accepts that premise, the deformities and deaths associated with LOS are to be expected as the inevitable wages of the sin of pride. From this point of view, if cloning technology were applied to humans, the same wages would have to be paid.

Therefore, the idea that human reproductive cloning would *not* result in LOS runs contrary to the expectations of many people. For this reason alone, the idea is not what those people *want* to hear or believe about cloning. It amounts to an arrogant assertion that the boundary between human and divine can be transgressed with impunity. Worse, the idea that scientists may be able to clone humans more easily and safely than cows or sheep turns biblical doctrine on its head. God gave human beings dominion over other animals[55] but not dominion over themselves. Any research that implies such dominion smacks of heresy.[56]

3. The Role of Reprogramming

Not every problem found in cloned animals is associated with LOS.[57] There is another possible explanation for both low success rates and birth defects that has proven to be very popular with the media and policymakers. Before describing it, I offer more scientific facts as a helpful background for the reader.

All genes necessary to healthy life – including the genes that control fetal development – exist within every cell of an adult animal. However, most cells in adults have gone through the process of differentiation and have taken on specialized roles. For example, in a skin cell, only those genes relevant to skin are expressed. Proteins cover and supress the remaining genes.

Let us suppose that a skin cell is selected as a source of nuclear DNA. The original parental imprints must be intact so that they can guide embryonic and fetal development. Some adult cells lose their imprints during the course of cellular division over the lifetime of the donor animal. Scientists have speculated that some cloning attempts fail as the result of lost or damaged imprints.[58]

Even if the imprints are intact, another challenge remains. To function properly as skin, the cell only needed certain genes to be expressed. Now without damaging the imprints, the egg must "reprogram" the DNA in the cell so that all of the genes necessary for proper embryonic and fetal development are expressed.[59] Many scientists and policymakers have speculated that reprogramming is the basic challenge involved in cloning an adult mammal. According to this hypothesis, although such reprogramming is not impossible, it is extremely difficult and thus is likely to produce many failures for every success.

As explained in the opening section of this chapter, the majority of cloning failures occur at a very early stage in the process. Some embryos do not develop to the point of being mature enough for transfer to the uterus, and most embryos that are transferred stop growing soon thereafter.

In 2003, Dr. Rudolph Jaenisch and other scientists reported the results of their research into this conundrum. Working with blastocysts cloned from adult mice, the scientists investigated the expression of Oct4 and 10 related genes that they believed to be essential for proper embryonic development.[60] They found that 62 percent of the blastocysts expressed all tested genes correctly. The remainder did not express one or more of the tested genes and thus lacked the ability to develop properly.[61] The scientists noted that the reason for this failure was unclear. Epigenetic mechanisms affect the expression of genes in embryos, but scientists do not know much about how epigenetic reprogramming works in the context of normal development and cloning.[62]

Faulty reprogramming could explain why most cloned embryos do not develop or implant. However, for some scientists, that is only the beginning. Dr. Jaenisch has become one of the best known advocates of the view that faulty reprogramming of imprinted and nonimprinted genes is also responsible for the miscarriages, birth defects, and deaths observed in cloned animals. More damningly, he has asserted that *all* cloned animals – even those that appear healthy – are, in fact, riddled with invisible reprogramming errors.

To understand this aspect of the debate over human reproductive cloning, it helps to place scientific theory in a political context. On 28 March 2001, Dr. Ian Wilmut and Dr. Rudolph Jaenisch published an editorial entitled "Don't Clone Humans!"[63] The editorial was intended as a response to news reports that some fertility doctors were trying to clone babies for infertile couples.[64] Drs. Wilmut and Jaenisch made their political stance very clear at the outset, stating that they opposed human reproductive cloning for social and ethical reasons.[65] But the main point of their editorial was to warn that cloning is not safe. Cloning requires that the donor nucleus be reprogrammed quickly within a matter of minutes or hours. The two scientists speculated that faulty reprogramming could lead to errors in gene expression and might be the cause of the physical flaws observed in some cloned animals. They warned that even clones that appeared normal could have epigenetic defects lurking inside them.[66]

On that same day, Dr. Jaenisch provided testimony before the Subcommittee on Oversight and Investigations of the Committee on Energy and Commerce in the House of Representatives, which was considering whether legislation should be introduced to ban human reproductive cloning. Dr. Jaenisch stated his hypothesis that deaths and birth defects in animal clones are due to reprogramming errors. He reasoned that even apparently healthy animal clones might have epigenetic defects too subtle to detect; thus, there probably were no "normal" animal clones. Similarly, he maintained that human cloning is dangerous because any one of 30,000 genes could be subject to reprogramming errors.[67]

A few months afterwards, Dr. Jaenisch and coauthors published two papers on cloning. The first paper reported the results of original research on mice cloned from embryonic stem cells. The experiment investigated the expression of imprinted genes and found that few of the embryonic stem cell clones showed normal expression of all imprinted genes.[68] The paper speculated that the abnormal fetal growth found in some of the mice was due to the cumulative action of many improperly expressed genes even though there was no significant correlation between the abnormalities and any single gene.[69] The experiment showed that even healthy mice also had some improperly expressed genes; on the basis of this evidence, the paper admitted that mammalian development may be more tolerant to epigenetic abnormalities than some scientists had supposed. Despite this good news, the paper concluded with the warning that clones could suffer from subtle physiological abnormalities that could be difficult to detect.[70]

The second paper, published a month later, canvassed the scientific literature on cloning and drew wide-ranging conclusions regarding the status of the technology.[71] Consistent with the prior editorial, the second paper hypothesized that faulty reprogramming of the genome was to blame for deaths and birth defects in cloned animals.[72] The paper observed that some mice cloned from embryonic stem cells suffered from imprinting errors.[73] Even though mice cloned from adult cells did not have the same imprinting errors, the paper rejected the implication that adult cell nuclei were faithfully reprogrammed after transfer into the egg. Instead, the paper reasoned that the early death of most adult cell clones at the embryonic stage might be due to failure to reprogram the genes needed for embryonic development.[74] From this, the paper leapt to the conclusion that cloned animals that managed to survive to apparently healthy adulthood were, in fact, abnormal at the epigenetic level.[75]

These views made a big splash in the media. Carrying headlines like "Researchers Find Big Risk of Defect in Cloning Animals," newspaper, magazine, and television reports disseminated his hypothesis that there are no normal clones and that clones are subject to sudden and unexpected health problems.[76] To illustrate the point, one article published a photograph of a cloned mouse that was normal until it became obese at middle age.[77]

Within months, however, the scientists at Advanced Cell Technology stepped forward to defend animal cloning. In an article entitled "Cloned Cattle Can Be Healthy and Normal," they reported the results of their extensive examinations of 24 Holstein cows that had been cloned from adult cells.[78] The cows were vigorous at birth and remained alive and healthy 1 to 4 years later. The cows were normal in every respect: physical condition (including weight), blood chemistry, urine chemistry, immune function, social interaction, conditioned responses, fertility, and reproduction. Although some of the cows experienced pulmonary hypertension and respiratory distress at birth, the researchers did not observe genetic defects, immune deficiencies, gross obesity, or other abnormalities.[79]

A team of Japanese scientists sought to investigate the hypothesis that abnormalities in cloned animals are the result of epigenetic alterations in imprinted genes. In January 2002, they published the results of their work in an article entitled "Faithful Expression of Imprinted Genes in Cloned Mice."[80] The article stated that the scientists had examined mice cloned from a variety of adult and fetal cells and had found that over 90 percent of the newborn pups were healthy. The team tested cloned fetuses and associated placentas and found that paternal and maternal imprints on genes that direct embryonic development were faithfully maintained.[81] The team also found that expression of imprinted genes was normal in the cloned fetuses. However, placentas of cloned mice at term were larger than normal and did exhibit some alterations in the expression of imprinted and nonimprinted genes.[82]

The Japanese team concluded by noting that Dr. Jaenisch had cloned his abnormal mice from embryonic stem cells, which are much less stable epigenetically than adult cells. The abnormalities he found most likely were due to epigenetic mutations (e.g., loss of imprints) accumulated during in vitro culture of the donor cells rather than biological effects inherent to cloning.[83]

What the Japanese team had to say should have been big news. The article indicated cloning might be inefficient but that cloned animals that survived to birth were normal. Moreover, the article suggested that the epigenetic defects observed in some cloned animals were due to the use of an unstable type of donor cell. This was a correctable, rather than an inherent, problem.[84]

The article, however, did not receive much media attention. As Dr. Lee Silver commented shortly after the article was published:

> Now the amazing thing to me is that this paper that said that cloning was safer than previously thought ["Faithful Expression of Imprinted Genes in Cloned Mice"] was published in a top scientific journal, Science, and it didn't even make it into the newspapers. As I said, Dolly sneezes and its [sic] on the front page of the New York Times, but this paper saying clones are okay doesn't go anywhere. People don't want to hear this. They want to hear cloning is bad.[85]

Around the same time Dr. Silver gave this talk, the ACT scientists published another article entitled "The Health Profile of Cloned Animals." The scientists made it clear that they, too, were frustrated. In their view, the media and some scientists opposed to human reproductive cloning had overemphasized cloning defects and abnormalities.[86]

Seeking to set the record straight, the ACT scientists reviewed data from published experiments in the cloning of cattle, sheep, goats, pigs, and mice and reported that an astonishing 77 percent of live born animals were healthy.[87] The scientists admitted that the rate of embryonic and fetal attrition was high in these experiments. However, they asserted, most fetuses that miscarried were normal but malnourished. These losses, along with many stillbirths and neonatal deaths, were attributable to abnormal placentas. Simple interventions, such as keeping newborns warm, or providing them with glucose or oxygen, compensated for the malnourishment and allowed newborns to become normal within a few hours. Research could develop new methods that might reduce or even eliminate miscarriages and neonatal losses.[88]

Like the media, policymakers paid scant attention to this and other reports that presented animal cloning and clones in an optimistic light. For example, the President's Council on Bioethics extensively discussed faulty reprogramming[89] in its chapter on science; however, it devoted only one sentence to the article "Cloned Cattle Can Be Healthy and Normal"[90] and did not mention the article entitled "Faithful Expression of Imprinted Genes in Cloned Mice." The California Advisory Committee on Human Cloning also expressed concern about reprogramming errors and repeated Dr. Jaenisch's speculation that there were few, if any, normal clones.[91]

It is not surprising that the media and policymakers have embraced the faulty reprogramming theory. To understand why, it is necessary to evaluate the theory in the light of other objections to cloning that are not based on safety. First, the theory identifies a problem that goes to the very heart of cloning. This jibes with the notion that cloning is a form of scientific hubris. The inability to reprogram properly shows that cloning exceeds the human grasp; only God and nature can accomplish such miracles. Moreover, if reprogramming cannot be done properly, human reproductive cloning is never likely to occur – at least not on a large scale. This thought is likely to be very comforting to anyone who fears that cloning is a method of replication that could compromise his or her individuality.

Second, the faulty reprogramming theory asserts that epigenetic defects are embedded deep in the organism itself. This means that, even when we see an outwardly healthy animal, defects *are* present. This aspect of the theory also fits with the view that cloning is a form of technological hubris that inevitably must fail. The hidden defects are an epigenetic prophecy of doom that must surely come to pass.

By contrast, the assertion that cloned animals can be healthy and normal is deeply threatening and thus unwelcome. It raises the possibility that humans can clone themselves safely and might do so soon. This, in turn, triggers other deep-seated fears about cloning and human clones. For many religious people, the bare admission that human cloning can be done safely is prideful and presumptuous. For leftists who reject cloning, safe human cloning is a reprehensible triumph of the technological over the natural. Finally, for people who think that human clones are copies, safe human cloning raises the terrifying prospect that anyone, including them, could be duplicated soon – perhaps in multiple versions. It is much more comforting to believe that reprogramming errors are inherent and insoluble.

There is some movement on this scientific front, however, and it comes from a surprising source. Dr. Wilmut and his colleagues strongly oppose human reproductive cloning, but they are interested in cloning human embryos for use in medical experiments and therapies. Unfortunately, epigenetic abnormalities could undermine the validity and utility of such experiments and therapies. For example, epigenetic abnormalities could invalidate experiments designed to identify differences in how people with different genotypes metabolize drugs. Also, although doctors dream of curing their patients with transplanted embryonic stem cells, there is a risk that cells with epigenetic abnormalities could develop into tumors.[92]

In a recent article, these scientists called for a new approach to experiments that would shift the focus from retrospective analysis of cloning failures to the design of prospective, controlled studies that can isolate possible causes of reprogramming errors and identify ways to eliminate them.[93] They noted that clones may suffer from imprinting errors and other epigenetic abnormalities for a variety of reasons and advised researchers to design experiments that can "disentangle" factors such as donor cell type, culture media, embryo manipulation, and nuclear transfer protocols from factors that are specific to nuclear transfer as such.[94]

In sum, scientists who are concerned about reprogramming errors and other abnormalities in cloned embryos are motivated to ferret out the causes and improve the technology through further experimentation. Once scientists learn how to create healthy embryos without epigenetic defects, reproductive cloning will be safer. This is a happy prospect that the media and policymakers seldom convey.

4. The Telomere Scare

The final safety argument brings me back to Dolly. From the time her birth was announced, some critics speculated that she was older than her chronological age.[95] Once again, to explain this charge, I must provide a brief explanation of the relevant biology.

Telomeres are repetitive DNA sequences that protect chromosome tips.[96] As an animal gets older, its telomeres tend to get shorter. Scientists believe this happens because telomeres wear down over the course of repeated cell divisions. At some point, the telomeres shrink to nothing and the cell dies.[97]

Dolly was cloned from nuclear DNA taken from a 6-year-old donor sheep. If Dolly inherited that sheep's shortened telomeres, her lifespan could be shortened, too. She might look like a lamb, but at the DNA level, she would be the equivalent of a 6-year-old sheep.[98]

In 1999, the worst of these fears was seemingly confirmed. Dr. Wilmut and his associates published a letter in *Nature* magazine stating that they had measured Dolly's telomeres and found them to be about 20 percent shorter than those of other sheep her own age.[99] The scientists admitted that this difference could be within the range of natural variation in the telomere lengths of sheep.[100] The scientists did not mention a second weakness in their findings: telomeres are so small that measuring their length is difficult. The difference between the length of Dolly's telomeres and "normal" telomeres was within the range of experimental error.[101]

On the basis of these data, the scientists speculated that Dolly's telomeres were shorter because she had been cloned from a 6-year-old sheep (whose telomeres were already shortened consistent with her age) and also because the donor cells had been cultured for a period of time before cloning.[102] The scientists conceded, however, that they did not know whether the shorter telomeres indicated that Dolly was physiologically older than her chronological age – particularly given that veterinary examinations had confirmed that she was healthy and typical for a sheep of her breed.[103]

Despite the tentative nature of these findings, the media quickly picked up on the most sensationalistic aspects of the research.[104] Most reports emphasized the scary idea that clones were prematurely aged without mentioning the important qualifications that the scientists had placed on their data and its interpretation.[105]

Meanwhile, researchers at Advanced Cell Technology studied the telomeres of several cows that had been cloned from cells that were nearing the end of their life spans. In 2000, they reported that the resulting cattle had telomeres that were significantly longer than those of regular cows of the same age.[106]

In another experiment that same year, Japanese researchers succeeded in the reiterative cloning of mice. In other words, they cloned mouse pups from other cloned mice out to six generations. Their paper, "Cloning of Mice to Six Generations," reported that the mice showed no outward signs of premature aging. Telomeres were not shortened; rather, they had increased slightly in length.[107]

In 2001, Dr. Rudolph Jaenisch reported that telomere length adjustment was faithfully accomplished following nuclear transfer and would not be expected to impair survival of cloned animals.[108]

Policymakers resisted this good news. Although the National Academies admitted that the possibility of shortened telomeres was not a major concern,[109] the California Advisory Committee on Human Cloning asserted that the question of telomere shortening and consequent premature aging remained unresolved on the basis of the Dolly study. The committee acknowledged that scientists had succeeded in the reiterative cloning of mice but did not note that lengthened telomeres and normal behavior had been observed in the mice. Instead, it observed that the reiterative cloning "might suggest that telomere shortening will not be a problem, but the normal lifespan of a mouse is only two years, and the scientists did encounter progressive difficulty in creating clones with each succeeding generation."[110] The committee did not report that lengthened telomeres had also been observed in cloned cattle.[111]

Unfortunately, the charge that Dolly was old beyond her years persisted. When she developed arthritis in her left hip and knee at age 5½ years, many people speculated that cloning was to blame.[112] However, Dr. Wilmut was more cautious. He pointed out that the arthritis could have developed because Dolly stood on her hind legs to greet the many admiring tourists who came to see her.[113] Also, 5½ is relatively old for a sheep; joint disease is sometimes seen in sheep that age.[114]

On February 14, 2003, Dolly was put to sleep at the age of 6 years. At the time, she was suffering from a contagious lung disease that was spreading among the sheep at the Roslin Institute.[115] According to Dr. Wilmut, her illness and death probably had nothing to do with the fact she was a clone. Sheep that live indoors (as Dolly did for security reasons) are prone to developing lung infections of this kind.[116] Nevertheless, many news reports strongly implied that Dolly had died from premature aging by reminding readers about her arthritis and allegedly shortened telomeres.[117]

While the media and policymakers cling to the telomere scare, good news continues to roll in on the scientific front. In 2004, Japanese researchers reported that they had cloned two generations of offspring from a stud bull. Significantly, their data showed that both generations seemed healthy and had normal telomere lengths.[118]

Now that several research teams have demonstrated that telomeres in cloned animals are normal, the telomere scare should be over. However, the way in which the media reported Dolly's death shows that the scare has enormous staying power. Why should there be such a persistent preoccupation with telomeres and premature aging?

Once again, the scientific picture has been distorted by nonscientific concerns. A leading culprit behind the telomere scare is the identity fallacy. The identity fallacy teaches that a clone and DNA donor are, in effect, one and the same. If a news reporter or a policymaker accepts this premise (whether consciously or subconsciously), he or she is more likely to cling to the false belief that the age of the DNA donor must be inherited. Of course, this is false: whether animal or human, a clone is a new individual with a new lifespan that is not determined by the lifespan of the DNA donor.

Another culprit behind the telomere scare is the belief that cloning is a form of scientific hubris that offends God and nature. An animal (or human) born with shortened telomeres and a restricted lifespan would suffer from a physical deformity. Some people may expect cloned animals (and humans) to be deformed in this way because they believe that fallible humans cannot create life from scratch in the same way that God or nature can. (Indeed, it is a sin just to make the attempt.) From this point of view, clones are shoddy work products that are doomed to break down early and disintegrate back into the clay from whence they came. The wages of the sin of pride are shortened telomeres, premature aging, and death.

5. Stereotypes

The problem with safety arguments that are riddled with errors, speculations, or overgeneralizations is that they can have real and continuing consequences for innocent people. This section explains how each argument is based on, or is likely to inspire, harmful stereotypes about human clones.

a) Inefficiency

First, opponents have argued that animal cloning has been inefficient. From this, they argue that human cloning must also be inefficient.

If not overregulated or prohibited, the science of cloning is likely to improve with time, resulting in improved efficiency. Even today, the vast majority of failures in animal cloning occur at a very early embryonic stage; moreover, later miscarriages, birth defects, and deaths associated with LOS probably will never occur in humans. Given the way the science has been reported, however, the public has been conditioned to believe that every healthy human birth will come at the expense of countless miscarriages, birth defects, and dead newborns and mothers. This is an objection to cloning technology as such. Although the public cannot hold human clones responsible for initiating the use of the technology, it may perceive them as having survived at the expense of others or their own mothers. This perception would associate human clones with danger, violence, and even homicide.

It is particularly unfortunate that so little of the cloning debate has been devoted to better educating the public on the harsh realities of sexual reproduction.[119] Policymaking reports do sometimes compare asexual reproduction with sexual reproduction – usually for the purpose of demonstrating that asexual reproduction is currently *more* inefficient and dangerous.[120] What the reports *should* emphasize, however, is that this difference remains one of degree and not of kind.

In sexual reproduction, many are called, but few are chosen. Not every release of eggs and sperm results in fertilization, and not every embryo implants successfully in the uterus. Even when embryos implant and grow, many miscarry. Thus, as noted in Section 1 of this chapter, up to 75 percent of human embryos conceived through sexual intercourse never make it to birth.[121]

Some fetal deaths occur late in pregnancy. The National Center for Health Statistics reported that, in the year 2000, for every 1,000 live births, 6 fetuses died after 20 or more weeks of gestation and 3 fetuses died after 28 or more weeks of gestation.[122] These statistics, however, understate these late-term losses significantly, for not all fetal deaths are reported – even when the law so requires. For example, a study of one chain of hospitals in California found that only 10 percent of deaths at 20 to 27 weeks were reported, whereas 79 percent of deaths at more than 28 weeks were reported.[123]

Birth does not guarantee survival or good health. Again, in the year 2000, approximately 7 infants under 1 year of age died for every 1,000 live births in the United States.[124] The average rate of serious birth defects ranges from 4 to 12 percent (the higher end of this range applies when a baby is born to a mother over the age of 40).[125] But this is just an average. The rate can rise to 25 percent when both parents carry a gene for an autosomal recessive disorder, like cystic fibrosis, or 50 percent if even one parent carries a gene for an autosomal dominant disorder like Huntington's disease.[126] Furthermore, the average rate only incorporates defects that are diagnosed and reported. Defects that are not discovered or diagnosed until adulthood (for example, infertility) are left out.

Women who engage in sexual reproduction risk their health and their lives. One hundred years ago in the United States, for every 1,000 live births, 6 to 9 women died of pregnancy-related complications.[127] Today, that rate has been cut significantly, but deaths do occur. In 1997, death certificates alone documented 327 maternal deaths in the United States; however, experts believe that the actual numbers are two to three times higher.[128] Leading causes of maternal death include hemorrhage (bleeding to death), pregnancy-induced hypertension (toxemia), and embolism.[129]

In short, everything that could go wrong with asexual reproduction already goes wrong with sexual reproduction. All of us alive today are the survivors of a bloody and inefficient process that has left many embryos, fetuses, newborns, and mothers injured or dead; we just do not think of ourselves and the process that way.

In this context, the novel *Frankenstein* once again is relevant. As discussed in Chapter 1, the novel is often interpreted as a warning to scientists not to play God. Less often noted is the connection between Mary Shelley's own bad experience with sexual reproduction and the inspiration for her book. When Shelley was only 17 years old, she gave premature birth to an illegitimate daughter who died after only 2 weeks. After the death, Shelley was depressed; she had nightmares in which she rubbed the baby and it came back to life.[130] Fifteen months later, she imagined a scientist reanimating a corpse; this vision became the kernel of her novel.[131] One expert on Shelley and her works has theorized that the novel expresses the anxieties women feel about their pregnancies.[132]

b) Large Offspring Syndrome

Second, consider the charge that cloning leads to LOS. There are good reasons to believe that LOS will not affect human clones. Nevertheless, media and policymaker reports have primed the public to anticipate the birth of oversized, grotesque, and deformed babies.

This is a statement about the traits of human clones, and it is advanced as a reason they should not exist. This stereotype could be exacerbated by the analogies that the media and policymakers constantly draw between cloning and the novel *Frankenstein*, for the "creature" in that book was also oversized (8 feet tall) and grotesque in appearance.

c) Reprogramming

Third, consider the argument that human cloning cannot be permitted because *all* animal clones are flawed at the epigenetic level. This argument prejudges the health of human clones. It overlooks the fact that many cloned animals are healthy and normal and encourages the public to believe that every human clone will have health problems.

This stereotype can have serious consequences for human clones. It could unfairly compromise their contractual relationships. Employers may deny employment; life and health insurers may deny insurance. Moreover, the stereotype may compromise social relationships.

Although epigenetic defects are not contagious or heritable, if human clones are associated with illness, birth defects, or death, many people will ostracize them out of fear of contamination.[133] Potential sexual, marital, and reproductive partners may veer away from persons that they imagine to be the carriers of heritable defects.[134] This is particularly unfortunate given that the offspring of cloned animals have proven to be fertile and normal.[135] Because those who associate with disabled individuals are themselves stigmatized, human clones may find it hard even to make friends.[136]

Again, it is ironic that many people who are born through sexual reproduction find this argument compelling when their own genetic and epigenetic health is unknown and far from guaranteed. All humans, and not only those born through cloning, face the risk that health problems may crop up later in life. Indeed, because reproductive cloning will draw on the existing genomes of humans who have survived to adulthood, the risk of unforeseen genetic problems ultimately may prove to be greater for humans whose chromosomes are produced through the random chance of sexual reproduction. As for epigenetic problems, to paraphrase Dr. Jaenisch's testimony before Congress, one could say that any of the 30,000 genes in a human conceived through sexual reproduction could also be a target for unpredictable errors in gene expression.

d) Telomeres

Finally, consider the charge that animal clones have shortened telomeres. Although this charge is untrue, opponents assert it as yet another reason human clones should not exist.

At a minimum, this stereotype teaches that human clones are aged and decrepit. Moreover, the idea that a young person is, in fact, very old, may cause the public to develop related stereotypes that extend far beyond physical deformity. To illustrate, suppose I show you a photograph of a pretty 16-year-old girl and tell you that she is functionally the age-equivalent of a 50-year-old woman. What emotions do I provoke in you? Perhaps you shudder in revulsion at the girl's hidden age, for aging can be associated with death. Perhaps you experience the girl, who is not what she appears to be, as a fraud. Note the resulting associations: human clones are grotesque, deceitful, or both.

6. The Dangers of Excessive Caution

To some readers, the fact that some scientists, the media, and poli-cymakers have done all they can to accentuate the safety hazards of cloning may seem unremarkable and even commendable. Given the risks, it may seem that it pays to err on the side of caution – at least for now. After all, can we not count on science to set the record straight eventually? Surely, experiments will continue. Time will deter-mine which safety theories are correct and which are not.

Every public policy, however, including caution, has its dangers. In this book, I have argued that the safety arguments unfairly stereotype an entire category of human being. This is a significant cost that deserves to be recognized in the cloning debate.

Moreover, it is naïve to believe that we can count on science to set the record straight and debunk the stereotypes. For one thing, some the-ories may not be accurate and yet may be inherently hard to disprove. The hypothesis that cloned animals are flawed at the epigenetic level cleverly asserts its own defense: even if scientists measure the physi-cal attributes of cloned animals and find them to be normal, the mea-surements cannot disprove the hypothesis because epigenetic flaws are difficult to detect and may not produce negative effects for years.

For another thing, most people are not scientists and do not grasp the distinction between hypothesis and scientific fact. Thus, if the me-dia or policymakers embrace certain scientific theories prematurely, or present those theories one-sidedly, it may become difficult to dislodge those theories from the imagination of the public later on. For example, people continue to believe that cloning produces prematurely aged an-imals despite scientific evidence to the contrary. This belief may linger because most people are not educated or interested in science and pay attention only to the most widely reported and sensationalistic science stories. Or, perhaps the belief lingers because premature aging is con-sistent with other notions such as the idea that cloning is a sin of pride destined to produce shoddy products or that a clone is a duplicate that continues the lifespan of the original animal. In either case, the end re-sult is that, even after scientific theories are proven wrong, they may live on for years, decades, or even centuries in the public mind.

Finally, there is no guarantee that scientists in the United States will have the freedom they need to conduct the experiments that *could* set the record straight. As Part 2 explains, exaggerated safety arguments have been used to justify the enactment of flat bans on human cloning (including research cloning). These laws threaten to stop the very research that is necessary to find out what the truth is. If we enact inflexible laws today, we will reap what we sow tomorrow in the form of scientific ignorance, and the perpetuation of harmful stereotypes about the health of human clones.

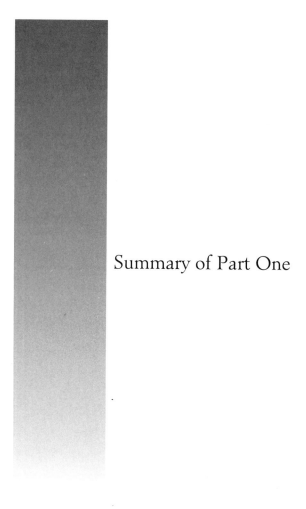

Summary of Part One

Part 1 of this book documented five objections to human reproductive cloning and subjected them to critical analysis. What this analysis revealed is the fundamental weakness of those objections. Some objections are religious or moral arguments that, by definition, cannot be proven. Other objections are susceptible of proof, but cloning opponents have put forward little or no social, psychological, or scientific evidence to support them. Many of the arguments are rooted in a single, gross scientific error, namely, the false notion that human clones are copies of their DNA donors. Even safety concerns have been greatly overstated; with time, as cloning technology improves, they may disappear altogether.

In Parts 2 and 3, I will return to this critique of the five objections, and use it to explain why anticloning laws not only are bad public policy but also are unconstitutional.

Part 1 has also shown how the five objections reflect, reinforce, and inspire stereotypes about human clones. I am now in a position to provide a concise summary of those stereotypes.

First, the warning that cloning offends God is an objection to hubris rather than to a particular type of human. However, the objection encourages the religious right to believe that human clones are evil. Similarly, the related objection that cloning is unnatural encourages the environmentalist left to conclude that human clones are unnatural, abnormal, strange, artificial, and inferior. Frequent references to *Frankenstein* and its warning against scientific meddling with nature imply that human clones are grotesque, immoral, and dangerous.

Second, the objection that cloning treats humans as if they were manufactured products is an objection to cloning technology and its practitioners rather than to human clones as such. When argued loosely (as it frequently is), however, this second objection quickly shades into an argument that human clones *are* manufactured products. This, in turn, encourages the false belief that human clones are soulless, inert, unfeeling, and inferior.

Third, the objection that human clones are copies is a direct protest against their existence based on their presumed traits. The identity fallacy leads to other stereotypes about human clones, who will be perceived as evil, unoriginal, fraudulent, inferior, zombielike, constrained, pathetic, disturbed, disgusting, identity thieves, destroyers, a threat to democratic values, and subhuman.

Fourth, it is argued that human clones will cause overpopulation, diminish genetic diversity, and facilitate programs of eugenics or genetic engineering. To the extent these doomsday arguments are rooted in the identity fallacy, they are based on the stereotype that human clones are copies. But that is not all; the doomsday arguments also imply that human clones are multitudinous, rapacious, dirty, diseased, dangerous, criminal, superior, arrogant, unfair, and capable of destroying humanity.

Fifth, some argue that human clones should not be born because they would be grotesquely oversized, deformed, flawed at the epigenetic level, and prematurely old. These, too, are stereotypes. Because some of these defects would not be apparent to the naked eye, the safety objection also implies that human clones are deceitful.

Cloning opponents also emphasize the inefficiency of reproductive cloning. False and dated information associates human clones with danger, violence, and the destruction of others.

Part 2 will explain how anticloning laws validate these untrue and unfair stereotypes, thereby injuring human clones. Before taking on that task, however, I must first explain what the laws say and do and trace their origins to the five objections.

ANTICLONING LAWS ARE BAD
PUBLIC POLICY

In Part 2 of this book, the focus shifts from human reproductive cloning to *laws* against human reproductive cloning.

Chapter 6 addresses laws against cloning that have been proposed, applied, and enacted in the United States, and Chapter 7 demonstrates how the laws are based on the five objections.

Chapter 8 explains that laws against cloning do more than ban an unpopular technology. The laws are intended to ensure that an unpopular class of humans never comes into existence. Reasoning by analogy to antimiscegenation laws, which once banned interracial marriages as a means of avoiding the birth of mixed-race children, I explain how laws against cloning implement a policy of existential segregation against human clones.

Chapter 9 presents an analysis of the costs and benefits of laws against cloning. The discussion begins with costs and emphasizes those that human clones are likely to bear. Next, drawing upon my critique of the five objections, I examine purported benefits and find that they are not substantial enough to justify the laws. I therefore conclude that the laws are bad public policy.

CHAPTER SIX

What Anticloning Laws Say and Do

The United States does not yet have a national law against human reproductive cloning. However, several bills have been introduced in Congress, and the Food and Drug Administration (FDA) has applied some general regulatory laws to prevent human reproductive cloning – at least for now. Meanwhile, many states have enacted laws that make human reproductive cloning a crime or civil offense.

This chapter discusses these bills, regulatory actions, and state laws and explains how these anticloning laws[1] could be enforced – not just against scientists and doctors but also against parents who want to have a child to raise and love.[2]

1. Federal Bills

a) Efforts to Ban All Cloning

In 2001, during the 107th Congress, Representative Dave Weldon (R-Fla.) introduced a bill known as H.R. 2505. The bill would have criminalized both research and reproductive cloning. H.R. 2505 passed the House of Representatives by an overwhelming margin of 263–162.[3] However, this early effort to impose a total ban failed because some senators did not want to ban research cloning.[4]

In 2003, as soon as the 108th Congress began, Representative Weldon introduced a nearly identical bill, and the entire debate began over again. The 2003 Weldon bill made it unlawful for any person knowingly to perform, attempt to perform, participate, or attempt to participate in human cloning within the United States. "Human cloning" was defined as human asexual reproduction accomplished by introducing nuclear material from a human somatic cell into an egg "so as to produce a living organism (at any stage of development) that is genetically virtually identical to an existing or previously existing human organism."[5] This broad definition criminalized research as well as reproductive cloning.

The 2003 Weldon bill was not consumer protection legislation designed to protect patients against exploitation by arrogant scientists or maverick doctors. Its ban on performing or participating in cloning applied to "any person," including parents.

For those who think I am exaggerating, I offer the following vignette. On July 24, 2001, the Committee on the Judiciary for the House of Representatives held a business meeting on H.R. 2505, a nearly identical bill that preceded the 2003 Weldon bill.[6] Representative Robert Scott (D-Virginia) offered an amendment he termed the "Family Preservation Exemption." The Scott amendment provided that the law would not apply to a woman who received a cloned embryo into her uterus with the intention to initiate a pregnancy. In support of the amendment, Representative Scott stated, "I would hope that we would not jail and fine women who are trying to get pregnant."[7] Speaking against the amendment, Representative Lamar Smith (R-Tex.) retorted, "Although this amendment may appear benign at first glance, it serves to protect women who knowingly participate in the unethical experimentation on a child to be."[8] The amendment failed on a voice vote,[9] indicating that most members of that committee were perfectly willing to throw infertile women in prison if they attempted to overcome their medical disability through reproductive cloning.

The 2003 Weldon bill was draconian in yet another respect: its reach was not limited to actions taken within the United States. The bill made it unlawful for any person knowingly and for any purpose to import an embryo[10] produced by human cloning or any "product" derived from such an embryo.[11] This provision closed a loophole in the general ban by making it a crime to engage in research or reproductive cloning abroad and then bring the "product" home. For example, a scientist could not travel to Britain, where research cloning is legal, create cloned embryos there, and bring the embryos home for research in the United States. Nor could a patient travel to Britain, commission the creation of a stem cell therapy based on his or her own nuclear DNA, and then bring the "product" of cloned embryos, that is, the therapy, back to the United States for use in his or her medical treatment. Most radical of all, the 2003 Weldon bill also made it unlawful for a woman who traveled to an offshore cloning clinic and got pregnant there to return to the United States with the "product" of a cloned embryo, that is, a fetus or baby.[12]

Finally, the 2003 Weldon bill imposed severe penalties. Anyone who violated its provisions, including a parent, could be sent to prison for 10 years, subjected to fines under Title 18 of the U.S. Code, or both. In addition, anyone who made money from the violation (as a fertility doctor might) faced civil fines of one million dollars or twice the amount of money he or she made, whichever was greater.[13]

One might expect that such a radical bill would die a quiet death in committee. On the contrary, on February 27, 2003, the House of Representatives enthusiastically passed the 2003 Weldon bill by a lopsided vote of 249–155.[14]

Only one obstacle remained: the Senate also had to pass a total ban. Senator Sam Brownback (R-Kans.) introduced a companion bill in the Senate,[15] but it was not enacted. This failure did not reflect support for reproductive cloning; rather, some senators wanted to preserve the right of scientists to engage in research cloning.

As this book went to press, supporters of a total ban introduced new anticloning bills in the House (H.R. 1357) and Senate (S. 658) on

17 March 2005. The new proposals mirror the provisions of the 2003 Weldon bill.

What might happen if Congress enacts a law like the 2003 Weldon bill?

Suppose that an infertile man and his wife live in the United States and decide to have a baby through cloning. If the man contributes the nuclear DNA for the procedure and the wife contributes an egg and gestates the baby, both have participated in cloning and are guilty of a crime. If the wife is the infertile one and she obtains an egg from a donor and uses her own nuclear DNA and womb to conceive and carry a cloned child, her husband can be prosecuted as a person who aided and abetted her crime. As such, he is punishable as a principal, that is, he serves the same sentence as if he had committed the crime himself.[16] Also, both he and his wife can be prosecuted for conspiracy. The two of them plotted to clone (together with any scientist or doctor who may have assisted them); beyond that, all the law of conspiracy requires is that at least one of them had taken one step toward that impermissible goal. Conspiracy is a separate crime that carries a separate, 5-year prison sentence.[17]

Can the couple escape this outcome by traveling to a Caribbean island nation where cloning is legal and undergoing treatment at a clinic there? If they try to reenter the United States with a cloned pregnancy or child, they can be charged with the crime of importing a "product" of cloning. Both can also be charged with conspiracy to import a product of cloning.

b) Efforts to Ban Reproductive Cloning Only

Some representatives and senators have pursued what they imagine to be a more moderate approach: enactment of a federal law that would ban reproductive cloning only.

For example, Senator Orrin Hatch (R-Utah) introduced a bill during the 108th Congress. The 2003 Hatch bill did not prohibit nuclear transplantation. However, the bill did make it unlawful for any person to conduct "human cloning," which was defined narrowly as implanting the product of nuclear transplantation into a uterus or the functional equivalent of a uterus.[18] The upshot was that scientists could clone human embryos for research but would face jail time if they implanted the embryos and gave them a chance at life.

Like the 2003 Weldon bill, the 2003 Hatch bill was not consumer protection legislation. By proclaiming that it was unlawful for "any person" to conduct human cloning, the bill applied not only to scientists and doctors but also the parents of a cloned child.

The penalties of the 2003 Hatch bill were severe. Violators were subject to 10-year prison sentences and fines. They also faced civil penalties of one million dollars or, if pecuniary gain resulted from the violation, three times the gross pecuniary gain, whichever was greater. Real or personal property derived from or used to commit a violation was subject to forfeiture.[19]

The 2003 Hatch bill was never put to a vote in the Senate and was not enacted into law during the 108th Congress. The reason for its failure was clear: many representatives and senators believe that the destruction of human embryos is tantamount to murder. From their point of view, any law that permits embryos to be cloned for research but makes it a crime to introduce those embryos into the womb is an immoral "clone then kill" law. President George W. Bush embraces this latter view and has stated in the past that he would veto a law banning reproductive cloning but permitting research cloning.[20]

Advocates of research cloning have not given up the fight. On 21 April 2005, they introduced a new bill against reproductive cloning (S. 876) that replicates the Match bill.

What might happen if Congress enacts a law like the 2003 Hatch bill?

Suppose a lesbian and her life partner live in the United States. They desire to have children without involving the DNA of strangers. The first woman donates the nuclear DNA for cloning and her partner provides the egg. Using the DNA and egg, a doctor creates a cloned embryo and transfers it to the womb of the partner.

Is the doctor guilty of "implanting the product of nuclear transplantation into a uterus"? From a scientific perspective, the embryo "implants" itself into the uterus, but because an embryo cannot be charged with a crime, lawmakers must intend that the language be interpreted broadly enough to cover what the doctor did.

Arguably, that broad interpretation also covers the conduct of the woman who received the embryo into her womb. If so, she faces a 10-year prison sentence and fines, a civil penalty of one million dollars, and the loss of any real or personal property used to commit the violation (for example, a house in which the embryo transfer took place).

Under the law of aiding and abetting, the DNA donor is punishable as a principal because she helped the embryo recipient commit the crime. She, too, faces a 10-year prison sentence.

Even if the embryo recipient did not "implant" the embryo, both she and the DNA donor helped the doctor and thus can be punished as principals. In addition, both women can be prosecuted as co-conspirators who helped to plot the cloning and took at least one step toward that impermissible goal.

c) The Commerce Clause

On the assumption Congress does enact a ban on reproductive cloning, there is one more point that deserves mention here. Congress does not have unlimited authority to legislate; it must act pursuant to a constitutional grant of authority. Although some legal scholars believe that Congress can ban cloning pursuant to its authority to regulate interstate commerce,[21] the Supreme Court has limited the reach of the Commerce Clause in recent years. In *United States v. Morrison*, the Court held that Congress had exceeded its authority in enacting a federal civil remedy for the victims of gender-motivated violence.[22] Congress could regulate intrastate activities that had substantial effects on interstate commerce, but only when those activities were economic in nature.[23] The Court refused to hold that Congress could regulate noneconomic, violent criminal conduct based solely on its cumulative effect on interstate commerce.[24] Otherwise, Congress could regulate any activity that might have some impact on the economic productivity of individual citizens, including matters traditionally subject to state authority such as crime, education, and family relations.[25]

Thus, under *Morrison*, the question is whether reproductive cloning is a commercial or economic activity. Some argue that cloning deserves to be recognized as commercial because it is a service that scientists and doctors will provide in exchange for money.[26] This, however, is not necessarily true. Scientists or doctors might provide cloning for free to advance their research interests[27] or ideological agendas. Moreover, prospective parents with friends or relatives who have medical training and laboratory access will be able to "do it themselves." Thus, although cloning involves the use of technology, it is not inherently commercial any more than sexual reproduction is. For individuals who cannot reproduce effectively or safely through sexual intercourse, cloning is simply an alternative means of having a child. It is asexual reproduction.

Congressional attempts to ban reproductive cloning have been consistent with this latter view. The 2003 Weldon bill defined human cloning as human asexual reproduction.[28] Both it and the 2003 Hatch bill banned human reproductive cloning outright. These bills did not seek to regulate providers of medical services; they made it a crime for anyone, including parents, to engage in cloning for any reason whether fees were charged or not and whether state lines were crossed or not. Moreover, the underlying policy rationales for these proposed laws, as reflected in the five objections,[29] had nothing to do with commerce.[30]

Cloning opponents might argue that, whether reproductive cloning is inherently commercial or not, the use of the technology is likely to have substantial effects on commerce, for clinics must purchase equipment and supplies, and doctors, employees, and patients will sometimes travel.[31] This argument, however, ignores the teachings of *Morrison*. Sexual reproduction could also have substantial effects on interstate commerce; men and women purchase beds, sheets, blankets, and pillows and sometimes use cars, taxis, buses, trains, and planes to reach each other. It does not follow that Congress has the authority to regulate sexual reproduction under the Commerce Clause. Similarly, the cumulative effects of reproductive cloning do not justify the exercise of Congressional authority over that means of reproduction.

Morrison also teaches that the Supreme Court is more likely to object when Congress tries to regulate areas traditionally subject to state regulation such as crime, education, or family relations. Interestingly, sexual reproduction is not an area that the states regulate extensively in part because there is a constitutional right to privacy that protects reproductive decisions from governmental interference. As explained in Chapter 9, the states probably cannot regulate asexual reproduction either[32]; however, on the assumption that they can, if one believes in basic principles of federalism, it makes sense to leave moral decisions about cloning to the states.[33]

In sum, Congress might not have the authority to regulate reproductive cloning under the Commerce Clause. One possible solution is to do what Representative Weldon did and draft a bill that includes an express jurisdictional element restricting application to persons or entities "in or affecting interstate commerce."[34] This strategy has its limitations. An express jurisdictional element could save a federal anticloning law from outright invalidation,[35] but, at the same time, the element would restrict the scope of the law and permit a great deal of reproductive cloning to go forward without any regulation.

2. FDA

Although Congress has not yet enacted a federal law directed specifically at cloning, the FDA has stepped in to fill the regulatory gap.

Several months after Dolly's birth was announced, an eccentric physicist named Richard Seed announced his intention to clone a human being.[36] Even though Dr. Seed was not a fertility doctor or expert in biotechnology, and even though he lacked any affiliation with a university or research laboratory, the media showered him with attention.[37] In January 1998, FDA Commissioner Michael Friedman responded by asserting that the FDA had the authority to regulate human reproductive cloning pursuant to the Federal Food, Drug, and Cosmetic Act.[38] According to Commissioner Friedman, a scientist like Dr. Seed who wanted to attempt human reproductive cloning would have to file an investigational new drug (IND) application with the agency and await its approval to proceed. Commissioner Friedman threatened legal action against anyone who attempted to clone without first obtaining the FDA's approval.[39]

Several months later, in October 1998, the FDA sent a "Dear Colleague" letter to the institutional review boards of America's medical and research institutions.[40] The letter reiterated that the agency had authority to regulate human reproductive cloning pursuant to the Public Health Service Act and the Federal Food, Drug, and Cosmetic Act.[41] It also stated that anyone pursuing clinical research using cloning technology to create a human being must submit an IND application.[42] However, in the next breath, the FDA made it clear that submitting an application would be a waste of time. "Since FDA believes that there are major unresolved safety questions pertaining to the use of cloning technology to create a human being, until those questions are appropriately addressed in the IND, FDA would not permit any such investigation to proceed."[43] Readers of the vaguely worded letter were left to wonder whether the agency sought to regulate only clinical trials designed to lead to live births, or, more broadly, any research intended to advance the science of human reproductive cloning, including preliminary experiments with embryos.[44]

Three years later, on 28 March 2001, Dr. Kathryn C. Zoon testified on behalf of the FDA before Congress. She asserted that "[t]he use of cloning technology to clone a human being would be subject to both the biologics provisions of the Public Health Service (PHS) Act and the drug and device provisions of the Federal Food, Drug, and Cosmetic (FD&C) Act."[45] She attempted to reassure Congress that the FDA would stop human reproductive cloning: "Because of the unresolved safety questions pertaining to the use of cloning technology to clone a human being, FDA would not permit any such investigation to proceed at this time."[46] Thus, the FDA argued that it had the authority to regulate human reproductive cloning attempts but slammed the door by asserting that it would not approve any such attempts.

About the same time, Dr. Zoon sent a second letter to scientific organizations and their members reminding them that the FDA asserted jurisdiction over clinical research using cloning technology to clone a human being. The letter again asserted that, owing to major unresolved safety questions, the FDA would not permit cloning to proceed.[47]

The FDA took stronger action against two scientists in the United States who had asserted their plans to clone humans: Dr. Panayiotis Zavos, a fertility doctor, and Dr. Brigitte Boisselier, a member of the Raelian religious sect. Both received a letter warning them that failure to comply with FDA regulatory requirements could lead to enforcement action.[48] A federal grand jury in Syracuse, New York, initiated an investigation into the cloning activities of the Raelian sect, and FDA agents visited Dr. Boisselier's laboratory and ordered a halt to any human cloning experiments. Dr. Boisselier responded by moving her cloning efforts offshore.[49] Dr. Zavos is also conducting his research offshore.[50]

Thus, the FDA's regulatory program to date has consisted of several intimidating steps: first, the issuance of strong public statements asserting the authority to regulate cloning and threatening legal action against scofflaws; second, the en masse dispatch of letters to scientists and researchers who might be in a position to clone explaining how to apply for permission to clone while indicating that permission will be refused; and third, agent visits to at least one laboratory and a grand jury investigation.

The FDA's regulatory program seems to have stopped cloning efforts in the United States, or, at least, driven them entirely underground. This is true even though most violations of the relevant provisions of the Federal Food, Drug, and Cosmetic Act and the Public Health Service Act seem to be misdemeanors and are subject to relatively short prison sentences and low civil fines.[51] Of course, even 1 year in federal prison is 365 days too many for most people, and the expense of defending oneself throughout the grind of criminal investigation, indictment, trial, and sentencing is high enough to make it cost-effective to move operations offshore.

Researchers could follow the designated path and submit an IND application to the FDA requesting its approval for experiments in cloning humans. However, there have been no reports of any such application.[52] This, too, is not surprising because the agency has already said it will reject such applications.

So far, the FDA has limited its enforcement efforts to doctors and other individuals who have announced their plans to help parents produce babies. This should not be taken to imply that parents are exempt from liability. If the FDA believes a scientist has cloned in violation of the laws that fall within its jurisdiction, it could choose to prosecute the parents who commissioned the cloning on the ground that they aided or abetted the crime and are punishable as principals.[53] Alternatively, or in addition, the FDA could prosecute the parents for the separate crime of conspiring to commit a federal offense (though the penalty for conspiring to commit a misdemeanor cannot exceed the maximum provided for the misdemeanor).[54]

The FDA's assertion of authority over human reproductive cloning has attracted much criticism. Politicians have questioned the wisdom of treating human embryos as "drugs" subject to federal regulation.[55] Lawyers have gone further, arguing that the FDA simply does not have the statutory authority to regulate human embryos as "drugs," "devices," or "biological products."[56] Moreover, given that the FDA had never sought to regulate human embryos before,[57] its assertion of authority over human reproductive cloning significantly extended its jurisdiction and altered the legal environment for cloning research.[58] Yet, the FDA did not issue a new federal regulation or substantive rule, nor did it comply with the procedural requirements (including prior notice and public comment) that the Administrative Procedure Act imposes on administrative lawmaking.[59]

Thus far, there have not been any lawsuits challenging the FDA's statutory authority to regulate cloning or the questionable manner in which the FDA has chosen to assert its authority – if it exists.[60]

Even if a federal court upheld what the FDA has done, the agency's ability to stop cloning would be limited. Its regulatory authority is limited to the United States; it has no authority to control what happens offshore. Moreover, the agency has admitted that its jurisdiction extends to scientific concerns, not moral or ethical ones.[61] During her testimony before Congress, Dr. Zoon admitted that the FDA could not and would not attempt to prevent a human cloning experiment that had been shown to be safe for the child and gestational mother.[62] This means that, over the years, as technology improves, the FDA's ability to control reproductive cloning will become weaker and weaker until it finally fails altogether.

3. State Laws

Many states already have enacted laws prohibiting human reproductive cloning. Although I cite every state law in this section, I do not discuss them all in detail. Rather, I have devoted the bulk of the discussion to a few laws that are particularly illustrative and interesting.

Like Congress, state legislatures have struggled to achieve a consensus on the morality of research cloning. This struggle has produced a split between states that ban all cloning and states that ban reproductive cloning only.

Let us begin with states that have enacted comprehensive bans. At the time this book went to press, states with bans in place[63] included Arkansas,[64] Iowa,[65] Michigan,[66] North Dakota,[67] and South Dakota.[68]

Michigan was one of the first states to ban cloning. As such, its laws are worthy of special mention. The basic prohibition is disarmingly simple: an individual shall not intentionally engage in, or attempt to engage in, human cloning.[69] "Human cloning" is broadly defined as the use of human somatic cell nuclear transfer technology to produce a human embryo.[70] Thus, potential violators include not only fertility doctors and their patients but also scientists who want to make, study, and harvest stem cells from cloned embryos. Human cloning is a felony punishable by imprisonment for up to 10 years, a 10 million dollar fine, or both.[71] In addition, doctors and other health professionals who engage in human cloning can have their licenses revoked[72] and are subject to a civil penalty of 10 million dollars.[73]

The Arkansas, Iowa, North Dakota, and South Dakota laws are similar (but not identical) to the 2003 Weldon bill. For example, Arkansas makes it a crime to perform, attempt to perform, or participate in an attempt to perform human cloning.[74] "Human cloning" is defined as human asexual reproduction accomplished by introducing the genetic material from one or more human somatic cells into an enucleated egg[75] so as to produce a living organism at any stage of development that is genetically virtually identical to an existing or previously existing human organism.[76] Violators are guilty of a felony and are subject to a minimum fine of $250,000 or twice the amount of any pecuniary gain, whichever is greater.[77]

Many other states have banned reproductive cloning but not research cloning. At the time this book went to press, these states included California,[78] New Jersey,[79] Rhode Island,[80] and Virginia.[81]

In 1997, California became the first state in the nation to enact anticloning legislation. Its 5-year moratorium on human reproductive cloning was set to expire on 1 January 2003, unless extended.[82] In late 2002, the California State Legislature declared that it was state policy to permit research cloning.[83] In the same session, it enacted a law that eliminated the sunset provision and transformed the moratorium into a flat ban on reproductive cloning.[84] As discussed in Part 1 of this book, this action was consistent with the recommendation of the California Advisory Committee on Human Cloning.

Thus, in California, "no person shall clone a human being or engage in human reproductive cloning."[85] California law defines "clone" narrowly as the practice of creating or attempting to create a human being by transferring the nucleus from a human cell into a human or nonhuman egg cell from which the nucleus has been removed for the purpose of, or to implant, the resulting product to initiate a pregnancy that could result in the birth of a human being.[86] The law limits "human reproductive cloning" to the creation of a human fetus that is substantially genetically identical to a previously born human being.[87] California does not impose criminal penalties on violators, but civil penalties are steep: corporations, firms, clinics, hospitals, laboratories, or research facilities can be fined one million dollars; individuals (such as fertility doctors and their patients) can be fined $250,000.[88] If the violation resulted in pecuniary gain, the penalty is increased to twice the amount of the gain.[89] Medical professionals who violate the law are guilty of unprofessional conduct[90] and can have their business licenses revoked.[91]

New Jersey offers another example of proresearch and antireproductive cloning zeal. In 2003, its legislature enacted a law declaring it is the public policy of New Jersey to permit research involving the derivation and use of human embryonic stem cells from any source, including somatic cell nuclear transplantation (i.e., research cloning).[92] At the same time, the legislature made it a crime of the first degree (punishable by up to 20 years in prison) for a person knowingly to engage or assist, directly or indirectly, in the cloning of a human being.[93] The law defines "cloning of a human being" as the replication of a human individual by cultivating a cell with genetic material through the egg, embryo, fetal, and newborn stages into a new human individual.[94] Prolife critics have complained that this is an aggressive "clone then kill" law that permits researchers to create and destroy cloned human life up to the very moment of birth.

In sum, nine states have produced nine laws so far. The laws tend to fall into one of two categories: either they ban all cloning, or ban reproductive cloning only.

More and more states can be expected to enact laws against human reproductive cloning. (Credible reports of human births would be sure to accelerate this trend.) Unless Congress acts decisively and relieves state legislatures from political pressure, all 50 states eventually could ban reproductive cloning. This would amount to a national ban but with some interesting glitches. There may be a few cases that fall between the cracks of a patchwork of anticloning laws. For example, as just noted, New Jersey makes it a crime for a person knowingly to clone a human being but defines the crime as the replication of a human individual by cultivating a cell with genetic material through the egg, embryo, fetal, and newborn stages into a new human individual.[95] Now, suppose that a scientist creates a cloned embryo in New Jersey knowing that his or her patient plans to take it to Michigan and transfer it to her uterus there. There might not be a crime in New Jersey because the crime of cloning seems to presuppose a completed biological process and no child was born in New Jersey. There is no crime in Michigan either because that state only outlaws the creation of cloned embryos and not their transfer into a uterus.[96] Of course, prosecutors and courts might construe the New Jersey statute to reach the conduct of the scientist and the patient – perhaps by reasoning that their initial steps taken in New Jersey had "assisted" in the cloning of a human.

4. Possible Legal Futures

The discussion in this chapter suggests that at least three legal futures are possible.

First, Congress could enact a federal ban on human reproductive cloning. Despite philosophical divisions and recent legislative failures, I think this outcome is likely for two reasons. First, many countries have already enacted legislation against reproductive cloning. The United States finds itself in the embarrassing position of having no national policy and has come under increasing political pressure to develop one. Second, the membership of Congress is not static. Sooner or later, one side or the other in this determined struggle will gain the upper hand in an election and have enough members to ram through a new federal law. No matter which side prevails, the law will ban reproductive cloning at a minimum.

Federal legislation would create a uniform ban across the entire nation. The legislation might explicitly preempt state laws; otherwise, state anticloning laws would continue to provide an additional arsenal of penalties that state prosecutors could persist in enforcing independently.

Second, if Congress remained deadlocked, the FDA could continue to apply existing regulatory laws to stop human reproductive cloning. This would operate as a national ban until and unless someone sued the FDA and obtained a court ruling that the agency lacked the statutory authority to regulate cloning in general or that the agency lacked the statutory authority to regulate cloning because it had been proven safe. In the meantime, states would also continue to enact and enforce their anticloning laws.

Third, if Congress and the FDA were inactive or ineffective, state anticloning laws would become the sole vehicle for controlling the technology and its "products." All 50 states could eventually enact a ban on cloning with a prohibition on reproductive cloning likely to emerge as a bare national minimum.

None of these futures necessarily involves an *effective* ban on human reproductive cloning. There are always some people who violate any law, no matter what the penalties, because they are strongly motivated to engage in the prohibited activity, do not expect to get caught or punished, or both. In the case of cloning, in which the prize is a much desired baby, the motivation to defy the law will be particularly strong. Moreover, parents have an even better alternative: they can travel abroad, get pregnant, and quietly bring their cloned pregnancies and babies back into this country. The FDA has no authority to regulate or prohibit such activities. To close this loophole, Congress would have to enact a law (like the 2003 Weldon bill) that made it a crime to bring the "product" of human cloning into the country.[97]

CHAPTER SEVEN

The Five Objections Have Inspired
Anticloning Laws

What could have inspired the draconian anticloning laws discussed in Chapter 6? This chapter documents the influence of the five objections on federal and state legislators and regulators.

1. Federal Law

I begin with federal law. As explained in Chapter 6, the Food and Drug Administration (FDA) claims that it has the authority to stop human reproductive cloning in the United States. Human reproductive cloning also faces strong opposition in both houses of Congress. Efforts to ban human reproductive cloning have foundered to date, but only because the House and Senate cannot agree on whether the ban should include research cloning.

Why have regulators and legislators opposed human reproductive cloning?

When Dr. Zoon testified before Congress in 2001, she admitted that the FDA could regulate human reproductive cloning only on safety grounds. However, she added that the National Bioethics Advisory Commission (NBAC) had issued a report identifying social and ethical problems with reproductive cloning. She added that the FDA unequivocally opposed reproductive cloning.[1]

Similarly, when advocating the enactment of anticloning laws, members of Congress frequently have cited the 1997 NBAC report[2] and the 2002 reports of the National Academies and President's Council on Bioethics.[3] Thus, these three reports should help to explain why regulators and legislators have opposed human cloning.

The NBAC argued that cloning should temporarily be banned for 3 to 5 years – in large part on safety grounds but also because the NBAC had identified other serious ethical concerns that deserved further public deliberation.[4] These other concerns included the warning not to play God (hubris),[5] manufacture of human beings,[6] the identity fallacy,[7] and eugenics.[8]

The National Academies report considered only scientific and medical issues. That report recommended a ban on safety grounds that could be reevaluated after 5 years.[9] Later that same year, however, the President's Council on Bioethics recommended that human reproductive cloning be permanently banned.[10] The Council began by pronouncing human reproductive cloning to be impermissible on safety grounds;[11] it went on to describe additional objections that at least some of its members found persuasive.[12] These included concerns that cloning treats humans as products,[13] impairs identity,[14] and facilitates eugenics.[15]

As this brief overview demonstrates, the NBAC, National Academies, and President's Council on Bioethics discussed the five objections as grounds for prohibiting human reproductive cloning. By relying on these reports, regulators and legislators implicitly have relied on the five objections.

To document further the influence that the five objections have had, I present a sampling of explicit statements that presidents, members of Congress, and regulators have made to justify their opposition to human reproductive cloning.

Most of the statements presented below come from Congressional debates on proposed anticloning legislation. Because no specific law has been enacted yet, I present these statements not as legislative history per se but rather as general evidence of the influence that the five objections have had on Congress.

For clarity's sake, the five objections are presented in the same order as in Part 1 of this book. Statements have been organized by topic, though some statements could fit into more than one category.

a) Cloning Offends God and Nature

Representative John Sullivan (R-Okla.): "When debating this issue, we must ask the ethical question: Are we created in God's image, or are we created in our own? Today, this House has a unique opportunity to shut the door on . . . an affront to humanity. I urge my colleagues . . . to set a precedent for morality and the sanctity of humanity."[16]

Representative Rick Renzi (R-Ariz.): "The issue here is human cloning. The issue has to do with us playing God and allowing human embryos to be produced."[17]

Representative Carolyn McCarthy (D-N.Y.): "As Members of Congress, we need to impose very strict penalties to prevent scientists from making the jump from doing important research to playing God."[18]

b) Cloning Treats Humans as Products

President George W. Bush: "Life is a creation, not a commodity. Our children are gifts to be loved and protected, not products to be designed and manufactured. Allowing cloning would be taking a significant step toward a society in which human beings are grown for spare body parts, and children are engineered to custom specifications, and that's not acceptable."[19]

Representative Marilyn Musgrave (R-Colo.): "[C]loning cheapens all human life by making it a commodity, an object to tinker with, to alter, to change to a scientist's preset specifications."[20]

Representative J. Randy Forbes (R-Va.): "Cloning diminishes human reproduction from a loving act between two parents to a cold exercise of producing parentless children. Life is a gift. It is not ours to manufacture to our predetermined criteria. I shudder to think of the consequences of turning the creation into the creator."[21]

Representative Lamar Smith (R-Tex.): "Cloning is a manufacturing process – a scientific assembly line – devoid of procreation. Efforts to improve humanity should never spin out of control and devalue humanity, which is precisely what human cloning does."[22]

Representative Lee Terry (R-Neb.): "[C]hildren could be manufactured with specific genetic traits, making them commodities rather than precious gifts from God."[23]

c) Human Clones Are Copies

President Bill Clinton: "My own view is that human cloning would have to raise deep concerns given our most cherished concepts of faith and humanity. Each human life is unique, born of a miracle that reaches beyond laboratory science. I believe we must respect this profound gift and resist the temptation to replicate ourselves."[24]

Representative James Greenwood (R-Penn.): "It is wrong to create a human being through cloning. It is probably physically cruel to do that, because of the likelihood of defect; and it is emotionally, I believe, cruel to do that because no one should be brought into life as a duplicate of another."[25]

Representative David Price (D-N.C.): "[R]eproductive cloning would threaten individuality and confuse identity, confounding our very definition of personhood, and it would represent a giant step toward turning procreation into manufacture."[26]

Representative Jim DeMint, (R-S.C.): "Mr. Speaker, you and I and every other person on the face of this earth have unique features – things that make us not only human, but individuals. Our fingerprints are like snowflakes – there is not, nor has there ever been, an exact replica of another human being.

Cloning is a whole new world.... What is the identity of a clone?"[27]

Representative Bernard Sanders (I-Vermont): "While I support stem cell research, the cloning of a human being for any purpose raises the deepest and most profound ethical and moral questions: questions about the sanctity or the uniqueness of each human person; questions about the evil of eugenics and genetic engineering in humans; and, equally important, questions about the ownership and use of cloned humans by an unregulated corporate biotechnology industry motivated almost exclusively by their quest for venture capital, short-term profits, and higher stock prices."[28]

d) Human Clones Could Destroy Humanity

Representative Dave Weldon (R-Fla.): "Might I also add that there are some people who want to allow this research to move forward so that they can some day be able to do reproductive cloning....And what will happen, what will be next with that? I contend that the age of eugenics will have arrived. There will be people who will then want to manipulate these embryos for the purpose of creating a human with preintended [sic] specifications, specifying size, height, weight, athletic performance, intellectual capabilities...."[29]

Representative Mike Pence (R-Indiana): "Human cloning is morally wrong....It is a dark path leading to the nightmare of eugenics, and it is a path upon which those in the 20th century embarked too often."[30]

Representative Todd Tiahrt (R-Kansas): "It does not take a fan of science fiction to imagine the scenarios that would ensue from legalized cloning – headless humans used as organ farms, malformed humans killed because they were viewed as an experiment not a person, gene selection to create a supposedly inferior species to become slaves, societal values used to create a supposed superior species."[31]

Representative J.C. Watts (R-Okla.): "Cloning is an insult to humanity. It is science gone crazy, like a bad B-movie from the 1960s. And as bad as human cloning is, it would lead to even worse atrocities, such as eugenics."[32]

Representative Joseph Pitts, (R-Penn.): "The Nazis may in fact have been able to create a race of healthier and more capable Germans if they had been allowed to proceed, but eugenics and cloning are both wrong."[33]

Representative Melissa Hart (R-Penn.): "There are so many very serious questions that human cloning raises, questions about conducting experiments on a human being bred essentially for that purpose; questions about the evils of social and genetic engineering; questions about the rights and liberties of living beings, of human beings."[34]

e) Cloning Is Unsafe

For the safety objection, I have selected statements that emphasize worst-case scenarios or fail to represent the science accurately and completely. More particularly, these statements do the following:

- Misrepresent the Dolly experiment,
- Incorrectly assert that cloned animals are old beyond their years,
- Emphasize the high rate of cloning "failures" without admitting that the vast majority involve the loss of eggs or embryos that never implant in the uterus,
- Incorrectly suggest that all or nearly all cloned animals are abnormal, and
- Insinuate that miscarriages, birth defects, and deaths are inherent to cloning without acknowledging alternative causes such as laboratory culture or the DNA source.

President George W. Bush: "Others have announced plans to produce cloned children, despite the fact that laboratory cloning of animals has led to spontaneous abortions and terrible, terrible abnormalities."[35]

Representative Joseph Pitts (R-Penn.): "The history of cloning is replete with defects, deformity, and death. Dolly the sheep was the 277th try. By now, everyone knows of the euthanized death of Dolly. She died . . . at the age of 6, half the normal life expectancy for sheep."[36]

Representative Ron Paul (R-Tex.): "Are you aware that it took 277 attempts to clone Dolly the sheep, and when she finally was born, she was defective and died soon after?"[37]

Representative Lamar Smith (R-Tex.): "Those in favor of cloning humans often downplay that it took 277 stillborn, miscarried or dead sheep to make one Dolly."[38]

Representative John Sullivan (R-Okla.): "The fact is, in animal cloning trials, 95 to 98 percent of all cloning attempts have ended in failure, and almost all successfully cloned animals have genetic abnormalities. In fact, Dolly, the infamous cloned sheep, died this past Valentine's Day of a lung disease she acquired before she was even born, and lived only half of the normal life expectancy for a sheep."[39]

Dr. Kathryn C. Zoon (FDA): "It took 276 failed attempts before Dolly was born. Since the time of Dolly, additional animals have been cloned. However, the success rate remains low and numerous abnormalities in the offspring and safety risks to the mother have been observed."[40]

2. State Law

Tracing the origin of state anticloning laws can be difficult owing to the relative paucity of recorded legislative history in many states. It is beyond the scope of this book to develop a legislative history for every state law that bans human reproductive cloning.

However, California law provides an interesting example. California enacted the first anticloning law in the United States back in 1997. As explained in Chapter 6, this original law placed a 5-year ban on human reproductive cloning but permitted research cloning. At the same time, the California State Legislature asked the California Department of Health Services to appoint an advisory committee to evaluate the medical, social, legal, and ethical implications of human reproductive cloning and advise the legislature and governor.[41] The California Advisory Committee on Human Cloning (committee) was charged with the responsibility of preparing a report and sending it to the legislature by 31 December 2001.[42]

As early as August 2001, *San Francisco Chronicle* science reporter Tom Abate was predicting that the committee would recommend a ban on reproductive but not research cloning.[43] On 7 January 2002, State Senator Dede Alpert (D-San Diego) introduced a bill to eliminate the sunset provision in California's original law and continue the ban on reproductive cloning indefinitely.[44] Four days later, on 11 January 2002, the committee published a report that was consistent with Senator Alpert's efforts. Its report recommended that the legislature enact a flat ban on reproductive cloning with no expiration date.[45]

All members of the committee concluded that reproductive cloning is too unsafe to perform. Beyond safety, different members found different arguments against the technology persuasive.[46] Three of the five objections were prominently featured among those arguments: hubris,[47] manufacture,[48] and the identity fallacy.[49] The report also included arguments that cloning could lead to overpopulation,[50] reduce genetic diversity,[51] and encourage genetic engineering.[52]

On 15 January 2002, the committee presented the report to Senator Alpert and the other members of the Senate Select Committee on Genetics, Genetic Technologies and Public Policy.[53] The legislature enacted Senator Alpert's bill in August 2002, and Governor Gray Davis signed the law into effect on 23 September 2002.

Thus, California went from a temporary ban on human reproductive cloning to an outright ban with no sunset clause. Given the political hazards of repealing anticloning legislation, this ban is likely to stand until a successful court challenge is made.

On the basis of this history, it seems fair to conclude that the committee's report must have influenced the legislature because the legislature ultimately followed the recommendation of the committee. It can be inferred that the five objections, which played such a prominent role in the committee's report, must have influenced the legislature in reaching its decision.

CHAPTER EIGHT

Anticloning Laws Reflect a Policy
of Existential Segregation

Chapters 6 and 7 explained that federal and state lawmakers believe
human reproductive cloning should be banned. However, anticloning
laws do far more than ban the use of a disfavored technology. The laws
also reflect a policy of existential segregation; that is, they are intended
to prevent the birth and existence of human clones. Four factors lead
me to this conclusion.

First, consider the language and impact of anticloning laws. The
2003 Weldon and Hatch bills did not become law, but they merit close
examination; both will serve as templates for the next round of proposals to ban cloning at the federal level.

The 2003 Weldon bill made it a crime for any person to perform
or participate in human cloning.[1] The bill defined "human cloning"
as human asexual reproduction accomplished by introducing nuclear

material from a somatic cell into an egg "so as to produce a living organism (at any stage of development) that is genetically virtually identical to an existing or previously existing human organism."[2] This language was broad enough to prevent scientists from creating and experimenting on cloned human embryos. More importantly for our purposes, however, the language made it a crime to produce a living organism *at any stage of development*. Thus, it is logical to infer that this language was designed to deter and prevent the birth of human clones.

As noted in Chapter 6, the 2003 Weldon bill also made it a crime to import the "product" of cloned embryos. Given the historical context of the cloning debate, in which maverick doctors and religious cultists have asserted their determination to clone offshore, this provision seems to have been intended to close a loophole in the general ban on cloning. It was worded broadly enough to make it a crime for American citizens to patronize cloning clinics abroad and return home with pregnancies or babies. This, too, was an attempt to deter and prevent the birth of human clones.

The 2003 Hatch bill made it a crime for any person to conduct or attempt to conduct "human cloning,"[3] which the bill defined as "implanting or attempting to implant" a cloned embryo into a uterus or its functional equivalent.[4] Because the ordinary biological consequences of embryo implantation are gestation and birth, the logical inference is that the bill was designed to ensure that human clones not be born.

The Food and Drug Administration (FDA) has followed an administrative path to the same end. In media statements, warning letters, and testimony before Congress, the agency has consistently stated that it seeks to prevent the use of cloning technology *to create or clone a human being*. The nature and timing of its most vigorous regulatory actions are consistent with this purpose. In 1998, and again in 2001, when mavericks based in the United States stepped forward to declare their intention to clone, the agency responded quickly and vigorously with warning letters, threats of legal action, and laboratory and grand jury investigations. These actions had the desired effect of bringing reproductive cloning efforts to a halt in the United States.

State laws against human reproductive cloning are similar in their language and apparent purpose. For example, Michigan prohibits the creation of cloned embryos.[5] Certainly, its laws prevent the creation of cloned embryos for research, but they also prevent the birth of babies who could be generated from those embryos. As another example, Arkansas makes it a crime to introduce nuclear material from a somatic cell into an egg so as to produce a living organism at any stage of development that is genetically virtually identical to an existing or previously existing human organism.[6] This language indicates that Arkansas wants to prevent the creation of human clones at any stage of development, including live babies. California prohibits the implantation of cloned embryos into the womb for the purpose of initiating a pregnancy that could result in the birth of a human being.[7] Here, the statute is explicitly targeted at actions that could lead to unwanted births. Lastly, New Jersey prohibits the cloning of a human being, which is defined as the replication of a human individual by cultivating a cell with genetic material through the egg, embryo, fetal, and newborn stages into a new human individual.[8] This law permits the cloning of embryos and fetuses for research purposes but draws the line at the cloning of a newborn baby.

Second, in seeking to justify anticloning laws, lawmakers and regulators persistently rely on arguments that disparage human clones.[9] The identity fallacy and the safety objection both focus on the nature and characteristics of human clones. They teach that human clones are copies – and physically damaged ones at that. Because these bad traits are inherent and cannot be changed, human clones must not be allowed to exist.

Doomsday scenarios go even further, arguing that multitudinous, duplicative, and superior human clones are a menace to the rest of us. Given the dire consequences of their presence on the planet, human clones must not be allowed to exist.

Realistically, the options that lawmakers and regulators can employ to deal with this menace are limited. They could enact laws making it a crime for people to exist as human clones, but the laws would be ineffective. Human clones are unlikely to commit suicide to satisfy their detractors. Some human clones might flee the United States (just as Jews once fled Nazi Germany). However, because there is no way to identify a human clone just by looking at him or her, many others would remain behind and in the closet.

Also, a law that criminalized the *status* of being a human clone probably would be unconstitutional. The Supreme Court has held that a law criminalizing the status of being addicted to drugs (as opposed to the use of drugs) is an infliction of cruel and unusual punishment in violation of the Eighth and Fourteenth Amendments.[10] Similarly, years before the Supreme Court recognized that the right of privacy included the right of gays and lesbians to engage in consensual sex,[11] the U.S. Court of Appeals for the Fourth Circuit opined that a statute that criminalized the status of being gay or lesbian would be unconstitutional.[12]

Thus, legislators and regulators opposed to human clones have chosen the logical alternative of nipping the "problem" in the bud. They have enacted laws that prohibit *actions* that lead to the existence of the members of the objectionable class. This strategy does not change the fact that human clones are the target.

Third, lawmakers make slippery-slope arguments against *research* cloning that also indicate that their true purpose is to prevent the birth of human clones. Congressmen have argued that, so long as there are "stockpiles" of cloned embryos around, there is a terrible danger that some embryos will be introduced into wombs and born in violation of law. The following comment from Representative Chris Smith (R-N.J.) is typical:

> Once stockpiles of cloned human embryos are created for research, how realistic will it be really to have an implementation ban? Not only is allowing research cloning immoral, it would also not work. We do not fight the war on drugs by telling the public to manufacture as much cocaine as possible, pile it up in warehouses, but make sure to destroy it before anyone can smoke it or inhale it. If anyone suggested that strategy on the floor of the House, they would be criticized from here to breakfast; but that is exactly what the proponents of human cloning for research are advocating and with a straight face.[13]

The "stockpile" argument is telling because it presents the birth of human clones as the ultimate evil. Like nuclear weapons (which are stockpiled) or illegal drugs, human clones must be stopped at their inception, even at the cost of stopping research that could one day cure deadly diseases.

Fourth, and finally, what is going on in legislatures and agencies across the country is not an entirely new phenomenon. It has an ugly precedent, one that is seldom mentioned in the cloning debate, but should be. To understand the purpose and effect of anticloning laws fully, it is necessary to place them in historical context.

1. Antimiscegenation Laws

Most Americans are familiar with the basic history of racial segregation. Laws prohibited blacks from sharing public accommodations, transportation, schools, and other facilities with whites.[14] The invidious purpose was to separate blacks from whites physically.

However, fewer Americans are aware that many states once made it a crime for a person of one race to marry a member of another race.[15] Thus, it was a crime for a white person to marry a black person, and vice versa. States prohibited various other racial combinations, depending on regional and local prejudices.[16] The history of these laws is complex; for the sake of simplicity, I limit my comments here to the prohibition on black and white marriages.

Professor Rachel Moran has noted that antimiscegenation laws helped to distinguish blacks from whites based on color.[17] At first, color served to distinguish slaves from nonslaves; after the Civil War, color made segregation work.[18]

The laws enforced color distinctions in two ways. First, the laws physically separated the races from one another within marriage. This had to be done; if blacks and whites had begun to share their affections and assets within the institution of marriage, blacks would have acquired a social status that was inconsistent with their continued subordination.[19]

Second, although most states did not make it a crime to have a mixed-race child,[20] they did try to prevent such births by enacting antimiscegenation laws.[21] In theory, if interracial couples could not marry, mixed-race children would not be born.

Stopping such births was important because mixed-race children posed a serious threat to racist institutions that depended on color distinctions. Mixed-race children threatened to undermine the institution of slavery; light-skinned slaves could run away from masters and, if caught, argue that their white ancestry entitled them to freedom.[22]

Even after slavery ended, moreover, mixed-race children threatened the practice of racial segregation; without a clear color line, it would be hard to know who should have access to segregated facilities. Finally, mixed-race children threatened white economic privilege; if legitimate children were born of interracial marriages, they could begin to inherit property from their white parents.[23]

Antimiscegenation laws served as a first line of defense against such threats to white power and privilege. Of course, despite antimiscegenation laws, and related laws against interracial sex,[24] plenty of mixed-race children were born anyway. Thus, to maintain a clear color line, the states resorted to a second line of defense: laws establishing the infamous "one drop rule," which defined mixed-race children as black if they had any African ancestry.[25] Even though the birth of mixed-race children could not be prevented altogether, the law could choose to treat those children as if they did not exist by refusing to recognize their white heritage.

To summarize the discussion thus far, antimiscegenation laws tried to prevent the birth of mixed-race children because such children threatened the viability of racist institutions.

But that was not all. White society viewed mixed-race children themselves as inherently inferior. Antimiscegenation laws were a conscious attempt to stop the birth of these children, who were considered unworthy of existence. In other words, the laws were eugenics laws that implemented a policy of existential segregation.

For example, in 1869, the Georgia Supreme Court upheld an antimiscegenation law that had been challenged under the state constitution.[26] The court reasoned in part:

[The antimiscegenation law] was dictated by wise statesmanship, and has a broad and solid foundation in enlightened policy, sustained by sound reason and common sense. The amalgamation of the races is not only *unnatural*, but is always productive of deplorable results. Our daily observation shows us, that the offspring of these unnatural connections are generally *sickly* and effeminate, and that they are *inferior in physical development and strength*, to the full blood of either race.[27]

Proponents also argued that antimiscegenation laws protected mixed-race children from the social consequences of their unfortunate existence. For example, in 1959, the Louisiana Supreme Court held that a law making it a crime for whites and blacks to marry or cohabitate did not violate the Equal Protection Clause.[28] In an ironic passage, the court quoted *Brown v. Board of Education*[29] in support of its decision:

> A state statute which prohibits intermarriage or cohabitation between members of different races we think falls squarely within the police power of the state, which has an interest in maintaining the purity of the races and in preventing the propagation of half-breed children. *Such children have difficulty in being accepted by society,* and there is no doubt that children in such a situation are burdened, as has been said in another connection, with *"a feeling of inferiority* as to their status in the community that may affect their hearts and minds in a way unlikely ever to be undone."[30]

As this last case suggests, after the Fourteenth Amendment was ratified in 1868, the antimiscegenation laws attracted their fair share of legal challenges. Despite this, the laws survived for a long time. Three basic arguments supported the laws. First, it was argued that the statutes did not violate the Equal Protection Clause so long as they applied with equal force to members of each race. Because antimiscegenation laws denied not only blacks but also whites the right to marry outside their own race, the laws had to be valid. Second, proponents of the laws argued legislative history supported their claim that Congress did not intend the Fourteenth Amendment to eliminate prohibitions on interracial marriages. Third, it was argued that the regulation of marriage was a matter left to the states under the Tenth Amendment.[31]

The first successful constitutional challenge to antimiscegenation laws had to wait until the California Supreme Court confronted the issue in 1948. The facts of the case were clear enough. Andrea Perez, a white woman, and Sylvester Davis, a black man, applied to the County clerk of Los Angeles County for a certificate of registry and a license to marry.[32] The clerk refused, citing a statute that provided "no license may be issued authorizing the marriage of a white person with a Negro, mulatto, Mongolian or member of the Malay race."[33] This statute implemented the basic antimiscegenation statute in California, which rendered marriages between whites and "negroes, Mongolians, members of the Malay race, or mulattoes" illegal and void.[34]

The couple brought a proceeding in mandamus, seeking to compel the clerk to issue the certificate of registry and license to marry. They argued that the antimiscegenation statutes unconstitutionally prohibited them from freely exercising their religion (Roman Catholicism) by denying them the sacrament of marriage.[35]

The California Supreme Court reasoned that the regulation of marriage was a proper function of the state. If the statutes under attack employed a reasonable means to prevent a social evil, they would be valid despite incidental effects on religious exercise. However, if the statutes were discriminatory and irrational, they unconstitutionally restricted not only religious liberty but also the liberty to marry.[36]

The clerk defended the constitutionality of the antimiscegenation statutes, arguing that they served several legitimate legislative objectives: (1) preventing the birth of mixed-race children who would be physically inferior,[37] (2) preventing the Caucasian race from being "contaminated" by races whose members were physically and mentally inferior,[38] and (3) protecting mixed-race children from the stigma of inferiority and rejection by members of both races.[39]

The California Supreme Court rejected each of these arguments in turn. First, the court reasoned, modern experts agreed that mixed-race children are not inferior. Even if they were, the antimiscegenation statutes did not evince a clear policy against the birth of mixed-race children because they permitted whites to marry Native Americans, Hindus, and Mexicans and permitted nonwhites to intermarry freely.[40] Second, the court continued, the contention that nonwhites are inherently physically or mentally inferior was without scientific proof.[41] Third, the court rejected the argument that mixed-race children would suffer from the stigma of inferiority: "If they do, the fault lies not with their parents, but with the prejudices in the community *and the laws that perpetuate those prejudices by giving legal force to the belief that certain races are inferior.*"[42]

Therefore, the court concluded, California's antimiscegenation statutes lacked the compelling justification that would be required to uphold such discrimination.[43] The laws violated the Equal Protection Clause by impairing the right of individuals to marry on the basis of race alone and by arbitrarily and unreasonably discriminating against certain racial groups.[44]

Ten years after *Perez* was decided, two residents of Virginia, Mildred Jeter, a black woman, and Richard Loving, a white man, had the temerity to get married in the District of Columbia. When they went home and took up residence together, a grand jury charged them with violating Virginia's antimiscegenation laws.[45] These laws included a statute that made it a crime for a white person and colored person to go out of Virginia to get married and come back home to cohabitate.[46] Mr. and Mrs. Loving pleaded guilty to the felony charges and were sentenced to 1 year in jail. However, the trial judge suspended the sentences for 25 years so long as Mr. and Mrs. Loving left Virginia and did not return together or at the same time for 25 years.[47]

The trial judge made some statements in his opinion that are worth repeating here – not only because they are relatively recent (dating to 1959) but also because they are reminiscent of arguments that cloning should be banned because it violates the will of God: "Almighty God created the races white, black, yellow, malay and red, and he placed them on separate continents. And but for the interference with his arrangement there would be no cause for such marriages. The fact that he separated the races shows that he did not intend for the races to mix."[48]

Mr. and Mrs. Loving moved to the District of Columbia. A few years later, they challenged their convictions and sentences on the ground that Virginia's antimiscegenation laws violated the Fourteenth Amendment.[49] The Supreme Court of Appeals of Virginia upheld the antimiscegenation laws and affirmed the convictions,[50] relying on its earlier decision in *Naim v. Naim*. Eleven years before, *Naim* had upheld the antimiscegenation laws on the following reasoning: "We are unable to read in the Fourteenth Amendment... any words or any intendment which prohibit the State from enacting legislation to preserve the racial integrity of its citizens, or which denies the power of the State to regulate the marriage relation *so that it shall not have a mongrel breed of citizens*. We find there no requirement that the State shall not legislate to prevent the obliteration of racial pride, but must permit *the corruption of blood even though it weaken or destroy the quality of its citizenship*."[51]

Confronted with this brick wall of precedent, Mr. and Mrs. Loving had to carry their appeal all the way to the U.S. Supreme Court in order to obtain relief. There, in *Loving v. Virginia*,[52] the Supreme Court reversed their convictions and held that antimiscegenation laws were unconstitutional on two grounds. First, the laws had no legitimate purpose independent of invidious racial discrimination and thus violated the Equal Protection Clause of the Fourteenth Amendment.[53] Second, the laws infringed the fundamental right of the individual to marry and thus deprived Mr. and Mrs. Loving of liberty without due process of law in violation of the Due Process Clause of the Fourteenth Amendment.[54]

The *Loving* decision put a stop to both marital apartheid and the attempt to segregate mixed-race children at the existential level. However, it is worth noting that the Supreme Court did not decide the case until 1967 – more than 100 years after the Civil War ended. Marriage and reproduction were the last significant battlefields in the fight to end legalized racial segregation.[55]

2. Anticloning Laws in Historical Context

Let us now return to the anticloning laws. The purpose of such laws is to ensure that human clones are never born. *By working to prevent the birth of human clones, the laws seek to enforce a policy of existential segregation just as the old antimiscegenation laws did.*

With the history of antimiscegenation laws firmly in mind, the reader is now equipped to realize that most of the arguments against cloning and human clones are not new but, rather, eerily familiar. There once was a time when lawmakers thought mixed-race unions violated the laws of God and nature; today, lawmakers assert that cloning violates the laws of God and nature (first objection). There once was a time when politicians believed individuals of mixed race to be sickly and physically inferior; today, politicians speculate that human clones would suffer from birth defects – both visible and invisible (fifth objection). There once was a time when the state asserted that mixed-race individuals should not exist because they would suffer prejudice at the hands of others; today, the state asserts that human clones should not be born because others would treat them as copies (third objection). Although society can never replicate a human being, it seems to have no trouble in replicating prejudicial attitudes.

There is another interesting historical parallel between antimiscegenation laws and anticloning laws. As discussed in the previous section, by preventing mixed-race marriages (and births) from taking place within its own borders, Virginia attempted to effectuate a policy of physical segregation within marriages and existential segregation for mixed-race children. However, Virginia understood that there was a loophole: mixed-race couples could easily travel to neighboring states, get married, come home, and have children. Thus, Virginia made it a crime to get married elsewhere and come home. In this way, Virginia not only deterred mixed marriages but also discouraged mixed couples from returning home, where they might do something unseemly like live together openly (contrary to the state's policy of physical segregation) or give birth to mixed-race children (contrary to the state's policy of existential segregation). The suspended sentences of Mr. and Mrs. Loving were consistent with this strategy; the couple was allowed to avoid jail time so long as they removed their inconvenient selves and marriage from the soil of Virginia.

Similarly, suppose that Congress does indeed make it a crime to "import" the product of cloned embryos, as specified in the 2003 Weldon bill. As explained in the opening of this chapter, the apparent purpose of such a provision is existential segregation. It closes a loophole in the general ban on cloning. It seeks to deter American citizens from traveling abroad to conceive babies.

To summarize the foregoing discussion bluntly, anticloning laws send the message that, when it comes to human clones, we do not want their kind around here. This is an ugly public policy. As demonstrated in the next chapter, its costs are significant.

CHAPTER NINE

The Costs of Anticloning Laws
Outweigh Their Benefits

Antimiscegenation laws were bad public policy. Their costs outweighed their putative benefits.

The laws injured the men and women who were denied the fundamental right of marriage. The laws also injured the children of mixed-race couples by subjecting them to existential segregation and stigmatizing them as inferior. In addition, the laws denied mixed-race children legitimacy and the legal and social benefits of that status.

The legislatures that enacted antimiscegenation laws, and the courts that upheld them, disregarded these costs in favor of flimsy and speculative "evidence" regarding the supposed degeneracy and inferiority of mixed-race unions and children. This evidence included scientific studies purporting to establish that blacks are physically and mentally inferior to whites and that racial mixing leads to children who are inferior.[1]

Today, most people recognize and acknowledge that antimiscegenation laws were bad public policy. Unfortunately, they have not recognized or acknowledged that laws against human reproductive cloning are bad public policy. Policymakers and lawmakers have emphasized the putative benefits of these laws and minimized or ignored their costs.

In this chapter, I seek to reverse this trend and provide a fresh public policy analysis of laws against human reproductive cloning. The chapter first identifies the costs that such laws impose – not only upon existing adults *but also upon the innocent children who will be born through cloning technology.*

Unfortunately, policymakers and lawmakers have virtually ignored the costs that anticloning laws will impose on human clones. To fill this gap, this chapter emphasizes those costs, which include injuries resulting from the prosecution of the parents[2] of human clones.

After completing the discussion of anticloning law costs, I go on to analyze their putative benefits and conclude that these benefits are not substantial enough to justify the high costs of the laws.

1. The Costs of a National Ban on Cloning

A national ban on human reproductive cloning would impose the widest possible range of costs and thus is a logical starting point for discussion. To lay a foundation for the analysis that follows, I must remind the reader what a national ban is likely to do, and why.

Arguably, a national ban already exists. The Food and Drug Administration (FDA) has asserted its authority to regulate reproductive cloning. Although the FDA has not explained the basis of its authority, it has consistently stated that it seeks to prevent the use of cloning technology to create or clone a human being. As discussed more thoroughly in Chapter 8, the FDA's evident purpose is to prevent the birth of human clones.

Those who defy the FDA could be subjected to criminal sentences and civil penalties.[3] So far, the agency has gone after those who have offered cloning services as opposed to the parents who paid for those

services. However, if the FDA believes a scientist has committed a criminal violation of the laws that fall within its jurisdiction, it could, in the
future, choose to prosecute the parents on the ground that they aided
or abetted the crime or conspired to commit it.[4]

However, the FDA can regulate only what happens in the United
States. It does not have the power to stop scientists from offering or
providing cloning services in offshore clinics. It does not have the power
to stop parents from traveling abroad to obtain those services and returning home with pregnancies or babies.

Congress is contemplating a more drastic solution. The 2003 Weldon
bill shows the form that federal legislation is most likely to take in the
future. Passed by an overwhelming margin in the House of Representatives, the bill sought to make it a federal crime for any person to perform
or participate in human cloning within the United States. The bill defined "human cloning" as human asexual reproduction accomplished
by introducing nuclear material from a somatic cell into an egg "so as
to produce a living organism (at any stage of development) that is genetically virtually identical to an existing or previously existing human
organism."[5] This language made it a crime to produce a human clone at
any stage of development. The bill was a deliberate attempt to ensure
that human clones would not be born. Violators faced a 10-year prison
sentence; parents were not exempted. Those who derived a pecuniary
gain from the violation (as doctors might) faced a minimum fine of one
million dollars.

To support its goal of existential segregation, the 2003 Weldon bill
also made it a crime for any person to travel abroad for cloning services
and come home with the "product" of a cloned embryo such as a fetus
or baby. Parents were not exempted.

There is an alternative form that federal legislation could take. The
2003 Hatch bill made it a crime for any person to implant a cloned
embryo into a uterus. Again, the purpose was to prevent the birth of
human clones. The sanctions were even broader than those in the 2003
Weldon bill. Violators faced a 10-year prison sentence, a civil penalty
of at least one million dollars (imposed even if there was no pecuniary
gain), and the forfeiture of real or personal property derived from, or
used to commit, the violation. Parents were not exempted.

a) First Cost: Violation of Procreative Freedom

If human reproductive cloning is banned in the United States, men and women who cannot reproduce safely or effectively via sexual reproduction will lose the chance to have children who are genetically related to them. This is more than a personal loss. The U.S. Supreme Court has recognized a constitutional right to privacy that includes reproductive freedom. This freedom includes the right to procreate through cloning when that is the only option.

A brief history will help to explain this conclusion. In 1942, in the landmark case of *Skinner v. Oklahoma*, the Supreme Court first identified procreation as a fundamental right deserving of special protection.[6] In that case, the Court invalidated an Oklahoma law that mandated sterilization of certain criminals but not others who had committed offenses of comparable seriousness. The Court held that the law violated the Equal Protection Clause of the Fourteenth Amendment. The Court subjected the law and its meaningless distinctions among crimes and criminals to strict scrutiny because procreation was at stake.

> Marriage and procreation are fundamental to the very existence and survival of the race. The power to sterilize, if exercised, may have subtle, far-reaching and devastating effects.... There is no redemption for the individual whom the law touches. Any experiment which the State conducts is to his irreparable injury. He is forever deprived of a basic liberty.[7]

Constitutional scholars have identified this case as the beginning of the development of the constitutional right of privacy (even though the *Skinner* court never used that particular term of legal art).[8] The reader is probably more familiar with cases like *Griswold v. Connecticut*, which recognized that the right to privacy includes the right of married couples to use contraception,[9] or *Roe v. Wade* and its progeny, which recognized the right of a woman to have an abortion up to the point of fetal viability.[10] Recent cases such as these have focused on the right of fertile men and women *not* to reproduce because laws threatened that right. Since *Skinner*, there have been few cases that directly addressed the right to procreate largely because the government has very seldom interfered with that right in recent years. In vitro fertilization (IVF) was never outlawed despite the public outcry over "test-tube babies" when it was a new technology. For the most part, the government has left infertile men and women free to pursue their medical treatments without interference.

However, one antiabortion law in the state of Illinois did make some fertility doctors very nervous. The law prohibited experimentation on fetuses but expressly permitted IVF. Nevertheless, the vaguely worded statute left the doctors uncertain whether variations on the basic IVF technique were illegal or not, and they brought suit challenging the law. In *Lifchez v. Hartigan*, a federal district court granted them an injunction against enforcement of the law on two grounds: (1) the law's vague language and uncertain applicability violated principles of due process; and (2) by restricting access to fertility technologies, the law violated a woman's fundamental right to make reproductive choices free of governmental interference. The court reasoned that "it takes no great leap of logic to see that within the cluster of constitutionally protected choices that includes the right to have access to contraceptives, there must be included within that cluster the right to submit to medical procedure that may bring about, rather than prevent, pregnancy."[11]

For a man who has no functional sperm or a woman who has no functional eggs, sexual reproduction is not possible even with the benefit of IVF. If reproductive cloning develops to the point at which it is safe and effective, it could provide many infertile men and women with the only means possible of having genetically related offspring.

On the basis of this reality and cases like *Skinner* and *Lifchez*, a growing number of attorneys and legal scholars have argued that reproductive freedom should include the right to employ cloning – at least for infertile men and women who cannot reproduce sexually.[12] The same argument could be made on behalf of carriers of heritable diseases for whom sexual reproduction is too hazardous. Arguably, the liberty to clone should also be granted to gays and lesbians, who can have genetic children through sexual reproduction but only if they accept gametes from persons who are not their sexual partners.

Any law that infringes on the fundamental right to reproduce is subject to strict scrutiny. In other words, the government must prove a compelling interest in support of the law and show that it is narrowly drawn to vindicate that interest.[13] In a fair fight, the government would not be able to make this case for anticloning laws.

As I explain at greater length below and also in Chapter 12, most of the five objections to cloning are weak or incapable of proof and cannot rise to the level of a compelling interest. Safety is the one exception, but, as Chapter 5 explains, the risks involved in cloning have been grossly exaggerated. Even if safety concerns were compelling, a flat ban on cloning goes much further than necessary to protect the safety of children and other participants because cloning technology is bound to become safer over time.[14]

Of course, few fights are fair. The Supreme Court might hesitate to recognize a right to clone for political reasons. The Court has taken much abuse over the years for extending the privacy right to include abortion. It might be reluctant to issue another opinion that could be as controversial as *Roe v. Wade*.

What if the Supreme Court refuses to hold that the right to privacy includes a right to clone? If no right to clone exists, how could a national ban injure reproductive freedom?

The answer is simple. The right to privacy is not stated expressly in the U.S. Constitution. Some of its applications, notably the right to an abortion, are unpopular with the public and many legislators. Once the Supreme Court starts to chip away at reproductive freedom, further erosions become more likely.

Professor John Charles Kunich has made an intriguing argument along these lines. In his view, a "moderate" law that permits research cloning but bans reproductive cloning could serve as a Trojan Horse to overturn *Roe v. Wade*. Such a law would require researchers to destroy cloned embryos; any attempt to give them life by implanting them in a womb would be a crime. When confronted with such a repugnant "clone then kill" law, the Supreme Court might be motivated to rethink the entire question of whether nascent human life deserves protection against destruction. If it does, the right to abortion logically must come into question.[15]

The costs of a national ban, moreover, would not be limited to the erosion of reproductive freedom as such. If the Supreme Court holds that there is no right to clone, even for those who cannot reproduce by other means, the Constitution will stand for the proposition that men and women who are fertile, healthy, and heterosexual enjoy greater procreative freedom than men and women who are infertile, disabled, or homosexual. This antiegalitarian outcome would devalue the humanity of infertile, disabled, and homosexual men and women. Further, among these victims, such unjust treatment would breed contempt for the Constitution itself. These, too, should be counted among the costs of a national ban on cloning.

b) Second Cost: Loss of Scientific Freedom

A national ban on human reproductive cloning could infringe not only on reproductive freedom but on scientific freedom as well.

To date, the U.S. Supreme Court has not held that there is a constitutional right to conduct scientific research.[16] Legal scholars, however, have attempted to locate protection for scientific research under the First Amendment. Some contend that, if the First Amendment protects the dissemination of scientific information, it also must protect the scientific research that creates the information. Otherwise, the government could control ideas by choking them off at the source.[17] Others argue that scientists who experiment are like protesters who burn flags; their conduct is symbolic speech that merits First Amendment protection.[18]

Although a complete analysis is beyond the scope of this book, it is interesting to think about how these theories might apply to human reproductive cloning. For example, the research necessary to perfect human reproductive cloning, including clinical trials that insert cloned embryos into the wombs of willing participants, may be protected as a precondition to the publication of scientific information regarding human reproductive cloning. A flat ban on human reproductive cloning can be characterized as a content-based restriction on knowledge. As such, the law would violate the First Amendment unless it was the least restrictive means of achieving a compelling interest.[19] However, as explained in this chapter and in Chapter 12, most objections to cloning are weak rather than compelling. Even safety concerns will wane over time as scientists involved in animal and research cloning continue to advance our knowledge and technical proficiency. Moreover, a flat ban goes further than necessary to protect children and other participants in cloning and can be challenged on the ground that it is not the least restrictive means of ensuring safety.

Alternatively, reproductive cloning might be protected as symbolic speech. For example, one author has argued that the act of cloning expresses the idea that there should be no limits on science.[20] Any law designed to stop scientists from "playing God" relates to this idea and could be an unconstitutional attempt to suppress symbolic speech.[21] The act of cloning also challenges prevailing views of human individuality.[22] Any law that banned cloning to protect such views would be an unconstitutional attempt to suppress symbolic speech.[23]

The government might claim that it wants to ban cloning for reasons unrelated to the suppression of speech. A national ban could pass constitutional muster if these governmental interests were important and the incidental restriction on symbolic speech was no greater than essential to further those interests.[24] Again, however, most of the five objections to cloning are weak, and safety concerns will dwindle over time.

Although the foregoing arguments show some promise, their success is not guaranteed. Given the lack of precedent protecting scientific research, it is hard to predict how the Supreme Court would react if confronted with the claim that there is a First Amendment right to engage in reproductive cloning. The public and media are likely to view any scientist who wants to clone as a crank or worse. The Court might be reluctant to champion such an unpopular person or cause and could uphold a national ban on reproductive cloning.

To many readers, this might not seem like a significant loss. Few mainstream scientists or doctors are interested in pursing human reproductive cloning. However, a case about reproductive cloning could have a broader impact because it would force the Supreme Court to address the question of whether the First Amendment protects scientific research and, if so, to what extent. To justify upholding a ban on reproductive cloning, the Court might adopt a narrow view of the First Amendment and its protections for scientific experimentation. If this occurs, the ban on reproductive cloning will have damaged scientific freedom more generally. Ultimately, this would hurt not just scientists but also the rest of society; whenever scientific experimentation is limited, we forfeit not just knowledge but also all the useful technologies that could have been derived from that knowledge.

c) Third Cost: Loss of Human Resources

On the assumption it can survive constitutional challenges brought under the right to privacy or the First Amendment, a national ban on human reproductive cloning is likely to be somewhat effective. The criminal and civil penalties are so extreme that many people will be deterred from using the technology to have children. As a result, many perfectly normal babies will not be born. This is the core goal of existential segregation, of course, but it has costs – not only for families who lose valuable members but also for society, which loses the many physical, intellectual, and emotional contributions that the babies would have made throughout their lives.

However, a national ban on cloning will not be entirely effective. In this book, I have identified three groups that may have an interest in reproductive cloning: infertile men and women who lack viable gametes, carriers of heritable diseases, and gays and lesbians. In addition to the powerful urge to reproduce, these individuals may feel contempt for the laws that have discriminated against them and see no reason to obey the laws so long as detection and punishment can be avoided.

This raises the question of how these individuals might gain access to cloning services. Fertility doctors are not likely to offer reproductive cloning in defiance of a legal ban and its penalties. They can make plenty of money from legal technologies like IVF (which can be offered together with donor eggs or sperm to patients who lack viable gametes). The fact remains, however, that there are thousands of fertility doctors, technicians, clinics, and laboratories in the United States with the expertise and equipment required to harvest eggs, perform nuclear transfer (using micromanipulation equipment that is a standard feature in many laboratories), cultivate embryos, and transfer them to the womb. Some people who want to have a child through cloning will belong to this group of professionals or have spouses, relatives, or friends who do, and thus will have access to the expertise and equipment necessary to "do it themselves."

Another possible scenario is that research scientists could be fooled by "patients" who pay them to clone embryos ostensibly to obtain stem cell therapies but in fact to obtain embryos that can be used for reproductive purposes. Scientists engaged in research cloning will have the eggs, equipment, and expertise to create healthy embryos. Once created, the "patients" could transfer the embryos to fertility clinics, lie about the origins of the embryos, and have them transferred to the womb.

Finally, American citizens who want to reproduce asexually might flock to offshore fertility clinics and come home with cloned pregnancies or babies.

In short, if human reproductive cloning is possible, and safe enough to attract clients, many babies will be born through cloning no matter what the law says. Thus, I proceed to consider the costs that a national ban would inflict on human clones.

d) Fourth Cost: Exclusion of Citizens at the National Border

As the 2003 Weldon bill suggests, Congress might make it a crime to import the "product" of a cloned embryo. If so, some parents who clone abroad might never dare to return to the United States with their offspring. Because babies and children cannot travel without caretakers, a national ban could exclude some cloned citizens from what should have been their homeland – banishing them, in effect.

It seems likely, however, that most people who clone abroad would not elect to stay there. Rather, they would come back quietly, while the mother was still pregnant, but not obviously so.[25] This is the best way to avoid unwanted attention, detection, and prosecution, and it has the added advantage of ensuring that the baby be born on American soil and be able to claim citizenship under the Fourteenth Amendment[26] without having to rely on a favorable interpretation of federal statutes that grant citizenship to American parents when children are born abroad.[27]

Thus, from this point onward, I address the costs that a national ban would impose on cloned babies, children, and adults residing within the United States. To prepare for the coming discussion, I first note some of the conceptual complexities that existential segregation involves.

Owing to our sorry national experience with racial segregation, most Americans are already familiar with the concept of physical segregation through which one disfavored group is kept apart from a privileged group. By its very nature, physical segregation is easy to conceptualize. It presumes an existing person, whom the law excludes from a certain location. Because the person exists, there is no doubt that he or she can be the victim of discrimination.

By contrast, existential segregation seeks to prevent the members of a disfavored group from coming into existence in the first place. To achieve this goal, a law must prohibit actions that are taken *before* a person is born. Thus, for example, anticloning laws can prohibit activities such as the creation, implantation, and gestation of a cloned embryo. At the moment a person is born through cloning, the prohibitions of the law cease. For this reason, some might argue that human clones who are born despite anticloning laws *cannot* be victims of legal discrimination.

This is not correct, however. Even after their prohibitions cease to operate, anticloning laws impose penalties and other injuries that harm human clones born despite the laws. Here, I enumerate those negative consequences, beginning with the one that is most general and unavoidable, and working my way towards others that may or may not occur as determined by the specific facts of individual cases.

e) Fifth Cost: Legal Stigma

Social psychologists define a "stigma" as a sign or mark that designates the bearer as defective and less valuable than "normal" people. Categories of stigmatizing conditions include tribal identities (e.g., race, religion, or nation), blemishes of individual character (e.g., mental disorders or a criminal conviction), and abominations of the body (e.g., physical deformities or disease).[28] In addition to marking those who bear them as less worthy than others, stigmas often evoke social identity through the device of stereotypes regarding people who share the same stigma.[29]

Human clones bear the stigma of the "duplicative" genomes that they share with other humans who existed before them. This genetic stigma is not visible but is potent nevertheless. If the stigma is revealed, it links the bearer to all of the harmful stereotypes about "clones" discussed in Part I of this book.

Moreover, social psychologists have shown that individuals who bear a stigma are more likely to experience derision, exclusion, discrimination, and even violence at the hands of nonstigmatized persons. Victims of discrimination can lose jobs, housing, insurance, and other resources; victims of social exclusion can lose friends and romantic partners. Aware of their own devalued identities, many stigmatized individuals experience stress and a loss of self-esteem.[30] This research strongly implies that human clones are also likely to face discrimination, stress, and psychological damage on account of the genetic stigma they bear.

Anticloning laws will take this bad situation and make it much worse. To understand why, consider the historical root of the term "stigma." In ancient Greek society, criminals and traitors were cut with knives and burned with branding irons. The resulting mark, or "stigma," served as a potent symbol of their immorality and unworthiness. A person bearing a stigma was considered unfit for normal society.[31]

Today, laws can serve the same function as knives and branding irons. Laws are a powerful statement of what the majority of the people in a society believe and what is right and just. Laws can mark a certain class of human being as immoral or unworthy, thereby justifying others in abusing or discriminating against them.

Because this book is about law, this type of stigma is most relevant to my analysis. In this and remaining chapters, the terms "legal stigma" or "stigma" will be used to refer to the mark that discriminatory laws inflict on their victims.

The Supreme Court has recognized that legal stigma can do serious harm. In the landmark case of *Brown v. Board of Education*,[32] the Court invalidated laws that segregated blacks from whites in public schools. The key to the Court's ruling was its recognition that the laws imposed a stigma: "To separate [children] from others of similar age and qualifications solely because of their race generates a feeling of inferiority as to their status in the community that may affect their hearts and minds in a way unlikely ever to be undone."[33] Reasoning that separate was inherently unequal, the Court held that the segregation laws violated the equal protection guarantee.[34]

Sodomy laws provide another example of the damage that legal stigma can do. In general, these laws prohibited oral or anal sex, or both – even between consenting adults. In the United States, the majority of the laws applied to heterosexual sex as well as homosexual sex.[35] Most people, however, perceived the laws as prohibitions on homosexual sex.[36] The laws sent the message that gays and lesbians are criminals. This, in turn, caused gays and lesbians to suffer psychological damage; anxiety and self-loathing were the predictable consequences of such categorization.[37] Worse, the message that gays and lesbians are criminals was taken as a signal that they were entitled to less than equal treatment in the workplace and home. Bigots used the laws to justify employment and housing discrimination.[38] The laws also encouraged vigilantes to commit violence against gays and lesbians as a kind of informal enforcement mechanism.[39] In 2003, the Supreme Court finally eliminated this particular legal stigma by ruling that sodomy laws violate the constitutional right to privacy.[40]

Let us return to reproductive cloning and the legal stigma that a national ban would impose on human clones. Any time conception, implantation, or gestation took place within the United States in violation of the ban, the resulting baby would, by definition, be someone whom lawmakers did not want to exist. The same would be true of any baby born after parents "imported" a cloned embryo or fetus into the United States; if the import ban had worked, the parents would not have traveled abroad for cloning services, and the baby would not exist.

Thus, a baby born in defiance of the national ban would be marked as unworthy of existence. Moreover, to the extent a national ban would be based on the five objections, it would be based on the many stereotypes about human clones that underlie those objections. Thus, the ban would also incorporate and validate the stereotypes, presenting them as the *reasons* why human clones are unworthy of existence.

For example, on the basis of the opinions expressed in policymaking reports and Congressional debates, if Congress ever bans cloning, it will be, in part, due to the identity fallacy. Thus, a national ban would mark human clones as unworthy of existence *because they are copies*. The ban would validate not only this root stereotype but also all of the stereotypes that logically flow from it. It would mark human clones as evil, unoriginal, fraudulent, inferior, zombielike, constrained, pathetic, disturbed, disgusting, identity thieves, destroyers, a threat to democratic values, and subhuman.

Policymakers and lawmakers also seem to have been influenced by doomsday scenarios in which human clones threaten the survival of humanity. As explained in Chapter 4, all of these scenarios feed off of the notion that human clones are copies. Therefore, at a minimum, any national ban enacted as a response to the doomsday scenarios would stigmatize human clones as unworthy of existence *because they are copies that endanger humanity.* The law would validate related stereotypes, marking human clones as multitudinous, rapacious, dirty, diseased, dangerous, murderous, coercive, criminal, superior, arrogant, and unfair.

Safety concerns have played a dominant role in Congressional debates over cloning and form the sole basis of the FDA's regulatory ban. Repeatedly, lawmakers and regulators have asserted the stereotype that human clones are not physically healthy or normal. Thus, the FDA regulatory ban, or any anticloning law that Congress might enact on safety grounds, would stigmatize human clones as unworthy of existence *because they are oversized, deformed, flawed, and prematurely aged.* By accepting claims that invisible flaws exist at the epigenetic level, a national ban would also warn that human clones are abnormal, no matter how normal they might appear to be. This, in turn, would imply that human clones are deceitful.

In considering legislation, Congress has also been strongly influenced by arguments that go to the evils of cloning as a technology. For example, the objection that cloning offends God, nature, or both warns against the hubris of those who seek to transcend the human domain. The objection that cloning violates human dignity warns against those who treat human beings as a manufacturing project. The objection that cloning is an inefficient process warns against the risks to adult participants. Although not directed at human clones, these objections strongly imply that such persons have bad traits. A national ban based on these objections would imply that human clones are unworthy of existence because they are evil, unnatural, abnormal, strange, artificial, inferior, objectified, soulless, inert, unfeeling, dangerous, violent, and destructive.

In an ironic twist, a "moderate" law permitting research cloning but prohibiting reproductive cloning would impose the worst legal stigma of all. A law decreeing that cloned embryos are fit only for research and making it a crime *not* to destroy cloned embryos would express the sickening view that some forms of human life are so flawed that the only logical solution is to kill them.[41]

Reasoning by analogy to the experience of gays and lesbians with sodomy laws, we can see that the legal stigma of a national ban on cloning would have devastating consequences for human clones. By marking human clones as unworthy of existence, the ban would damage their self-esteem and cause psychological damage. Also, by marking human clones as unworthy of existence, the ban would send the message that they are not entitled to the equal treatment that humans ordinarily enjoy under the law. This would embolden bigots who already do not like human clones to perpetrate employment and housing discrimination. Finally, and most dangerously, any law that marks human clones as unworthy of existence would encourage vigilantes to kill them as a kind of informal enforcement mechanism.

f) Sixth Cost: Loss of Parents, Funds, and Assets

A national ban on cloning would impose another highly significant cost on many human clones: the loss of their parents and parental assets.

As explained at length in Chapter 6, anticloning bills pending in Congress have not exempted parents, no matter how sympathetic their circumstances. I expect this trend to continue. Thus, if an anticloning bill becomes federal law, men and women who have children through cloning in the United States will violate the law, aid and abet those who violate the law, conspire to violate the law, or be guilty of all of these activities. Some violations will be discovered; some men and women will be prosecuted, convicted, and punished.

To offer more specifics, I return to the hypothetical cases discussed in Chapter 6. First, consider the plight of an infertile man and his wife under any federal law modeled after the 2003 Weldon bill. If the man contributes the nuclear DNA for the procedure and the wife donates an egg and carries the baby, both have "participated" in human cloning and are guilty of a crime. Alternatively, if the wife is infertile, obtains an egg from a donor, and uses her own nuclear DNA and womb to conceive and carry a cloned child, she has "participated" and is guilty of the crime of human cloning. Her husband, who aided and abetted her actions, can be punished as a principal. Both could go to prison for 10 years.

In either case, both husband and wife are guilty of the separate crime of conspiracy because they plotted the cloning together and took steps toward that goal. The penalty for conspiracy is 5 years in prison.

Second, consider the case of a lesbian couple under a federal law modeled after the 2003 Hatch bill. One woman donates the nuclear DNA and the other provides the egg and womb. A doctor creates an embryo and transfers it to one of the women. The doctor is guilty of the crime of human cloning, but so is the woman who receives the embryo into her womb. She can be sent to prison for 10 years, fined one million dollars, and subjected to the loss of any real or personal property involved in her crime (for example, a house in which a clandestine embryo transfer took place). The DNA donor, who is guilty of aiding and abetting the crime, can also be sent to prison for 10 years. Once again, both women are independently guilty of conspiracy – a crime carrying a 5-year prison sentence.

Even if Congress does not enact a law against cloning, the FDA could prosecute parents for aiding and abetting the actions of the doctor who cloned their child[42] or conspiring with the doctor to commit a federal offense.[43] These crimes probably would be misdemeanors subject to relatively short prison sentences.

Given the public hysteria over cloning, I do not expect federal prosecutors to exhibit leniency and let parents go – at least, not in the short term. Far from it; zealous advocacy and the energetic pursuit of political careers virtually guarantee the prosecution of at least some couples.

Inevitably, some babies and children born through cloning are going to lose their parents to prison sentences. This is a terrible price that no person should have to pay in exchange for his or her existence. Indeed, because a child is not capable of providing for himself or herself, any law that takes parents away attacks the very existence of the child. Without love and financial support, a child cannot thrive physically or emotionally.

Some children may be taken in by relatives or friends of their parents; others may be placed in foster care. These children may have some of their physical and emotional needs met to a greater or lesser degree depending on the motivations and qualifications of the caretakers. (The inadequacies and outright failures of foster care in many states are a national scandal.[44]) Even those who are lucky enough to be placed in good homes for long periods, however, will have lost the people who loved and wanted them the most (even to the point of risking their freedom for them).

By taking a child away from parents, moreover, the law is likely to be taking the child away from someone who has a genetic link with that child. This follows because human reproductive cloning is *not* a method of copying others but *is* a method of having a child who bears a genetic link when sexual reproduction fails. If an infertile man or woman, or a carrier of a heritable disease, or a gay man or lesbian does not mind introducing the genes of a third party, he or she can employ donor gametes. If, instead, that person prefers cloning, the odds are that he or she is interested in having a child who is genetically related to him or her (or his or her partner).[45]

This loss, too, is a significant one. A child will learn more about his or her genetic heritage if the parent who donated the nuclear DNA is available. Moreover, the DNA donor also serves as a link to a larger pool of genetic relatives who may care about the child.

Even if parents are released from prison, their children will continue to suffer the consequences of the enforcement of anticloning laws. Children who have been forced to live without their parents for many years will find it difficult to establish the same sort of close relationship that other children enjoy with their parents. Moreover, parents who have criminal convictions will be denied some housing and jobs, thereby compromising the resources necessary to provide for their children. This could happen even when their convictions are misdemeanors, as would be the case if the FDA chose to prosecute parents for participating in cloning without agency permission. (Imagine having to disclose on a job application that one was convicted of human cloning in violation of the Federal Food, Drug, and Cosmetic Act!)

Finally, prison sentences are not the only deterrent that laws can inflict. Recall that, under the 2003 Hatch bill, violators faced a minimum civil fine of one million dollars and the forfeiture of any real or personal property used to commit the violation. All parents need money and other assets to raise healthy and well-adjusted children. A law that makes paupers out of parents will make paupers out of their cloned children.

g) Seventh Cost: Loss of Medical and Personal History

Not every parent is going to get caught. Some will protect themselves from prosecution by hiding the origins of their cloned children – even from the children themselves. This brings me to yet another cost of a national ban on cloning: the ban would deprive many children of access to their own medical and personal history. This is a significant loss for two reasons.

First, because some medical problems can be inherited, a child needs to know who his or her genetic parents are, or are not. If a child falsely believes that both parents have a genetic link, he or she may provide personal doctors with irrelevant medical histories and risk his or her own health. By contrast, if a child knows that he or she was cloned, a doctor can be informed of that fact. If the child knows the identity of his or her DNA donor, he or she can provide that information, thereby facilitating decisions as to what medicines and treatments are appropriate and safe. Moreover, to the extent there is any truth to the notion that cloning itself presents some unusual health risks (as discussed in Chapter 5), it is even more important that the child realize the means of his or her conception in order to be aware of those risks.

Second, psychologists believe that when parents keep important secrets, they damage the emotional health of their children.[46] Secrets bespeak a lack of trust, and without trust, there can be no true intimacy. This implies that a child deserves to know the truth about his or her origin in cloning. Otherwise, the secret itself will fester within the family, damaging the trust that should exist between parent and child. If, on the other hand, the child is told the truth, he or she will have the chance to understand what the parents went through to have him or her. The child will be better equipped to grasp his or her unique role within the family.

Some might scoff that the danger of prosecution is overblown and that anticloning laws cannot be blamed for parental silence. For one thing, after the statute of limitations expires, the parents cannot be prosecuted. Thus, even if parents hide the truth for a time, eventually, once the danger of prosecution has passed, they should be motivated to share the truth with their child.

Unfortunately, the statute of limitations is not likely to provide frightened parents with much relief. Both the 2003 Weldon and Hatch bills attempted to add provisions to Title 18 of the United States Code; laws modeled after these bills are likely to do the same. Under Title 18, indictments must be found within 5 years after the offense was committed except whenever a law expressly provides otherwise.[47] (Note that a state law against cloning would be subject to a different and perhaps longer statute of limitation in that state; statutes of limitation could vary widely from state to state.) However, even though it is relatively short, the federal statute of limitations is tolled during any period of time in which a criminal is "fleeing from justice."[48] Thus, if the parents fled the federal district in which they had committed their crimes with the intent of avoiding arrest or prosecution, the 5-year period would be suspended and the period of exposure to prosecution correspondingly lengthened. The statute would also be tolled if the parents did not flee the district but deliberately concealed themselves from authorities within it.[49]

People who are not lawyers, moreover, are not familiar with the concept of a statute of limitation. Thus, few parents who fear the consequences of their crimes will understand that the threat of prosecution has passed. Finally, even those who do understand may be reluctant to reveal the truth to children who might resent them for having lied for so many years. Once a national cloning ban triggers parental silence, the silence could become its own rationale and self-perpetuate.

Even leaving the threat of prosecution aside, a national ban would give parents another good reason to keep cloning secret, as the following account reveals.

On December 26, 2002, Dr. Brigitte Boisselier, a member of the Raelian religious sect, stunned the world by claiming that she had cloned a baby girl for parents who lived in Florida. Dr. Boisselier never offered any proof to support her claim; today, most people have concluded the claim was a hoax. At the time, however, one lawyer, Bernard Siegel, took the claim very seriously; he petitioned a Florida court to appoint a legal guardian for the baby on the grounds that she was being exploited and might have birth defects. Although Mr. Siegel denied that he wanted to take the baby away from her mother, parents who fail to respond to such petitions can lose custody.[50] Ultimately, the court dismissed Mr. Siegel's petition when Dr. Boisselier testified that the parents had taken the baby to Israel and out of the court's jurisdiction.[51]

Mr. Siegel's petition sent a clear message to anyone who might be interested in having a child through cloning: as determined by the breadth of state custody statutes, anyone, including a stranger with no relationship to your family whatsoever, can invoke the machinery of the state to interfere with your family, and perhaps seize your child. This threat provides a strong incentive to hide a child's origins in cloning.

At the time Mr. Siegel filed his petition, there was no federal or Florida statute against cloning. The existence of such a law would have strengthened his case.

For example, in custody disputes, sodomy laws have been used to support the claim that gay and lesbian parents commit crimes and make bad parents. Too often, the result has been that gay and lesbian parents have lost their children to angry exspouses or other relatives.[52] Similarly, a national cloning ban would brand the parents of cloned children as criminals whether they were prosecuted or not. This would make it easier for exspouses, relatives, and even complete strangers to attack a parent's fitness and seize the child. By weakening their position in custody disputes, a national ban would increase the risk of parents' losing their children. In this way, the ban would create further incentive for parents to hide the truth from everyone – even the children themselves.

h) Eighth Cost: The High Cost of Living a Lie

The foregoing analysis suggests that a national ban would encourage human clones who are aware of their genetic origins to hide them. Revelation of the truth might unleash zealous prosecutors on beloved parents. Beyond that, there is the harm of legal stigma and its consequences. Thus, a national cloning ban would cause some human clones to "pass" as the products of sexual reproduction just as some blacks pass as whites, or gays and lesbians pass as heterosexuals. Whenever the ban caused passing, it would have the following costs.

First, passing is a lie about exactly who and what a person is. Thus, a human clone who passes must sacrifice the intimacy and trust that would have come from sharing his or her truest self.[53] If the lie is ever exposed, relationships with loved ones or friends could founder – not because of cloning but because trust has been betrayed.[54]

Second, a human clone who passes must exercise a great degree of mental vigilance. He or she must steer clear of dangerous conversational topics and censor comments about the self. Unfortunately, social psychologists have found that concealed secrets tend to bubble to the surface, prompting further mental efforts to suppress the unwelcome thoughts. This cycle of intrusion and suppression places stress on the psyche and can even compromise physical health.[55]

Third, a human clone who passes loses the chance to interact with others who share his or her genetic condition and legal status. He or she loses valuable opportunities to enjoy social support, build relationships, exchange strategies for coping with prejudice, and find a respite from discrimination.[56]

Fourth, passing also forces the victim of discrimination to sacrifice his or her opportunity to fight back. As Professor Rachel Moran noted in writing about the black experience in America, passing helped individual blacks evade discrimination, but it did nothing to improve the status of blacks as a group. Rather, the very act of passing reinforced the fact that blacks occupied an inferior status.[57]

Similarly, in order to pass, a human clone must behave in a way that reinforces his or her own inferior status. He or she cannot challenge the social order; he or she must endure every bigoted movie, article, or joke about cloning in silence, leading to degradation and a feeling of powerlessness.[58] Nor can a human clone who passes challenge the legal order; the price of passing is complicity in his or her own oppression.

i) Ninth Cost: Isolation

There is one final cost that a national ban would inflict on human clones: isolation.

A national ban would discourage some prospective parents from using the technology. As a result, a ban would reduce the total number of human clones (the third cost). Moreover, some of those who were born would not know their genetic origins because their parents, intimidated by the threat of prosecution, would hide that information from them (the seventh cost). Others would pass to protect their parents from prosecution or themselves from legal stigma (the eighth cost).

Thus, a national ban on cloning would tend to isolate human clones from each other, which would be unfortunate.

Human clones are sure to face genetic and legal stigma. Therefore, they will have a strong psychological need to associate with others who can provide them with emotional support and social and economic relationships that are free of prejudice and discrimination. Moreover, human clones might want to organize in order to agitate for legislative changes that could improve their social and legal status. Isolation will make it harder for human clones to meet their psychological and political needs.

Again, I can cite the experience of gays and lesbians to support these conclusions. Sodomy laws inhibited the development of informal social networks because acknowledging one's sexuality could have led to criminal prosecution. The laws also inhibited the rise of political organizations devoted to fighting for the rights of gays and lesbians. Prospective members feared that the government might get a list of their names and start to arrest them. The net result was a profound isolation.[59]

The rise of the Internet may soften this isolation to a limited extent. Those who know of their technological origins but want to hide them in real-space interactions could find some emotional release and support by sharing their experiences and feelings with others in virtual space. Cloaking their true identities behind e-mail aliases, human clones could chat anonymously with each other online. However, if cloning is a crime, those who send e-mails or participate in chat rooms could be leaving behind the electronic evidence that prosecutors would need to pursue their parents. Detectives, insurers, employers, and others who claim an interest in the health or genetic status of specific individuals might also be expected to troll the chat rooms for evidence. Strong encryption could blunt these concerns if it remains available and legal to use within the United States.[60]

j) Tenth Cost: Undermining Egalitarianism

The foregoing analysis is bound to leave many opponents of cloning unmoved. If one believes that cloning is a sin, or a violation of human dignity, one is not going to worry about enacting a national ban that would restrict the reproductive freedom of some adults. Similarly, if one believes that human clones are dangerous and defective copies, one is going to perceive every cost that a national ban would impose on human clones, from nonexistence to legal stigma to passing to isolation, as entirely justified and a benefit to everyone else. To put it another way, if most of the costs of anticloning laws would fall on a small and unpopular group of human clones and their parents, who cares?

I would like to think, however, that at least some opponents have not yet recognized that some human clones are bound to born even if a national ban exists. These opponents may be surprised to realize that a national ban cannot be implemented without injuring an entire class of people (and children in particular) in the ways that I have described. Their war against cloning is not just a war against technology alone, nor is it just a preemptive strike against hypothetical beings. If cloning is possible, the war must inevitably inflict casualties on human beings – not the soulless duplicates of science fiction, but real, live people who can feel and suffer. This realization need not necessarily lead to approval of cloning, but it may be enough to inspire some cloning opponents to abandon their support for anticloning legislation as a solution to the problems they perceive with the technology.

For those who remain unmoved by costs that human clones and their parents suffer, I offer one final cost for consideration – one that society at large must endure.

Much has been made of the threat that human clones and their re-cycled lives supposedly pose to autonomy and democratic society. But too few have remarked on the threat that anticloning laws and their ugly message of inequality pose to egalitarianism. It would be ironic indeed if America managed to overcome its historical legacy of slavery and racism only to embrace a new form of discrimination marking some humans as less valuable than others based on their shared genomes.

Each and every time the law draws invidious distinctions between classes of humans, the basic principle of egalitarianism is undermined no matter how few people are affected. Each and every successful attack on the principle of egalitarianism invites further attacks as the government becomes emboldened to search out other unpopular groups and discriminate against them also.

Optimists might insist that a vital factor tends to safeguard egalitarianism despite such attacks: our common humanity.

Stereotypes can be hard to change; yet, they are vulnerable to experience. When people come into personal contact with members of a stigmatized group, they start to accumulate data that indicate the stereotypes could be untrue. Enough data may cause them to rethink and reject stereotypes.[61] Alternatively, simply bringing stigmatized individuals within a group can, by redefining boundaries between "us" and "them," give the nonstigmatized members of the group a strong psychological incentive to abandon the disparaging stereotypes they once held.[62]

Thus, for example, if we could get to know human clones at school, on dates, or in the workplace, we could develop enough facts to learn the truth. Contrary to the claims of their opponents, we would not find them to be unnatural, manufactured, copied, or deformed freaks. Also, if circumstances required us to include them openly in our classrooms, work groups, and other social organizations, we would have a strong incentive to recognize their humanity.

However, a national ban on cloning would deprive us of that opportunity. By reducing births and driving those who are born underground or into the closet, the ban would make it harder for us to gain experience with human clones. We would have fewer chances to learn that stereotypes about them are untrue and that we share a common humanity with the members of this supposedly subhuman class.

It might be argued that, even in the absence of personal contact, media accounts of human clones could help to dispel such false images. However, as Part 1 of this book discussed, the media has not been friendly to cloning. For every story that tells the truth about cloning, there are many others that misstate or exaggerate the facts in a manner calculated to titillate the public and sell more television advertisements, newspapers, or magazines. Given this history, the media cannot be counted upon to set the record straight. Even if the media reforms itself and tries to tell the truth, many people very sensibly will not trust what they see on television or read in the papers until they experience it for themselves.

Meanwhile, a national ban on cloning would take on a life of its own. By eliminating or greatly reducing personal experience with human clones, the laws would make it much harder for us to recognize that the arguments that inspired the laws were based on false stereotypes. In this way, the laws would tend to protect themselves against repeal. Moreover, opponents of cloning would be sure to assert that the very existence of the laws justified their premises and continued existence, further stacking the odds against repeal.[63]

In sum, a national ban on cloning would establish a new category of legally stigmatized humans; in so doing, it would undermine our society's commitment to egalitarian principles. This problem would be unlikely to correct itself. The national ban would drive unpopular and unwanted human clones underground or into the closet, making it hard for the rest of us to learn the stereotypes about them to be untrue. This, in turn, would make it harder to reject the stereotypes. Ignorance would perpetuate the ban and its antiegalitarian influence.

2. The Costs of State Anticloning Laws

Everything I have written so far about costs assumes that there is, or soon will be, a national ban on human reproductive cloning.

But, what if Congress simply cannot achieve the consensus on research cloning that seems to be a prerequisite to the enactment of a strict law against reproductive cloning? That would leave the FDA standing alone as a bulwark against human reproductive cloning. However, as I have mentioned, the FDA probably does not have the statutory authority to regulate cloning as a drug, device, or biological product. Someday, somewhere, someone may sue the FDA and cause an unwary judge to remark that the agency, like the emperor, has no clothes. Alternatively, even if the FDA does have statutory authority to regulate, it may lose the ability to stop cloning once the technology becomes safe.

Even if the federal government does absolutely nothing about cloning, the fact remains that many states have banned cloning already, and others plan to do so soon. Thus, it is necessary to examine the costs of these state anticloning laws.

To begin the analysis, let us first assume that the current state of affairs continues with some states banning cloning but others not. The costs of the anticloning crusade will be spread unevenly as dictated by where potential victims live.

People who live in states that outlaw cloning will incur essentially the same costs as I have described in my discussion of a national ban. Because Michigan was in the forefront of the drive to ban cloning, let us take it as an example. Some adult Michiganders will lose their procreative freedom (first cost), the state will forfeit the contributions of many worthwhile individuals who will not be born (third cost), and those children who are born as the result of actions that violate the law will suffer legal stigma (fifth cost). Some children will lose their parents to prison (sixth cost). Others will never learn of their genetic origins (seventh cost); alternatively, if they do learn, and choose to pass, they will suffer the physical and psychological costs of living a lie (eighth cost). Cloned children will be isolated from others who share their legal stigma and oppression (ninth cost). Finally, Michigan will have taken a step away from egalitarianism and toward a future in which some of its citizens are considered more worthy of existence than others (tenth cost).

Next, let us consider the fate of people who live in states that do not choose to criminalize human reproductive cloning. Suppose a man and his infertile wife live in Hawaii at a time when reproductive cloning is legal there. Utilizing cloning technology, the wife conceives and gives birth to a baby girl. The parents have not lost their reproductive freedom. Their baby was never targeted for nonexistence and does not face legal stigma on account of any laws that Hawaii has passed. Her parents are not subject to prosecution or asset forfeiture.

It does not follow, however, that the baby will live free of the damaging effects of anticloning laws. Laws in other states that make reproductive cloning a crime could have spillover effects on her. As the baby grows older, she may become aware of the other laws and experience a loss of self-esteem even if she lives in Hawaii. If she travels to the mainland for vacation, education, or employment, others could discriminate against or exclude her on the reasoning that she ought not to exist.[64] In other words, she could feel the sting of legal stigma (fifth cost) even though her own conception, gestation, and birth were perfectly legal and even though Hawaii never targeted her for nonexistence.

To protect the baby from these spillover effects, the parents may hide her origins from her (seventh cost). Alternatively, as she grows older and becomes aware of the stigma, the baby might hide her own origins even at the high cost of living a lie (eighth cost). Finally, if anticloning laws in other states create a powerful enough stigma, the baby could lose potential friends and political allies to parental silence or passing (ninth cost).

Some readers may wonder whether these costs make any difference in the context of the public policy analysis that this chapter seeks to encourage. When a state legislature weighs the costs and benefits of anticloning laws, there is a good chance that it will discount costs to nonresidents. To put it another way, Michigan may not care that its laws have spillover effects on residents of Hawaii. However, because this chapter seeks to enumerate the costs of anticloning laws, I feel that it is appropriate to mention their spillover effects here. (I will return to this topic in Chapter 11, when I discuss whether the Hawaiian baby should be allowed to assert spillover effects as a basis for her challenge to anticloning laws in other states.)

Now, let us take the final analytical step and envision a future in which all 50 states have enacted cloning bans. At that point, a patchwork national ban on cloning will exist even though each state law that is a component of the ban will vary in its particulars. Within each state, the procreative freedom of adults will be constrained. Within each state, human clones will be born as the result of actions that violate the anticloning laws. They will incur the costs of that violation, ranging from the loss of their parents to legal stigma to passing to isolation. In general, the foregoing analysis of the costs of a national ban applies and need not be repeated here.

However, there is one important difference between this patchwork ban and the national ban that Congress has the power to enact. As discussed in Chapter 6, the 2003 Weldon bill included a provision prohibiting any person from importing the "product" of cloning. In general, state anticloning laws do not include such a provision. Thus, even if there were a patchwork ban, parents could travel to offshore cloning clinics and return home with cloned pregnancies or babies. (Whether the mere act of continuing to gestate an established embryo or fetus would violate the anticloning laws of a particular state would depend on the language and intent of those laws.)

Let us consider the hypothetical case of a baby born in Michigan following conception offshore. Because the Michigan anticloning laws do not apply, it is hard to say that the state targeted this particular baby for nonexistence. However, there could be a different kind of spillover effect here. As a resident of Michigan, the baby faces an environment in which human clones are not wanted. The anticloning laws of that state impose a legal stigma on cloned residents that could lead to discrimination, exclusion, and damage to self-esteem (the fifth cost). In response, some parents might hide their children's origins in cloning (the seventh cost), and other children would choose to pass despite the high cost of living a lie (the eighth cost). Finally, by restricting births, silencing parents, and encouraging passing, Michigan's anticloning laws would isolate residents born through cloning from others who share their status and oppression (the ninth cost).[65]

3. The Benefits of Anticloning Laws

In the face of these significant costs, legislators and regulators should consider (or reconsider) whether anticloning laws have benefits to offer that outweigh their costs.

I believe that the benefits of such laws do not justify their costs. To explain why, I examine the purported benefits of anticloning laws in this section. For the sake of clarity, I will relate these benefits to the five objections and discuss the objections in the same order used in Part 1 of this book.

a) Keeping God and Nature Happy

First, as we have seen, some opponents argue that human reproductive cloning offends God. These people might argue that anticloning laws have the considerable benefit of keeping God happy.

However, as I explained in Chapter 1, there is no scientific proof that God exists. If God does not exist, then there is no benefit to be gained from anticloning laws. Even if God does exist, moreover, there is no objective way to know what God thinks about human reproductive cloning. If the technology does not offend God, there is no benefit to be gained from anticloning laws. Finally, even if cloning offends God, there is no way to know what the punishment for the sin of cloning would be, or who would feel the sting of that punishment. God could choose to condemn only the sinners who clone (i.e., scientists) and leave the rest of us alone. The less severe and widespread the punishment, the less benefit there is to be gained from anticloning laws.

A counterargument might run something like this: because we do not know whether God exists, or what God thinks about cloning, or what punishment God might impose, by far the safest course is to err on the side of caution and ban the technology outright. Moreover, no matter what God thinks, the fact remains that many people *believe* that cloning offends God. Therefore, anticloning laws are necessary, not just to keep God happy, but to keep some religious people happy also.

The problem with this counterargument is that these benefits do not come for free. Anticloning laws have costs, not just for sinners, but for the innocent children who are the inevitable fruit of the sin. The

possibility that cloning could provoke divine wrath and moral indigna-
tion in some humans is not enough to justify laws that take parents,
assets, self-respect, and equality away from these children.

Similarly, some opponents argue that cloning should be outlawed because it is unnatural. As I explained in Chapter 1, cloning (asexual
reproduction) is a part of the evolutionary heritage of humans and is
not "unnatural" in the strict sense of the term. Reaching for the deeper
moral question that underlies the "unnatural" label, one finds that there
is no clear answer to the question of how far humanity should go in en-
hancing its biological capabilities. What we are left with is the undeni-
able fact that many people *believe* that cloning goes too far. Laws that
validate this moral stance may make some people happy, but their sat-
isfaction comes at too high a price: harm to the physical and emotional
welfare of children born through cloning.

Finally, some opponents might argue that anticloning laws, like other
morals legislation, tend to affirm the democratic principle of majority
rule. The California Advisory Committee on Human Cloning hinted at
this approach:

> If no substantial rights are being infringed, a government might ban things
> solely because its citizens do not like them. . . . In 1998, California, by ref-
> erendum, banned the sale of horse meat for human consumption. The ar-
> guments for banning horse meat seemed mainly to have been a popular
> prejudice in favor of horses, but the "right" of people to eat horsemeat
> seemed weak. One might view human reproductive cloning similarly and
> so believe that, in light of weak arguments in favor of human reproductive
> cloning, the public's preferences should be respected.[66]

Again, however, this benefit does not come for free. Anticloning laws
do more than censure scientists and parents who dare to taste the for-
bidden fruit (or, should I say, horse meat?). They also condemn the children who are born through that technology as subhuman and unworthy
of existence. The public has plenty of other opportunities to reaffirm
the principle of majority rule; Congress and the states enact thousands of laws every year. Belief in the virtues of democracy does not require or justify the wholesale condemnation of an entire class of human
beings.

b) Ensuring that Humans Are Not Treated as Products

What about the objection that cloning treats human life as a manufactured product and violates human dignity? Is that argument weighty enough to support the enactment of anticloning laws?

As I explained in Chapter 2, this argument finds its roots in religious and moral concerns. Again, one could argue that anticloning laws provide the benefit of morals legislation generally; that is, people who believe that cloning is manufacture will feel gratified when anticloning laws are enacted to validate their moral values. This gratification is not enough to justify the high costs of anticloning laws – particularly to children.

Alternatively, the objection against manufacture can also be interpreted as a warning against bad consequences.[67] If parents would view cloned children as products, or if cloning would inexorably lead to the (misplaced) view that all humans are products, then one might worry that cloning could lead to an increase in human suffering.

Yet, as explained in Chapter 2 of this book, society has extensive experience with other assisted reproductive technologies – from IVF to donor gametes and surrogacy. Despite frequently asserted objections that such technologies treat children as products or commodities in the marketplace, the data show that children conceived and born through sperm donation or IVF are psychologically normal and loved by their families.[68] The same should hold true for children conceived and born through cloning. Each human is much more than his or her genome; it is biologically impossible for cloning to deliver a "designer" baby or predictable product. Thus, not only is there no evidence that cloning would lead to human suffering; the evidence we do have is very much to the contrary.

What if many people do not understand the basic biological premise that cloning cannot deliver specific products? What of the risk that some people may view human clones as products and lose faith in the preciousness of human life? This risk is speculative. However, even if we assume that this worst-case scenario is realistic, anticloning laws are not the solution. To the contrary, such laws are likely to produce the very result they seek to prevent because a ban on cloning strongly implies that the technology produces humans who are different from other humans – in effect, products who are subhuman.

c) Preventing the Birth of Copies

In Chapter 3, I explained that, as a matter of basic biology, humans cannot be copied. Any argument against cloning that is based on the identity fallacy is simply false. I will not recapitulate that entire analysis here, but I remind the reader of some key points:

- Hitler and other dangerous individuals can never be recreated,
- Human clones do not lack individuality and have their own autonomous lives to lead,
- The families of human clones are not condemned to dysfunction,
- Fathers are not destined to rape their cloned daughters,
- Human clones cannot steal the identities of existing persons, and
- Human clones do not threaten democratic institutions.

Although cloning is harmless, the identity fallacy is not. Human clones might suffer if they wrongly believe that they lack individuality or autonomy. They also might suffer if ignorant and prejudiced people treat them as copies. Humans born through sexual reproduction might be frightened at the false notion that an evil scientist could "clone" them. Most speculatively, some people might lose their faith in democratic institutions built on our core values of individuality and autonomy. Even if it is assumed that these concerns are real, anticloning laws should not be enacted. Such laws do nothing to dispel the identity fallacy that causes these harms. Rather, by legitimating the fallacy, the laws make the harms more likely and severe.

d) Saving Humanity

Human clones do not threaten the survival of the human species. As explained at greater length in Chapter 4, there are good reasons to believe that the average person will prefer sexual reproduction to asexual reproduction. Thus, cloning will not significantly increase the birth rate. It follows that human clones will not overpopulate the planet and cause famines, shortages, diseases, and pollution. Nor will human clones diminish the genetic diversity of our species, thereby reducing its ability to combat predators, parasites, and other environmental stressors. Finally, cloning is not a practical means of achieving eugenic goals. Thus, human clones are not the vanguard of a superior species that will extinguish our own. These speculative and improbable doomsday scenarios do not justify the costs of anticloning laws.

e) Safety

The last argument in favor of anticloning laws is that cloning must be stopped because it is unsafe. In theory, anticloning laws protect participants against the hazards of the technology and prevent the birth of children who would suffer from severe physical defects. There are, however, several reasons why this argument cannot justify anticloning laws.

Protecting Participants from Harm. In general, opponents have overstated the physical risks to participants in human reproductive cloning.

Egg Donors: Despite arguments that cloning could lead to the exploitation of women who donate eggs for the procedure,[69] the fact remains that egg donation involves minimal risks. The most serious risk confronted by any woman who uses fertility drugs (whether on her own behalf or for the purpose of donating eggs to others) is ovarian hyperstimulation syndrome, or OHSS. Only 0.8 to 1.95 percent of women who use fertility drugs suffer from moderate or severe OHSS.[70] Deaths from this condition are rare; they are limited to occasional case reports.[71]

Opponents have also warned that fertility drugs could increase the risk of ovarian cancer. A 1992 medical article sparked this concern by suggesting that women treated with fertility drugs were at a higher risk than the general population for ovarian cancer.[72] This article has been extensively criticized for its flawed methodology.[73] Subsequent scientific studies with more extensive data and improved methodology have failed to establish any link between fertility drugs and ovarian cancer.[74] A 2002 medical article found that fertility drugs do not put women at a higher than average risk of ovarian cancer; rather, certain diseases that cause infertility, such as endometriosis, are linked to a higher risk of ovarian cancer.[75]

In any event, the fact remains that fertility drugs are legal in this country, and many thousands of women choose to take them every year with the benefit of informed consent regarding potential risks. Neither the federal government nor state governments have seen fit to ban such drugs outside the context of cloning even though the risks are precisely the same when a woman takes the drugs to facilitate her own IVF cycle or to donate eggs to an infertile woman. The fact that fertility drugs are freely available and widely used undercuts any assertion that cloning must be banned to protect egg donors.

The President's Council on Bioethics argued that cloning poses a greater risk because it is so inefficient. It reasoned that many more eggs are required for a cycle of human reproductive cloning than for a cycle of IVF, and thus, many more women will be subjected to fertility drugs if cloning is allowed.[76] However, the minimal risks associated with fertility drugs do not increase for each individual woman simply because more women choose to take the drugs. What one ends up with is a larger number of women exposed to a risk that is still minimal.

Embryos and Fetuses: As I explained in Chapter 5, most attempts at animal cloning are unsuccessful. In terms of healthy births to embryos transferred, success rates in animal experiments currently range from less than 1 percent to 11 percent, meaning that anywhere from 89 to 99 percent of embryos never make it to birth.[77]

Most animal cloning failures occur early on, before a pregnancy takes hold, or even before an embryo is transferred.[78] Some cloned fetuses do miscarry, however. As is true of fetuses that are generated through sexual reproduction, most of these cloned fetuses miscarry owing to innate physical flaws (whether genetic, epigenetic, or developmental).

Opponents assume that human cloning would involve similar failure rates if undertaken today. In fact, we do not have enough data to know if that is true. More importantly, if human cloning is ever offered, it will be offered in the future after the technology has been sufficiently improved and tested to make it attractive to prospective clients. However, for the sake of analysis, I will assume that human cloning is as inefficient as animal cloning is today and will remain so. Must human cloning be stopped to protect embryos and fetuses from being created and lost in the process?

As noted in Chapter 5, sexual reproduction is also hazardous to embryos and fetuses. The vast majority (75 percent) of human conceptions do not make it to birth. Yet, no legislature has ever sought to outlaw sexual reproduction for that reason. As a society, we tolerate an enormous number of embryonic and fetal deaths to protect the freedom of the individual to procreate.

If 89 percent, or even 99 percent, of cloned embryos and fetuses are lost in the course of asexual reproduction, are those losses enough to justify anticloning laws? I do not think so. Although losses are somewhat heavier than in sexual reproduction, embryos and fetuses that partici- pate in cloning have, at the very least, a chance at existence. Anticloning laws take that chance at life away. Worse, the laws discriminate against the human clones who make it to birth. If the reproductive freedom of adults is enough to justify their participation in sexual reproduction, de- spite heavy embryonic and fetal casualties, egalitarianism and the need to treat all humans fairly, regardless of their genetic heritage, should be enough to counterbalance the embryonic and fetal losses involved in asexual reproduction.

Gestational Mothers: The vast majority of failures in animal cloning (83 to 99 percent) occur before a pregnancy is established.[79] Such losses do not threaten the health of gestating mothers, for in such cases there is no gestation. Once pregnancies are established, miscarriages do some- times occur in animal cloning.

Miscarriage is a risk that human mothers already face when they be- come pregnant through sexual reproduction. Most miscarriages do not place the health of the mother at serious risk. The National Academies acknowledged that miscarriages occur in human pregnancies but as- serted that most of these miscarriages occur in the first trimester, whereas animals gestating cloned offspring sometimes miscarry late in the pregnancy or are lost in the early neonatal period. Because late ges- tational fetal loss causes increased maternal morbidity and mortality, the Academies argued that human reproductive cloning posed a high risk, not only to fetuses and newborns, but also to the physical and psy- chological health of gestational mothers.[80]

However, there are two key distinctions between animal and human reproductive cloning. First, much fetal, neonatal, and maternal loss in animal experiments may be due to large offspring syndrome, or LOS. It is dangerous to give birth to oversized offspring. However, the govern- ment cannot prove that cloned human fetuses or offspring would suffer from LOS. Rather, the data suggest that the syndrome does not occur in human IVF and is unlikely to occur in human reproductive cloning for genetic reasons.[81]

Second, scientists have the power to require animals that gestate clones to carry fetuses to term no matter what the risks to them. The occasional death of a gestating animal mother is considered a cost of the experiment. By contrast, human mothers are independent agents who have a full range of options available to them to guard against the risks of a pregnancy initiated by cloning. These options include prenatal care and monitoring, abortion, drugs to prevent miscarriage, labor induction, and hospital delivery, including cesarean delivery. Thus, if a cloned fetus begins to develop in an improper or dangerous way, a human mother can protect her health by terminating the pregnancy. Alternatively, she may take medical steps to preserve the pregnancy while arranging birth for a time, method, and place that is safe for her and her infant. Human mothers do not face an unreasonably high risk of injury or death.

Preventing the Birth of Children with Physical Defects. Opponents of human reproductive cloning vigorously assert that the technology poses an unacceptable risk of producing babies and children with serious birth defects. Policymakers and lawmakers often act as if this argument is conclusive in and of itself.

However, animal research already has shown that some risks do not exist or are inapplicable to humans. For example, cloning does not produce prematurely aged animals with shortened telomeres.[82] Also, human babies do not suffer from LOS when conceived through IVF; there are good, genetic reasons to believe that they will not suffer from LOS when conceived through cloning either.[83]

Other safety risks remain unproven. As explained in Chapter 5, some scientists believe that reprogramming is very difficult – so difficult that clones (whether human or animal) inevitably are flawed at the epigenetic level. Other scientists argue persuasively that the vast majority of animal clones are healthy and normal, suggesting that human clones would be healthy and normal also.

I do not believe that speculative risks to the health of cloned babies and children can justify anticloning laws. To explain why not, I reason by analogy to sexual reproduction.

Children born through sexual reproduction face a risk of birth defects that is real and definable. Although the overall birth defect rate is relatively low, there are significant subgroups of births that are subject to rates as high as 12 percent (older mothers) or 25 percent (both parents are carriers of the gene for cystic fibrosis).[84] Yet, there are no laws that make it a crime for a 42-year-old woman to bear children or that make it a crime for carriers of heritable diseases to reproduce.[85] Why not?

Births to older mothers or carriers of heritable diseases pose safety concerns but do not implicate the first four objections. If a 42-year-old woman has a child through sexual reproduction, no one considers her venture to be an affront to God or nature. If a carrier of cystic fibrosis has a child through sexual reproduction, no one frets that the parent has objectified the child or that the child is a copy of the parent. Moreover, no one worries that births to these demographic subgroups may lead to destruction of humanity. The *only* objection that applies to older mothers and carriers of heritable or transmissible diseases is that their children may suffer from birth defects or disease. The fact that there are no laws against sexual reproduction, even when it is hazardous to offspring, indicates that society either (1) does not consider birth defects to be very important, or (2) believes that compensating factors, such as the need to protect the procreative freedom of adults, outweigh the harm of birth defects.

In Part 1 of this book, and again in this Chapter, I explained that the first four objections to cloning are based on scientific errors, or, at best, on religious and moral beliefs that cannot be proven. Thus, at this point in the analysis, it is reasonable to subtract them out. What we have left is the same thing that we have in the case of sexual reproduction: namely, the safety objection. But if real and proven risks to children are not enough to justify laws against sexual reproduction (even in high-risk cases), speculative risks to children should not be enough to justify laws against cloning. *This is particularly true given that the anticloning laws themselves stigmatize and injure the very children they seek to "protect."*

Risk-averse readers might not agree with me. They might point to the possibility that some of the speculative risks could turn out to be real and even substantial. Even then, however, anticloning laws are not the best way to protect children. Given that a market for reproductive cloning is going to exist, whether the technology is legal or not, a more sensible way to protect children (without stigmatizing or otherwise harming them) would be to fund research to improve the science and technology of cloning. This is how the government has treated other novel medical technologies to the great benefit of those who suffer from diseases and disabilities.

Unfortunately, executives and lawmakers have taken exactly the opposite approach. President Bill Clinton blocked the federal funding of human cloning experiments immediately after Dolly was born,[86] and federal and state legislators have worked to criminalize the technology. This is a counterproductive strategy that threatens to drive desperate people offshore and into questionable clinics. As lawyer and infertility patient advocate Mark Eibert has noted, "[i]f that happens, the anticloning laws themselves will be responsible for thousands of dead and deformed children."[87]

Finally, even if risks to cloned children turn out to be real, and even if policymakers insist that some level of regulation and control over human reproductive cloning is necessary to protect children, the fact remains that anticloning laws are bad public policy. The vast majority of such laws impose permanent bans with no sunset clause or provision for automatic review. Such flat prohibitions are excessive and not tailored to meet reasonable safety concerns. As discussed in Chapter 5, there is no reason to believe that reproductive cloning is an inherently imperfect technology or that the science and technology of cloning are incapable of improvement. Perhaps lawmakers have enacted permanent bans because they have been swayed by the other four objections; yet, as just noted once again, those objections have little merit and should carry little weight in the public policy analysis.

Opponents of cloning might point out that even a flat ban can be amended or repealed. However, relying on that solution is unfair to human clones. The statute books are packed with laws that have long since outlived their purposes and yet are not repealed.[88] Sometimes, outdated laws endure owing to inertia and apathy; other times, outdated laws survive because of their symbolic value.

Once again, antimiscegenation laws provide an instructive analogy. As explained in Chapter 8, the Supreme Court decided that antimiscegenation laws were unconstitutional in 1967. For decades afterward, states with antimiscegenation laws were slow to repeal them. Alabama was the last to do so. Its state constitution provided that "the legislature shall never pass any law to authorize or legalize any marriage between any white person and a negro, or descendant of a negro."[89] This provision survived until 2000, when it finally was repealed.[90] Even then, the public vote favored repeal by only 60 to 40 percent, suggesting that many Alabama residents would have preferred to preserve the antimiscegenation provision into the new millennium.[91]

When it comes to anticloning laws, repeal will be even harder to achieve. Even after the safety of the technology improves, social objections to cloning, no matter how unjust or scientifically unfounded, will linger in the public mind strongly reinforced by the laws themselves. Any elected representative who dares to suggest a repeal of anticloning laws will be viewed as an arrogant person who wants to play God, manufacture copies of existing persons, overpopulate the planet, and so forth. Given the ruinous political costs of favoring repeal, anticloning laws could remain on the law books for decades or centuries. Thus, even after cloning becomes safe, the laws will continue to stigmatize and otherwise injure human clones for no good reason whatsoever.

In summary, anticloning laws have significant costs. They deny reproductive freedom to adults who cannot reproduce sexually because of disability or sexual orientation. They threaten to undermine scientific freedom. Worse, they inflict a long list of injuries upon human clones, including exclusion at the national border, legal stigma, loss of parents and parental resources, loss of medical and personal history, passing, and isolation from other human clones. Lastly, by marking human clones as subhuman, the laws undermine the basic principle of egalitarianism.

The putative benefits of anticloning laws are insufficient to outweigh these costs. Most of the five objections to human reproductive cloning and human clones lack a scientific basis or amount to religious or moral arguments that cannot be proven. Remaining concerns about cloning technology and its "products" are minor, speculative, or better solved through alternative means. Therefore, I conclude that the anticloning laws that have been proposed, applied, and enacted are bad public policy.

Summary of Part Two

Part 1 of this book outlined five common objections to human reproductive cloning and human clones: (1) the technology offends God and nature; (2) the technology threatens to reduce human beings to the level of manmade objects; (3) human clones are copies; (4) human clones threaten the survival of the human species; and (5) the technology is unsafe for participants and produces human clones with serious birth defects. I explained how these objections are based on, and inspire, stereotypes about human clones.

Part 2 of this book moved on to public policy analysis. I described how anticloning laws work and how the five objections inspired the enactment of the laws. Next, reasoning by analogy to antimiscegenation laws, which once sought to prevent the birth of mixed-race children,

I explained that anticloning laws are just another attempt to impose existential segregation on another unpopular class of humans.

Construed narrowly, existential segregation simply excludes some human clones from existence. However, as Chapter 9 explained, this narrow interpretation does not do existential segregation justice. Existential segregation must be recognized as a broader form of discrimination that requires the government to injure the living deliberately.

Anticloning laws target human clones for nonexistence before birth. This stigmatizes those who are born in defiance of anticloning laws. The laws, moreover, cannot succeed in preventing births unless they deter offshore cloning and punish lawbreakers. Thus, the laws exclude some cloned babies and children at the national border and take parents and parental assets away from others. From these injuries, others flow. The laws encourage parents to hide medical and personal history from their children, induce passing, and isolate those born from human cloning from each other.

Against these substantial costs, I weighed the purported benefits of anticloning laws and found them wanting. Therefore, I concluded that anticloning laws are bad public policy.

Unfortunately, I have little confidence that Congress, the FDA, and state legislatures are going to heed my warning and stop proposing, applying, and enacting anticloning laws. Thus, the next part of this book discusses what might happen if human clones brought a lawsuit challenging the constitutionality of anticloning laws on equal protection grounds.

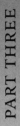

ANTICLONING LAWS VIOLATE THE EQUAL PROTECTION GUARANTEE AND ARE UNCONSTITUTIONAL

Part 2 explained how laws can be used to effectuate a policy of existential segregation against the members of disfavored classes of human beings. Chapter 8 offered antimiscegenation laws as a historical example of existential segregation, and explained how anticloning laws seek to effectuate a policy of existential segregation today. Chapter 9 outlined the harm that anticloning laws can inflict on parents and children and argued that anticloning laws should not be proposed, applied, or enacted.

Part 3 turns now to a different question: If anticloning laws are on the books, how can human clones and their families invalidate the laws?

One answer that readily comes to mind is that the parents of human clones could challenge the laws as a violation of their own fundamental constitutional rights. This is the strategy that has been used to combat existential segregation successfully in the recent past. As we have seen, antimiscegenation laws were intended, in part, to prevent the birth of mixed-race children. However, when the Supreme Court struck down those laws, it focused on the rights of the parents of such children, ruling that the laws infringed on their fundamental right to marry.[1]

In the context of anticloning laws, which seek to outlaw asexual reproduction, the fundamental right to privacy seems more relevant. As noted in Chapter 9, a growing number of lawyers and scholars have argued that the right to privacy includes a right to employ human reproductive cloning – at least for individuals who lack viable gametes and cannot reproduce in the usual sexual manner. Their arguments are logical and persuasive; there is no good reason why the Constitution should grant healthy Americans a reproductive freedom that is virtually absolute while denying disabled Americans the right to procreate in the only manner possible for them.

Unfortunately, the Supreme Court has never explicitly addressed the right to procreate via assisted reproductive technologies, let alone cloning. Parents who want to protect their cloned children from the harms of existential segregation can and should assert their privacy rights; however, they should not end their arguments there.

A second possible strategy would be to attack anticloning laws on the ground that there is a First Amendment right to conduct scientific experiments. This argument is intriguing, but the outcome is hard to predict; the Supreme Court has never recognized First Amendment protection for scientific experimentation. Moreover, scientists, and not parents, probably would be the ones with the standing to assert this sort of challenge.

A third possible strategy would be to argue that Congress does not have the power under the Commerce Clause to enact anticloning legislation. Although this argument is plausible, its success is not guaranteed. A Commerce Clause argument, moreover, does nothing to invalidate state anticloning laws; it simply shifts the battlefield from Congress to state legislatures.

Leaving the merits aside, I feel that the privacy, speech, and Commerce Clause arguments leave something important unexpressed. Human clones are the targets of these oppressive anticloning laws. They should be able to attack these laws by asserting their own rights and injuries rather than relying entirely on the privacy rights of their parents, First Amendment rights of scientists, or the limits on Congressional authority that the Commerce Clause imposes.

Moreover, human clones are not the only current target of existential segregation. There are other disfavored groups that are being subjected to existential segregation right now. This heightens the need for a new theory that can protect the rights of disfavored groups more directly and forcefully.

For example, in the last few years, some novel variations on standard IVF have attracted much negative press and governmental fire. In cytoplasm transfer, doctors inject the eggs of infertile women with fresh cytoplasm from third-party egg donors.[2] In the opposite technique, nuclear transfer, doctors transfer the nucleus of infertile eggs into enucleated donor eggs.[3] Both of these techniques challenge the standard genetic model for humans; by mixing the nuclear DNA of the patient with the mitochondrial[4] DNA of the egg donor, the techniques have the potential to create a child with two genetic mothers.

Twenty-three children were born through cytoplasm transfer in the United States before the FDA came down hard on American practitioners. In warning letters, the FDA told fertility clinics that they had to submit investigational new drug applications and receive agency approval before treating new patients. The FDA claimed that children should not be born from the techniques because they might be susceptible to mitochondrial disease;[5] moreover, the techniques involved genetic modifications to gametes that the children could pass on to future generations.[6] Such rationales are consistent with a policy of existential segregation; children who might be sick, or who embody heritable changes to the human genome, should not be born.

A recent report from the President's Council on Bioethics forecasts stormy weather ahead for novel assisted reproductive technologies. In *Reproduction and Responsibility*, the council recommended that Congress should prohibit attempts to conceive a child by any means other than the union of egg and sperm.[7] This sweeping recommendation encompasses technologies ranging from cytoplasm transfer[8] to reproductive cloning[9] to parthenogenesis.[10] The council also recommended that Congress enact laws to prohibit attempts to conceive a child by using sperm or eggs created from embryonic stem cells or harvested from fetuses.[11] In addition, the council advocated banning attempts to conceive a child by fusing two or more embryos.[12] In the council's view, all of these technologies are objectionable because they could "deny to children born with their aid a full and equal share in our common human origins, for instance by denying them the direct biological connection to *two* human genetic parents or by giving them a fetal or embryonic progenitor. We believe that such departures and inequities in human origins should not be inflicted on any child."[13] This amounts to a statement that children born through these technologies should not exist, for they would be less than fully human. Again, if Congress listens to the council, and passes laws banning these technologies, there is no guarantee that the courts will put a stop to the program of existential segregation by holding that infertile men and women have a right to reproductive freedom that includes the use of these technologies.

Second, consider the case of children born to, and reared by, gay and lesbian couples. Recently, the Massachusetts Supreme Court held that, consistent with the Massachusetts Constitution, the state could not deny civil marriage to same-sex couples.[14] This decision has sparked strong opposition, including an ongoing effort to amend the Massachusetts Constitution to define marriage as between a man and woman.[15] Other states have enacted laws that limit marriage to the union of a man and woman,[16] and there is an effort to amend the U.S. Constitution along the same lines.[17] One rationale that has been asserted for limiting civil marriage to heterosexual unions is that the state has a legitimate interest in promoting an "optimal" social structure for bearing and raising children.[18] The flip side of this rationale has the ring of existential segregation: same-sex couples should not be encouraged to bear and rear children because the children would lack either a father or mother figure or otherwise suffer emotional damage.[19] Because the U.S. Supreme Court has never ruled upon the question of whether gays and lesbians have the constitutional right to marry the partners of their choice, there is no guarantee that the right to marry protects against this form of existential segregation.

More speculatively, if genetic engineering does become scientifically possible in the future, Congress or the states could enact laws that make it a crime to reproduce through that technology as a means of preventing the birth of "super-babies." This, too, would be a program of existential segregation against an envied and despised class. Again, there is no guarantee that the fundamental right to procreate would be interpreted to encompass genetic engineering.

What this adds up to is a conclusion that an alternative legal strategy for attacking existential segregation is needed – one that focuses, not on the rights of parents, scientists, or others but rather on the rights of the children who have been targeted for nonexistence.

This task is undertaken in Part III of this book. Although I focus on human clones, the basic theory and reasoning presented can be extended to other disfavored classes confronted with existential segregation today and in the future.

I write on the assumption that, in the near future, humans will be born through cloning. If they live in the United States, those individuals will have a right to due process under the Fifth Amendment and equal protection under the Fourteenth Amendment.[20] I believe that anticloning laws violate this equal protection guarantee, giving the targets of existential segregation a constitutional claim that they can assert directly.

Chapter 10 describes the equal protection guarantee and explains that anticloning laws are subject to scrutiny under the guarantee because they reflect a discriminatory purpose. In the course of this explaination, moreover, I argue that the appropriate level of scrutiny is the highest level: strict scrutiny. This is so because human clones have the characteristics of a suspect class and require an extraordinary degree of judicial protection.

Chapter 11 identifies several injuries that anticloning laws inflict on human clones. In discussing these injuries, I explain why human clones should have the standing to challenge the laws – even in cases in which the core injury is one of legal stigma.

Finally, Chapter 12 analyzes the constitutionality of anticloning laws under a strict scrutiny standard. In that analysis, I conclude that the five objections (hubris, manufacture, identity, harm to the species, and safety) are not compelling enough to justify a policy of existential segregation against human clones. In addition, I explain that anticloning laws are not drawn or applied narrowly to address whatever legitimate concerns are embedded within the five objections.

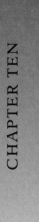

CHAPTER TEN

Anticloning Laws Classify Human Clones and Are Subject to Strict Scrutiny

The Fourteenth Amendment provides that no state shall deny any person within its jurisdiction the equal protection of the laws.[1] The Equal Protection Clause has been described as a direction that all persons who are similarly situated should be treated alike rather than differently.[2]

Although the Fourteenth Amendment does not apply to the federal government, the Fifth Amendment provides that no person shall be deprived of life, liberty, or property without due process of law. The U.S. Supreme Court has held that this Due Process Clause proscribes unjust legal discrimination.[3] Federal laws that classify individuals in a manner that would offend the Equal Protection Clause will be struck down on Due Process grounds, and the basic analysis and standard of judicial review is the same.[4] Therefore, for convenience's sake, I will use the phrase "equal protection guarantee" to describe the protection against discrimination that the Constitution grants to any person residing in the United States[5] under both the Equal Protection Clause of the Fourteenth Amendment and the Due Process Clause of the Fifth Amendment.

How is the equal protection guarantee relevant to a discussion of anticloning laws? This chapter answers this question in two steps: (1) it explains how such laws classify human clones and (2) it argues that this legal classification is suspect and triggers strict scrutiny under the equal protection guarantee.

1. Anticloning Laws Deliberately Treat Human Clones Differently from Humans Born through Sexual Reproduction

On their face, laws that ban human reproductive cloning do not classify human clones. Instead, the laws prohibit scientists, doctors, parents, and other individuals from engaging in reproductive cloning.

This does not mean, however, that the equal protection guarantee is irrelevant. The Supreme Court will invalidate a law that appears to be neutral but in reality is a subterfuge designed to impose hidden burdens on an unpopular class (such as a racial minority).[6]

To establish that a law is a subterfuge, a lawyer usually begins by showing that the law has a disparate impact on the unpopular class. The next section demonstrates that anticloning laws have a disparate impact on human clones.

a) Disparate Impact

I begin with an analysis of federal efforts to ban reproductive cloning. Although there is a political consensus that reproductive cloning is wrong, there is no federal law against cloning because representatives and senators cannot agree on whether research cloning should be banned. Sooner or later, the political balance will tip in one direction or the other and Congress will enact a law that is similar to either the 2003 Weldon bill, or the 2003 Hatch bill. Thus, in analyzing the disparate impact of federal anticloning laws, I will take these two bills as the basis for discussion.

The 2003 Weldon bill prohibited any person from performing or participating in human cloning. It defined human cloning as human asexual reproduction accomplished by introducing nuclear material from a somatic cell into an egg "so as to produce a living organism (at any stage of development) that is genetically virtually identical to an existing or previously existing human organism."[7] The "living organism" could be just an embryo; thus, the bill outlawed research cloning. But the bill did much more than that. The organism "at any stage of development" could also be a fetus or a baby. Thus, the bill prohibited scientists, doctors, and parents from engaging in reproductive cloning. In so doing, it sought to prevent the birth of human clones.

The 2003 Weldon bill also made it a crime to import the "product" of cloned embryos.[8] As noted in Chapter 6, this provision closed a loophole; it made it a crime to clone abroad and come home with the result. The provision was broad enough to make it a crime for a woman to travel to an offshore fertility clinic, get pregnant there, and return to the United States with a fetus or baby. Thus, the provision reinforced the ban on reproductive cloning.

The 2003 Hatch bill demonstrates another form that federal anti-cloning legislation might take. That bill made it a crime for any person to conduct human cloning, which was defined as implanting the product of nuclear transplantation into a uterus or the functional equivalent of a uterus.[9] The usual consequence when a human embryo is implanted in a uterus is the birth of a baby roughly 9 months later. Therefore, this bill prohibited scientists, doctors, and parents from engaging in reproductive cloning; in so doing, it sought to prevent the birth of human clones.

Although no federal law specifically addresses cloning, a national ban on cloning arguably exists. Relying on existing laws, the Food and Drug Administration (FDA) has asserted its authority to halt experiments to clone a human being. Thus, the agency opposes reproductive cloning and the birth of human clones. To date, the agency has chosen to limit its enforcement efforts to scientists and doctors. However, it could also choose to prosecute and punish parents who aid and abet cloning efforts or who conspire to clone.

Moving on to state legislative efforts, one finds that some laws ban research and reproductive cloning. For example, Michigan prohibits scientists, doctors, parents, and other individuals from creating human embryos through cloning.[10] Because no person can exist without first having been an embryo, the Michigan law bans not only research cloning but also actions that could lead to the birth of human clones. Similarly, Arkansas prohibits scientists, doctors, parents, or any other person from performing or participating in human cloning. Cloning is defined as introducing nuclear material from a somatic cell into an egg so as to produce a living organism at any stage of development that is genetically virtually identical to an existing or previously existing human organism.[11] Embryos are "living organism[s] at any stage of development," but so are fetuses and babies. Thus, the Arkansas law not only prohibits research cloning but also seeks to prevent the birth of human clones.

Other states ban reproductive cloning only. For example, California provides that no person shall clone a human being or engage in human reproductive cloning. Cloning is defined as implanting a cloned embryo to initiate a pregnancy that could result in the birth of a human being.[12] Thus, although the California law addresses the conduct of scientists, doctors, and parents, its underlying purpose of preventing the birth of human clones is clear. Similarly, New Jersey makes it a crime for scientists, doctors, parents, and others to engage or assist in the cloning of a human being but prohibits only cloning that proceeds through the egg, embryo, fetal, and newborn stages to produce a cloned baby.[13]

Human reproductive cloning is a reproductive technology. Therefore, as the foregoing discussion demonstrates, laws that ban reproductive cloning have the effect and purpose of preventing the birth and existence of some human clones.

Moreover, as explained in Chapter 9, anticloning laws cannot prevent the existence of some human clones without harming the many other humans clones who are sure to be born in defiance of the laws. Whenever a person is conceived, implanted, gestated, or born in violation of law, it is fair to say that the law targeted him or her for nonexistence. Impacts that follow from this targeting include legal stigma, loss of parents (who may be prosecuted for breaking the law), loss of medical and personal history, the injuries associated with passing, and isolation from other human clones. In addition, a law that prohibits parents from importing the "product" of cloning excludes babies and children who are American citizens at the national border.

All of this contrasts sharply with the position of humans born through sexual reproduction. Congress and the states do not prohibit or penalize sexual reproduction. The FDA has not asserted its jurisdiction over sexual intercourse even when it is dangerous for participants and the children who may result. Under the law, the children of coitus are free to increase in number. They do not face exclusion at the national border, legal stigma, loss of parents, loss of medical and personal history, the injuries associated with passing, or isolation.

In sum, anticloning laws have a disparate impact on human clones, treating them less favorably than humans born through sexual reproduction.

b) Discriminatory Purpose

However, the Supreme Court rarely invalidates a law on the basis of disparate impact alone.

> Sometimes a clear pattern, unexplainable on grounds other than race, emerges from the effect of the state action even when the governing legislation appears neutral on its face. The evidentiary inquiry is then relatively easy. But such cases are rare. Absent a [stark] pattern...impact alone is not determinative, and the Court must look to other evidence.[14]

Thus, it is important to continue the analysis, and identify further evidence that anticloning laws are intended to discriminate against human clones.

The sequence of events leading up to a law or administrative decision can help to establish that the responsible legislature or agency harbored animus towards the class and acted for discriminatory reasons.[15] In a lawsuit challenging a specific anticloning law, the circumstances preceding enactment of that particular law will be most relevant. For purposes of this book, it is enough to note that certain suspicious patterns of scientific action and political reaction have emerged during the past several years. As explained at greater length in the next section, every year or two, some scientist, doctor, or religious cultist pops up out of relative obscurity and asserts that he or she plans to clone humans or has done so already. Each time this happens, public and media hysteria boils over. In response, legislators and regulators try to ban cloning quickly to stop the (apparently) imminent birth of human clones. This reoccurring cycle reflects antipathy not just toward cloning as a technology but also toward human clones.

Evidence of a discriminatory purpose also can be gleaned from legislative or administrative history, including contemporary statements by lawmakers or regulators, minutes of meetings, and reports.[16] In Parts 1 and 2 of this book, I provided substantial evidence to show that anticloning laws are based on the five objections. This evidence included policymaking reports designed to advise lawmakers and the contemporary statements of legislators and regulators. Several of these objections – namely, the identity fallacy, destruction of the species, and the supposed physical defects of human clones – go directly to the negative traits of human clones or to the consequences that their presence on Earth could have for others. *To meet these objections, a law must be designed to eliminate this undesirable class of persons.*

As explained in Chapter 8, making it a crime for human clones to exist would not be an effective strategy for both constitutional and practical reasons. Status crimes violate the constitutional guarantee against cruel and unusual punishment. Moreover, human clones would not commit suicide to comply with such a law. Some might flee the country, but many others would remain underground. Lawmakers and regulators have taken the only logical alternative course – that is, they have acted to stop human clones from coming into existence and contact with the rest of us. Thus, anticloning laws deliberately discriminate against human clones.

Those who support anticloning laws will dispute this conclusion. I can imagine two arguments they might raise.

First, they might attempt to split the class of human clones into two subclasses. They might admit that anticloning laws seek to prevent the existence of human clones but argue that the laws are not intended to discriminate against or harm those human clones who manage to achieve birth despite the laws. By this reasoning, the injuries that the latter suffer are simply collateral damage of the war against the former.

This argument should be rejected as an attempt to exploit the conceptual quirks of existential segregation. Laws that seek to implement a policy of existential segregation necessarily must prohibit actions taken before a person is born such as the creation, implantation, gestation, or birthing of a cloned embryo. Nevertheless, the fact remains that any human clone born in defiance of anticloning laws must have been targeted for nonexistence before his or her birth, and this targeting lies at the root of all of the harms he or she suffers throughout life, as enumerated in Chapter 9. If there is to be meaningful recourse for existential segregation, it makes sense to view the target class as a whole and hold that the equal protection guarantee is relevant whenever there is intent to discriminate against that class, including animus directed at members of the class before their birth.[17]

Second, supporters might argue that legislators and regulators would have moved to stop human reproductive cloning even if they held no animus toward human clones. They might note that some of the five objections – hubris, manufacture, and the safety of participants in experiments – are directed primarily at cloning technology and those who would wield it but only indirectly at human clones.

It is not enough, however, to assert that there were nondiscriminatory reasons for enacting anticloning laws. So long as discrimination against human clones was a substantial or motivating factor, supporters must carry the burden of proving that anticloning laws would have been enacted even absent any discriminatory intent.[18] This they cannot do.

To demonstrate this point, I remind the reader of how our society has responded to complaints about hubris, manufacture, and participant safety in other reproductive contexts. Lawmakers have not banned IVF and other assisted reproductive technologies even though the technologies were considered unnatural when first discovered and even though many people continue to believe that these technologies are sinful today.[19] Similarly, IVF and other assisted reproductive technologies have remained legal despite complaints that the technologies violate human dignity and commodify children.[20] Concerns about hubris and manufacture have not been enough to produce bans on other reproductive technologies; by implication, these two concerns are not enough to produce a ban on cloning.

Similarly, sexual reproduction is hazardous for embryos, fetuses, and gestational mothers – particularly in cases in which the genetic parents carry heritable diseases or are older.[21] Yet, there has not been any drive to outlaw sexual reproduction even in cases in which it is very dangerous for participants. Participant safety has not been sufficient to produce legislation interfering with sexual reproduction; by implication, participant safety is not sufficient to produce a ban on cloning.

What, then, *is* sufficient to produce a ban on human reproductive cloning? Cloning is the *only* reproductive method that produces humans who are (falsely) believed to be copies of their DNA donors. This stereotype lies at the heart of all of the arguments against cloning described in Chapters 3 and 4. Moreover, as explained in Chapter 5, the safety objection centers on the (speculative) belief that human clones would be defective. Given the pervasive influence of the identity fallacy and the frequency with which lawmakers have asserted the need to prevent the birth of flawed children, supporters cannot *prove* that anticloning laws would have been enacted absent the obvious intent to discriminate against duplicative, dangerous, and defective human clones.

The analysis in this section may be summarized as follows: Anticloning laws might appear neutral on their face. Nevertheless, such laws classify human clones. Such laws are subterfuges designed to impose hidden burdens on human clones. This triggers the protection of the equal protection guarantee.

2. Strict Scrutiny Applies Because Human Clones Are a Suspect Class

Because anticloning laws classify human clones, the next step is to determine the level of judicial scrutiny such laws should receive.

Laws that classify individuals according to their race,[22] nationality,[23] and alienage[24] are considered inherently suspect and are subjected to strict judicial scrutiny. Such laws must be narrowly tailored to serve a compelling governmental interest; otherwise, the courts invalidate them.[25]

Are human clones a "suspect class" just as racial and national minorities are? If so, the Supreme Court must subject laws that classify human clones according to their genetic status to strict scrutiny.

Unfortunately, there is no simple test for what constitutes a suspect class. Throughout the years, in various opinions, the Supreme Court has noted several factors that mark the existence of a suspect class. The Court has never explained which of these factors are the most important or what relationship one bears to another (many seem to be intertwined). Scholars have debated the matter, but no universally accepted theory has emerged.

I do not propose to offer a general theory of suspect classification here. Instead, the relevant factors will be identified, adapted to the context of existential segregation, and applied to human clones as a group. If many markers are present, I will conclude that the Court should recognize human clones as a suspect class.

Before beginning, however, I wish to address one possible objection up-front. Some constitutional scholars believe that the Supreme Court is not going to identify any more suspect classes in the foreseeable future.[26] In support of this prediction, they point to the fact that the Court has not yet recognized women, illegitimate children, and gays and lesbians as suspect classes despite ample opportunities to do so.[27]

I believe this prediction is wrong for two reasons. First, it falsely assumes that the Court already has had the chance to evaluate and identify all suspect classes. That may be true of existing groups but it is not true of human clones. *Human clones are an entirely new group that will come into existence for the very first time during the twenty-first century.* The Court must evaluate this new group on its own terms, taking its unique biological and social characteristics into account.

Second, the prediction implicitly assumes that all discrimination is created equal. This, too, is incorrect. Granted, the law has discriminated against women, illegitimate children, and gays and lesbians in significant ways, but it has never mandated their wholesale elimination. Yet, that is precisely the fate that cloning opponents have in mind for human clones. Given the extreme degree of prejudice and discrimination that human clones face, there is a correspondingly greater need to provide them with the strongest form of judicial protection available by recognizing them as having a suspect status and strictly scrutinizing the laws that oppress them.

Under these circumstances, it would be a mistake to rely on the same old platitudes about the Supreme Court's unwillingness to recognize new suspect classes. Rather, it is time to take a fresh look at the relevant factors; the bottles may be old, but they can be adapted to the new wine waiting to be poured into them.

a) Disabilities, History, and Powerlessness: The Need for Extraordinary Judicial Protection

The Supreme Court has stated that a suspect class is one that is "saddled with such disabilities, or subjected to such a history of purposeful unequal treatment, or relegated to such a position of political powerlessness as to command extraordinary protection from the majoritarian political process."[28]

The "*majoritarian* political process" must refer to the legislative process, where raw numbers and political clout drive the outcome. Thus, what the Court is looking for is strong evidence that the class cannot protect itself against discrimination by participating in the legislative process. When such evidence is present, the Court is willing to take on the role of protector; it categorizes the class as "suspect" and subjects legislation that harms the class to heightened scrutiny.

To place this factor in context, it is helpful to take a look at the best-known suspect class: race. Blacks have been subjected to a "history of purposeful unequal treatment" in the United States. Stolen away from their homes in Africa, blacks were enslaved and forced to labor in the fields and homes of whites. Even after slavery was abolished, laws mandating segregation, together with the social prejudice that the laws reinforced, kept blacks from claiming the same rights, privileges, and social standing as whites. This history of unequal treatment was compounded by the "political powerlessness" of blacks. Blacks were fewer in number than whites and had fewer votes, making it hard for them to fight discrimination in the legislative branch of government. Centuries of slavery and discrimination also left blacks as a group without the same level of education, social standing, wealth, and influence as whites, making it harder for them to persuade whites to cast their votes in support of the black political agenda.

Now, consider the position that human clones will occupy within our society. On the basis of the evidence we have today, can we count on the legislative process to protect the class or should the judiciary step in and assume the role of special protector?

So far as we know, no human clones have been born yet. Therefore, there is no *history* of their unequal treatment in the literal sense. But a history of unequal treatment is just one type of evidence that demonstrates the need for extraordinary judicial protection. In the context of existential segregation, which involves an attempt to exclude an unpopular group from existence, the courts should place great weight on any *prehistory* of unequal treatment.

Here, the prehistory of human clones includes the record of public and political reaction to the mere possibility that human clones could be born in the near future. Let me briefly remind the reader of that record.

When scientists announced the birth of Dolly in 1997, human reproductive cloning – and human clones – became a realistic prospect.
The public was horrified.[29] The media cashed in with television reports
and news articles that portrayed cloning as capable of replicating existing persons. President Bill Clinton banned federal funding for research related to human cloning,[30] and the National Bioethics Advisory
Commission urged Congress to enact a moratorium on reproductive
cloning.[31]

In 1998, Richard Seed asserted his intention to clone a human baby.[32]
Despite his poor qualifications, hysteria intensified. Congress came
close to passing a ban on cloning as an *emergency* measure.[33] The FDA
announced that it had regulatory authority over human reproductive
cloning but would not grant permission for cloning experiments owing
to safety concerns.

Meanwhile, state legislatures lurched into action. As early as 1997,
California enacted a 5-year moratorium on human reproductive
cloning.[34] Michigan also acted quickly; its ban on research and reproductive cloning was signed into law in 1998.[35]

Time marched on. For a few years, the science of animal cloning advanced with little fanfare. However, in 2001, Dr. Panayiotis Zavos stated
that he planned to clone babies for infertile couples. Dr. Brigitte Boisselier, a member of the Raelian religious sect, made similar claims. Attitudes towards human reproductive cloning and human clones had not
improved in the new millennium,[36] and another wave of public hysteria
and media pandering followed.

Policymakers reacted strongly to the stated plans of Drs. Zavos and
Boisselier. In 2002, the National Academies, the President's Council on
Bioethics, and the California Advisory Committee on Human Cloning
all recommended that lawmakers ban reproductive cloning.[37]

Lawmakers agreed: in 2001, the House of Representatives passed a
ban on all cloning by an overwhelming margin. In late 2002, Dr. Boisselier announced that the first cloned baby had been born; the House
responded by passing another ban on all cloning in early 2003.[38]

In the new millennium, state legislatures also stepped up their efforts
to outlaw human reproductive cloning. Several states added new laws,
and California dropped its 5-year moratorium in favor of a permanent
ban.[39]

Thus, the prehistory of human clones shows a recurring pattern, and that pattern reflects antipathy toward the members of the class. Whenever the public believes that cloned babies are about to be born, or have been born, hysteria rises and politicians act to stop the threat by enacting legislation that seeks to prevent the birth of members of the class.

Moreover, the five objections are also a part of the prehistory of human clones. As explained in Parts 1 and 2 of this book, these objections are not limited to the evils of cloning technology or the arrogance of those who might use the technology[40] but also extend to the nature and characteristics of human clones themselves. Opponents have made it crystal clear that they believe human clones are deformed and dangerous copies who must not be allowed to come into existence.

This prehistory does not inspire confidence in the capacity of our democratic system to treat human clones fairly. Indeed, the anticloning laws enacted during this prehistory ensure that cloned babies and children will experience a *history* of discrimination and unequal treatment from the moment they are born. Owing to these laws, human clones will suffer all of the harms associated with existential segregation, including exclusion at the national border, legal stigma, loss of parents and parental resources, loss of medical and personal information, passing, and isolation from other human clones. Many of the harms (e.g., exclusion, legal stigma, and passing) are comparable to the injuries that racial segregation inflicts; all of the harms are substantial.

The prehistory and history of human clones are not the only indications that this class cannot protect itself through the legislative process. In addition, human clones will lack political power for three reasons.

First, the absolute number of human clones is going to remain very small for a long time. Not only is the technology likely to appeal to a relatively small demographic group of parents, but anticloning laws themselves are going to reduce the number of human clones. In a democracy, where votes count, human clones and their relatives and friends will have a very hard time making an impact.

Second, those who are the first to be born through cloning are going to be babies and children for many years. They cannot fight for their rights directly. Their parents face prosecution if they reveal the truth about their participation in cloning; therefore, they are unlikely to fight for the rights of their children.

Against this, it might be argued that a class does not lack political power and earn suspect status simply because it is a minority or even a closeted minority. There may be other evidence that the class has public and legislative support. For example, in ruling that the mentally retarded are not a suspect class, the Supreme Court noted that Congress had enacted many laws in their favor, thereby indicating that they had the ability to attract the attention and support of lawmakers despite their disability.[41]

However, when it comes to human clones, there is no evidence of public and legislative support; indeed, the record is very much to the contrary, as we have seen. This is the third reason human clones will lack political power: they are uniformly despised today and are likely to remain so for the foreseeable future. The attention they have attracted from Congress and state legislatures so far has been entirely negative – a fact that accurately reflects their utter lack of political power. Realistically, there is very little chance that human clones could work to repeal the anticloning laws that lie at the heart of their oppression. As noted in Chapter 9, given the hostile public attitude toward cloning and "clones," any legislator who votes in favor of repeal would be committing political suicide.

In sum, the prehistory of human clones, coupled with their lack of political power, present a strong case for judicial protection of the class.

b) Discrete and Insular Minorities

A related factor comes from what may be the most celebrated dictum in Supreme Court history. In *U.S. v. Carolene Products Co.*, the Court applied a minimal level of judicial scrutiny to uphold a federal law that prohibited shipment in interstate commerce of doctored milk.[42] In footnote 4, the Court suggested that a different, stricter standard of review might apply in other cases: "Nor need we enquire . . . whether prejudice against discrete and insular minorities may be a special condition, which tends seriously to curtail the operation of those political processes ordinarily to be relied upon to protect minorities, and which may call for a correspondingly more searching judicial inquiry."[43]

Read in context, a "discrete and insular" minority requires judicial protection because it cannot protect itself through the legislative process.

Human clones are going to be a minority in relation to the teeming hordes of humans born through sexual reproduction. However, are human clones a "discrete and insular" minority?

Human clones who live in the United States will not be separated from the rest of us in a *physical* sense. They will live together with their parents, relatives, and the rest of the masses born through sexual reproduction.

However, the concepts of "discrete" and "insular" apply in other ways. In a world in which most people are born through sexual reproduction and have individuated genomes, human clones, who are born through asexual reproduction and have shared genomes, are *biologically* distinct. Moreover, as Part I revealed, these biological distinctions also lead to *social* distinctions. The concept of the "clone" has become associated with stereotypes and stigma that mark human clones as inferior. Even before the class has come into existence, society has assigned its members to a lower rung of humanity. Finally, biological and social distinctions have triggered *legal* distinctions. Anticloning laws have marked human clones as a discrete and disfavored group, the members of which have no right to exist.

Perhaps most significantly, the characterization of human clones as a "discrete and insular" minority would be consistent with the policy underlying that factor – namely, the need to protect a minority that cannot protect itself through the legislative process. The biological distinctiveness of human clones does not directly affect their ability to participate in the democratic process. However, given that society and the law already have distinguished human clones as inferior – even subhuman – they are unlikely to command much attention or respect from a legislative process that runs on numbers, wealth, and social status.

c) Visible Characteristics

The Supreme Court has occasionally noted that members of suspect classes tend to be marked by visible or obvious characteristics.[44] The Court has not articulated consistent reasons for the relevance of this factor. Visibility could matter because it offers one way to define the members of a discrete group;[45] to that extent, it is just another way of articulating the "discrete and insular" test discussed immediately above. Alternatively, the Court has noted that visibility facilitates discrimination against members of the class.[46] This interpretation focuses on the vulnerability of class members to discrimination and their resulting need for judicial protection.

Birth through cloning is not a visible characteristic. Notwithstanding popular media portrayals of "clones" as carbon copies and chains of identical paper dolls, observers will have no way to know whether a person was conceived through cloning just by looking at him or her. The only way to be sure would be to conduct a genetic analysis and match the nuclear DNA of the suspect with that of some other person or persons. This makes it somewhat impractical (though not impossible) to subject human clones to physical segregation or legal discrimination once they are born and inside the country.

Visibility, however, is not an absolute prerequisite for suspect classification. It is not possible to determine the citizenship of a person at sight. Yet, the Supreme Court has granted suspect status to aliens.

Moreover, the relevance of visibility depends on the type of discrimination involved. Traditional methods of discrimination, such as racial segregation, require that those who enforce the law are able to identify members of the disfavored class and impose sanctions against them. In this context, visibility is a reasonable marker of vulnerability to discrimination.

However, existential segregation operates differently. Anticloning laws seek to eliminate human clones before their birth; toward this end, they ban the use of a particular reproductive technology. The laws can inflict substantial harms on human clones whether their genetic status is visible or not. Enforcers may prosecute parents based on evidence of involvement in cloning, and the child may feel the sting of stigma whether or not his or her genetic status is revealed to the world. Under these circumstances, visibility is a less reliable marker of vulnerability to discrimination and should not determine whether human clones qualify as a suspect class.

d) Immutable Characteristics

The Supreme Court also has noted that the members of suspect classes, such as racial minorities or disfavored nationalities, tend to have immutable characteristics determined by the accident of birth. This factor could be relevant for one or both of two different reasons.

First, immutable characteristics tend to define members of the class as a discrete group.[47] This helps to isolate them from the rest of society so that the majority has less reason to respect them or be concerned with their interests and needs.[48] From this point of view, immutability is similar to the concept of the "discrete and insular" minority; it serves as a marker for political impotence and a resulting need for judicial protection of the class.

Are human clones marked by an immutable characteristic in this sense? The answer appears to be yes. The defining characteristic of a human clone is genetic: he or she has nuclear DNA that is identical with that of the person who donated the nuclear DNA for the cloning procedure. He or she cannot do anything to change his or her nuclear DNA. Therefore, the defining characteristic of human clones is "immutable" just as race is.[49]

More importantly, the characteristic in question lies at the very heart of what bothers people about cloning and human clones. As we have seen, the public and lawmakers believe that human clones are copies of others. Their shared genomes relegate them to a subhuman category. There can be no greater isolation from the rest of society than this. Those who are subhuman are unworthy of consideration; there is no reason for the majority to be concerned with their interests and needs. Under such circumstances the potential for political oppression is profound and the need for judicial intervention acute.

There is a second way in which the Supreme Court has articulated the immutability of a characteristic as relevant to suspect classification. In some decisions, the Court has emphasized that an immutable characteristic is an "accident of birth."[50] To clarify the importance of this observation further, I move on to the next cluster of factors, which link immutability to other principles.

e) Fairness, Stereotypes, and the Ability to Contribute to Society

First, the Supreme Court has indicated that, when a law discriminates against the members of a class based solely on immutable characteristics that are accidents of birth, that law violates a basic principle of our legal system – namely, legal burdens should bear some relationship to individual responsibility.[51]

From this point of view, immutability is important because it is a marker for antiegalitarian injustice. In our democratic society, in which all men (and women) are supposedly created equal, it is unfair to impose burdens based on inborn traits that the individual cannot control or change.[52]

As discussed immediately above, the defining characteristic of a human clone is genetic: he or she bears nuclear DNA that is identical with that of the person who donated the nuclear DNA for the cloning procedure. This is an inborn trait; a person cannot change his or her nuclear DNA. Human clones are not responsible for their genetic condition, and it is unjust to discriminate against them on that basis.

Second, the Court has emphasized that the immutable characteristics of a suspect class bear no relation to the ability of individual members to perform or contribute to society.[53] From this point of view, immutability is important because it is a marker for unjust stereotypes. Legislating on the basis of stereotypes violates the ideals of individualism and egalitarianism.

All of the classes that the Supreme Court has recognized as suspect, or even quasi-suspect, exhibit this particular element. Race, nationality, alienage, gender, and illegitimacy are irrelevant to the ability of the individual to perform or contribute to society. Voters and legislators may be influenced by unjust stereotypes about blacks, disfavored nationalities, aliens, women, or illegitimate children. However, through the vehicle of suspect (or quasi-suspect) classification, the Court stops the electorate from imposing legal burdens based on such stereotypes.

Conversely, when a group is defined by characteristics that do affect ability to perform or contribute to society, the Supreme Court has declined to grant suspect status to the group. For example, in *City of Cleburne v. Cleburne Living Center, Inc.*, the Court refused to recognize the mentally retarded as a suspect class. It reasoned that the retarded, are, in fact, different from others. Their reduced ability to cope with and function in the everyday world gave the government a legitimate interest in dealing with and providing for them.[54] The Court also stated that it could not find any principled way to distinguish the mentally retarded from the aged (a group that the Court had already refused to recognize as suspect),[55] or from other groups with immutable disabilities such as the physically disabled, mentally ill, or infirm. In so reasoning, the

Court implied that it would withhold suspect status from these groups also.[56]

How does the class of human clones measure up against these principles? In the context of existential segregation, the relevant question is whether human clones have immutable characteristics that relate to their worthiness to exist. As explained in Part 1, the answer is no because the many stereotypes associated with human clones are unfounded. I do not wish to repeat that entire analysis here, but a few reminders are in order. Despite their origin in technology, human clones are not evil, nor are they manufactured products. Moreover, human clones are not copies simply because they share a genome with others who came before them. Rather, they are *individuals* just as identical twins are. Also, human clones are not dangerous to the survival of humanity.

Finally, even today, there is no proof that human clones are inherently flawed and doomed to a foreshortened life of physical disability.[57] By the time there are enough human clones alive to make an equal protection challenge a reality, the safety and reliability of cloning technology must necessarily have improved significantly; otherwise, parents would not have chosen to have children through the technology, and there would be no human clones. If cloning is safe, now or in the future, false beliefs about the physical condition of human clones cannot justify a policy of existential segregation against them.

f) Stigma and Opprobrium

Some scholars and judicial opinions have suggested that the stigma and opprobrium attached to membership in a class is another marker of a suspect class.[58]

To a large extent, stigma and opprobrium overlap with the other factors discussed in this chapter. For example, some visible or immutable traits (e.g., race and nationality) may be relevant to suspect status – in part because of the stigma associated with them.[59] Moreover, a class that is stigmatized is also likely to experience unequal treatment and political powerlessness.[60]

Parts 1 and 2 of this book detailed the stereotypes and stigma that human clones are going to face. Presumed to be dangerous and deformed copies, they have already been marked as inferior, subhuman,

and unworthy of existence. This renders them vulnerable to discrimination – existential and otherwise. If stigma and opprobrium are the
essential markers of a suspect class, human clones are such a class and
deserve extraordinary judicial protection.

g) Congressional Action and Political Realism

One final factor remains for consideration. Occasionally, the Supreme
Court has emphasized that Congress has acted to eliminate discrimination against the members of a class. For example, in *Frontiero v.
Richardson*, a plurality opined that gender should be recognized as a
suspect class. The plurality noted that Congress had legislated against
gender discrimination in employment and pay and had passed the Equal
Rights Amendment; thus, Congress itself had concluded that classifications based on gender are inherently invidious. The plurality argued
that this "conclusion of a coequal branch of Government" supported its
conclusion that gender is a suspect class.[61]

Congress has not legislated in favor of human clones; indeed, just
the reverse is true. As Chapter 6 explained, the House of Representatives twice has voted to make all human cloning a crime, and many
anticloning bills are pending in the Senate. As Chapter 7 made clear,
this attack on cloning has been motivated in part by animus toward
human clones, whom many lawmakers believe to be dangerous and deformed copies. Some might interpret *Frontiero* to mean that, because
Congress is poised to act against, rather than in favor of, human clones,
they should not be recognized as a suspect class.

However, another Supreme Court decision suggests a different outcome. In *City of Cleburne*, the Court emphasized that Congress had
enacted legislation to prohibit discrimination against the mentally retarded in federally funded programs. Congress had also recognized the
right of the retarded to receive treatment, services, and habilitation in
the setting least restrictive of personal liberty. Congress, moreover, had
directed states receiving federal funds to provide retarded children with
an education that integrated them with nonretarded children. It also
had exempted the mentally retarded from having to take a competitive
exam to enter the federal civil service. This legislative activity demonstrated not only that the retarded faced unique problems but also that
lawmakers had been addressing their needs in a manner that belied

prejudice and the need for intrusive judicial oversight.[62] For this reason and others, the Court declined to recognize the mentally retarded as a suspect class.

On the one hand, this reasoning in the *City of Cleburne* can be read as yet another sign that the Supreme Court wants to rule consistently with Congressional action. Through some of the cited legislation (e.g., exempting applicants for civil service from competitive examinations), Congress recognized that mental retardation *does* bear a relationship to performance. This implied that an element of suspect status was missing. By declining to find that the mentally retarded constitute a suspect class, the Court acted consistently with this judgment.

On the other hand, the Court also emphasized that Congress was working to address the specialized needs of the mentally retarded in a manner that *belied* prejudice and the need for intrusive judicial oversight. This implied that the outcome might have been very different if Congress had *not* supported the mentally retarded or had legislated in a manner that was actively hostile toward them. In that case, the Court might have recognized the mentally retarded as a suspect class.

This latter reading of the *City of Cleburne* makes good sense. Historically, state legislatures have been the source of laws oppressing racial minorities and other suspect classes, and Congress has acted to oppose such discrimination. However, this historical pattern does not guarantee that Congress can be counted on to protect disfavored minorities against discrimination in the future. (Indeed, as Chapter 6 revealed, the only reason Congress has not emerged as the most formidable perpetrator of existential segregation in the United States is because the anticloning bills before it have been bogged down in abortion politics.)

It is one thing for the Supreme Court to follow the lead of Congress when Congress seeks to protect a group against discrimination, as the *Frontiero* plurality did. It is quite another thing for the Court to follow the lead of Congress when it seeks to *discriminate* against a group. Such an interpretation of *Frontiero* is inconsistent with *City of Cleburne* and the entire purpose of judicial review, which is to ensure that Congress does not overstep its constitutional boundaries. When Congress exhibits animus toward a class such as human clones, the Supreme Court should grant suspect status to facilitate judicial protection of the class.

Although the foregoing argument makes good legal sense, politics could play a role in determining whether the Supreme Court recognizes human clones as a suspect class. Indeed, politics may be at the bottom of the reasoning in *Frontiero*. Perhaps Congressional action in support of a group matters because it gives the Supreme Court confidence that a judgment in favor of that group is within the political mainstream and will command respect and obedience. Perhaps the Court lacks the conviction and strength to oppose the judgment and power of Congress. If so, the Court is unlikely to recognize human clones as a suspect class.

The fact remains, however, that human clones display many of the hallmarks of a suspect class:

- A record of strong public and political opposition to their existence,
- Vulnerability to existing laws that will subject them to significant harms as soon as they are born,
- A tiny and closeted membership that is likely to be politically ineffective,
- Status as a "discrete and insular" minority,
- Immutable characteristics,
- A lack of responsibility for their genetic status,
- A lack of relationship between their genetic status and ability to contribute to society, and
- Stigma.

The Supreme Court invented the concept of "suspect class" to justify its intervention in the political process on behalf of victimized groups. If the Court expects to be taken seriously in this role, it must consistently stand as the last bulwark against majoritarian oppression – even when that oppression originates in Congress and even when the victims are unpopular human clones.

3. Summary

In this Chapter, I have reached two conclusions. First, anticloning laws do establish a classification. Even if the laws are neutral on their face, they are designed to implement a program of existential segregation against human clones. Because they establish a classification, the laws can be challenged on equal protection grounds. The next chapter describes the basic characteristics of some plaintiffs who will be qualified to bring that challenge.

Second, human clones display many of the hallmarks of a suspect class. Therefore, courts should subject anticloning laws to strict scrutiny.[63] That standard is applied in Chapter 12 to determine whether anticloning laws violate the equal protection guarantee.

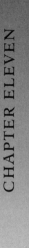

CHAPTER ELEVEN

Anticloning Laws Inflict Judicially Cognizable Injuries that Confer Standing

The last chapter presented the argument that laws banning reproductive cloning treat human clones differently than humans born through sexual reproduction. This discrimination triggers the equal protection guarantee.

It is not enough to conclude that such anticloning laws have put the equal protection guarantee into play in some abstract sense. Someone has to bring a lawsuit challenging the laws under the equal protection guarantee. This chapter examines how that might come about.

1. Basic Principles of Federal Standing

Under Article III, Section 2 of the U.S. Constitution, the federal courts have the jurisdiction to hear cases arising under the Constitution and the laws of the United States. Thus, if Congress enacts a federal anticloning law, the federal courts could hear an equal protection challenge to that law. Similarly, the federal courts could hear an equal protection challenge to the manner in which the FDA has applied federal law to stop cloning. Finally, if a plaintiff wants to challenge the constitutionality of a state anticloning law, he or she could bring that challenge in federal court subject to the limitations that the Eleventh Amendment imposes.[1]

Thus, it seems likely that an equal protection challenge to anticloning laws could end up in federal court. However, to proceed, the plaintiff must have the standing to invoke the jurisdiction of the federal courts.

Stating the test for federal standing is easy. Under Article III of the U.S. Constitution, a plaintiff must demonstrate that he or she has suffered an injury in fact, that this injury is fairly traceable to the actions of the defendant, and that a favorable court decision will redress this injury.[2] Unfortunately, applying the test is hard. Federal standing is a confused area of law rife with multiple and conflicting precedents.[3]

Ordinarily, if one wants to predict how the Supreme Court might handle a particular case, it is safest to rely on previous cases that presented the Court with similar facts and legal issues. Unfortunately, there are no cases that directly address the question of whether existential segregation violates the equal protection guarantee. Therefore, there also are no cases that explain the conditions under which a person has standing to challenge existential segregation. Of necessity, I frequently reason by analogy to cases that have involved challenges to racial segregation, which sought to separate the races from each other in a more physical sense.

This chapter provides several examples of human clones who could be injured by anticloning laws and explains why they should have standing to challenge the laws in federal court. The plaintiffs in these examples are babies or children, but this should not present any serious obstacle. In federal lawsuits, minors can be represented by legal guardians or others who have a significant relationship with them and wish to serve as "next friends."[4] When minors are not otherwise represented, courts have the discretion to appoint guardians *ad litem* to represent them.[5] In addition, as I will explain, parents who sue to vindicate their own constitutional rights may also have the standing to assert their children's rights.

These examples are intended as illustrations and not as an exhaustive account of all possible injuries or standing. The easiest cases are presented first before others that require more innovative analysis.

2. First Example: Exclusion at the National Border

For the first example, assume that Congress enacts a law like the 2003 Weldon bill, which makes it a crime to clone within the United States or to import the "product" of cloning. Despite the ban, a man and his infertile wife patronize a cloning clinic located in a Caribbean island nation where cloning is legal. With the help of an egg donor, the wife conceives, gestates, and gives birth to a cloned daughter ("Angela") abroad.

Because she was born to an American married couple, Angela is an American citizen even though she was born abroad.[6] The import provision, however, makes it impossible for her parents, or any other adult, to bring her home without committing a crime. Because Angela relies on her parents for financial, physical, and emotional support and cannot travel without the assistance of an adult, the law makes it impossible for her to enter the United States even though she is a citizen.

The family stays in the Caribbean and waits. Back in the United States, a relative or other close friend of the family hires an attorney. This "next friend" files a civil lawsuit on Angela's behalf in federal court. In the suit, Angela argues that the anticloning law excludes her from her homeland solely on the basis of her membership in the suspect class of human clones; therefore, it violates the equal protection guarantee of the Fifth Amendment.

An interesting threshold question arises: Do the Fifth Amendment and its equal protection guarantee provide protection to Angela given that she is not present within the United States? The Supreme Court has held that aliens outside the United States do not receive constitutional protections,[7] but these precedents are inapplicable because Angela is a citizen. There is some authority for the proposition that constitutional protections, including the Fifth Amendment and the equal protection guarantee, cover U.S. citizens abroad,[8] and so I will proceed on that assumption.

The next question is whether Angela has the standing to sue. The answer should be yes. As a baby, Angela depends on her parents for financial, physical, and emotional support and cannot travel without the assistance of an adult. Thus, by barring her parents and other adults from importing the "product" of cloning, the national ban on cloning *physically* excludes Angela from her homeland. Moreover, by excluding Angela, the ban stigmatizes her.

Angela's injuries (physical segregation and legal stigma[9]) are similar to the injuries that racial segregation inflicted on blacks for nearly one-hundred years after the Civil War ended. The laws of many states prohibited blacks from entering and using public facilities that were designated for whites. Beginning in 1954, the Supreme Court ruled that such physical segregation was barred in public schools,[10] parks and playgrounds,[11] and other public facilities.[12] The Supreme Court has recognized that racial discrimination and the stigma it inflicts can form the basis for standing.[13]

Reasoning by analogy, we can see that Angela has suffered cognizable injuries (physical segregation and legal stigma). Moreover, these injuries are directly traceable to the actions of the federal government in enacting the national ban on cloning with its draconian import provision. Finally, a favorable court decision will redress Angela's injury. If the ban is overturned, she can enter the United States and the stigma of her exclusion will be eliminated.[14] Because all three requirements are met, Angela has the standing to bring her equal protection challenge.

Unfortunately, the strategy outlined in this hypothetical case may be limited for two reasons in its ability to combat discrimination against humans born through cloning. First, it is possible that a court could redress Angela's injury in the narrowest possible manner by striking only the import provision. This would leave most of the national ban untouched and operational. Second, the hypothetical case presupposes parents who are brave enough to reveal what they have done and to remain abroad with the baby pending resolution of a very public lawsuit. It is far more likely that parents will choose to smuggle their cloned pregnancies and babies back into the country quietly. When some parents are caught and punished for the crime of importing the product of cloning, they and their children may be able to establish standing on different grounds as the next example illustrates.

3. Second Example: Prosecution of Parents

The second example presupposes there is a federal law against cloning and that parents are being prosecuted in federal court for violation of that law. (If there is a state ban on cloning and parents are being prosecuted in state court for violation of the ban, a similar analysis may apply on the assumption that the state follows federal principles of standing.)[15]

Suppose a lesbian couple has scientific expertise in cloning and access to a laboratory. Acting without the involvement of any outside doctors, May harvests some eggs from June, injects her own nuclear DNA into the eggs to create embryos, and transfers the embryos into June's uterus. Nine months later, a healthy baby girl ("Rose") is born.

Assume further that government authorities discover that the couple engaged in cloning. They arrest, indict, and prosecute May and June for cloning, aiding and abetting cloning, and conspiring to clone. If convicted, May and June face lengthy prison sentences, criminal fines, and asset forfeiture.

Logically, May and June would attempt to defend the prosecution by asserting the unconstitutionality of the anticloning law. They could assert that the law violated their own fundamental right to reproduce through cloning, rather than through sexual reproduction, which, unfortunately, is unavailable to them. As the defendants in a criminal prosecution, May and June would have the standing to assert this challenge to the anticloning law.[16]

In addition, to strengthen their case, May and June might claim that the anticloning law violates the equal protection rights of a third party – namely, their daughter, Rose.

For this strategy to work, May and June first must show that Rose meets the three basic elements of standing in her own right. Rose can demonstrate injury. As a baby, she depends on her parents for financial, physical, and emotional support. Unfortunately, the government has chosen to prosecute May and June for having Rose. If her parents are sent to prison, fined, and subjected to asset forfeiture, Rose will lose the love and money she needs to thrive.

Admittedly, Rose's injuries are indirect; they are sustained as a result of action taken against her parents rather than against her directly. However, granting standing to those who have suffered indirect injuries is consistent with case precedent. As the Supreme Court has noted, "[w]hen a governmental prohibition or restriction imposed on one party [e.g., May and June] causes specific harm to a third party [e.g., Rose], harm that a constitutional provision [e.g., the equal protection guarantee] or statute was intended to prevent, the indirectness of the injury does not necessarily deprive the person harmed of standing to vindicate his rights."[17]

There is a second and related injury: by seeking to prevent May and June from having Rose, the anticloning law has stigmatized Rose as unworthy of existence. These twin injuries (loss of parents and assets coupled with legal stigma) are directly traceable to the actions of the government that enacted the anticloning law. Moreover, a favorable court decision will redress Rose's injury. If the law is overturned, May and June will be released from prison and recover their assets; Rose can then live free of the stigma that the law inflicts with loving parents and the financial security that other children enjoy. Therefore, Rose has the standing to bring an equal protection challenge to the anticloning law.

Beyond demonstrating that Rose can meet these three basic elements of standing, if May and June want to assert the rights of Rose as a third party, they must also overcome prudential limitations that the Supreme Court has placed on the ability of litigants to assert the rights of third parties.

First, May and June must show they have suffered an injury in fact that gives them a concrete interest in the outcome of the issue in dispute.[18] Here, that is not difficult; May and June are being subjected to criminal prosecution. They have a strong interest in the success of the equal protection challenge and can be expected to advocate it vigorously.

Second, May and June must show that they have a close relationship with the third party. This, too, is not difficult; Rose is their daughter, and they love her. This parent–child relationship creates a congruence of interests. May and June are likely to be as effective in presenting Rose's claim as she would be herself.[19]

Third, the Supreme Court has indicated that the courts should not adjudicate the rights of third parties unnecessarily. Thus, standing is more likely to be granted when the activity that the litigant wants to pursue affects the ability of the third party to enjoy his or her right.[20] Here, May and June want to reproduce through cloning. If they cannot do so without going to prison, paying exorbitant fines, or suffering asset forfeiture, Rose cannot obtain equal protection under the law. She must forfeit the financial, physical, and emotional support that children born through sexual reproduction enjoy; moreover, she must endure legal stigma.

Fourth, the Supreme Court has indicated that, before a litigant can assert the rights of a third party, there must be some hindrance to the ability of that party to protect his or her own interests.[21] In this case, the hindrance comes from the fact that Rose is underage and cannot sue to vindicate her equal protection rights without the help of an adult. Rather than have May and June initiate an independent lawsuit on Rose's behalf, it is efficient to permit them to assert her constitutional rights in their own litigation.

4. The Need for a New Approach to Standing

The foregoing hypothetical examples apply existing principles of federal standing. However, there may be good reason to reconsider those principles and grant a broader standing in the context of existential segregation for the following reasons.

As noted in the first part of this chapter, when a law imposes physical segregation, existing persons are excluded from public facilities. Established law recognizes the exclusion as an act of discrimination and a cognizable personal injury.

By contrast, when a law imposes existential segregation, its objective is to prevent births. An anticloning law prohibits actions (such as the creation, implantation, or gestation of cloned embryos) that take place *before* birth. Yet, birth is precisely the point in time when a "person," in the Fifth or Fourteenth Amendment sense of that term, comes into being.[22] Those who are never conceived, or who are jettisoned or destroyed as embryos or fetuses during the course of research cloning, are not persons capable of asserting that their right to equal protection has been denied. They can never bring a lawsuit to redress their own injuries, nor can anyone sue for them.

At the moment a "person" with rights is born through cloning, the proscriptions (but not the effects) of the anticloning law cease. The person is not excluded from life because he or she has managed to achieve birth in spite of the law.

Does it follow that the authors of anticloning laws have found a way to discriminate with impunity? If the law holds that only the *unborn* are excluded from life but denies the unborn (and their representatives) the right to challenge anticloning laws because the unborn are not "persons," it might seem as if existential segregation, by its very nature, evades judicial review.

Two factors tend to protect against this undesirable outcome, but neither is entirely reliable.

First, as noted in Chapter 9, the privacy rights of adults should include the right to clone – at least when ordinary methods of procreation do not work for them. Thus, privacy rights should limit the government's ability to carry out a program of existential segregation. However, given that the Supreme Court has not yet ruled on the right to clone, it is wise to develop alternative strategies to combat existential segregation.

Second, if the law seeks to prevent the members of a disfavored class from coming into existence, it must prohibit scientists, doctors, and parents from acting to conceive, gestate, or give birth to members of the class. As my second standing example indicates, vigorous enforcement against parents will cause children to suffer injuries that are substantial enough to confer standing upon them to challenge anticloning laws. In more liberal federal districts or states, however, throwing infertile men and women into prison for the crime of having children could provoke a public backlash. Some prosecutors might prefer to enforce the laws only against "mad" scientists and "unethical" doctors who clone. This could make it harder for children born through cloning to establish federal standing and challenge the laws.[23]

There are no cases that consider the constitutional rights of children born in defiance of laws that seek to exclude them from life and no cases that explain the conditions under which such children have the standing to challenge existential segregation. This creates an opportunity to interpret principles of standing in a manner that respects the policies underlying those principles without unnecessarily obstructing reasonable efforts to combat existential segregation.

5. Third Example: Targeting and Legal Stigma

Therefore, a third hypothetical example is presented. It illustrates a fresh approach to injury and standing in the context of existential segregation.

Assume that a husband and wife live in the United States when cloning is banned at the federal level or in a state that makes cloning a crime. The man carries but does not express a heritable disease. The pair decides to conceive a son without the disease through cloning. They dupe a research scientist into creating cloned embryos using the husband's nuclear DNA ostensibly to serve as the source of stem cells; instead, the husband takes the embryos to a fertility doctor, who unwittingly implants them in the wife. The husband's crime is not discovered, the embryo develops successfully, and 9 months later, a healthy child ("George") is born.

Assume further that the parents are not subject to prosecution – perhaps because the statute of limitations has expired or perhaps because the relevant prosecutors have declined to indict them. Nevertheless, George (acting through a next friend or guardian *ad litem*) brings a lawsuit challenging the anticloning law as a violation of his right to equal protection.

At first glance, one might conclude that, because George was not excluded from life, he has not been subjected to an act of discrimination that is comparable to physical segregation. This seems to leave George with the claim that the anticloning law discriminates against him because it stigmatizes him.

There is authority for the proposition that legal stigma alone does not confer standing, though it is not directly on point. In *Allen v. Wright*,[24] parents of black public school children brought a nationwide class action complaining that the Internal Revenue Service had not adopted adequate standards and procedures to fulfill its obligation to deny tax-exempt status to racially discriminatory private schools. The parents argued, in part, that the government had denigrated them by granting financial aid (in the form of tax exemptions) to discriminatory private schools. However, the parents did not claim that their children had ever applied for entry into the discriminatory private schools. The Supreme Court held that the claim of denigration was not enough to confer standing; the parents had not alleged a stigmatic injury suffered as a direct result of having personally been denied equal treatment. The court reasoned as follows:

> If the abstract stigmatic injury were cognizable, standing would extend na-tionwide to all members of the particular racial groups against which the Government was alleged to be discriminating by its grant of a tax exemp-tion to a racially discriminatory school, regardless of the location of that school. All such persons could claim the same sort of abstract stigmatic injury respondents assert in their first claim of injury. A black person in Hawaii could challenge the grant of a tax exemption to a racially discrim-inatory school in Maine. Recognition of standing in such circumstances would transform the federal courts into "no more than a vehicle for the vindication of the value interests of concerned bystanders."[25]

Yet, George's case does not seem to present the abstract stigmatic injury that the *Allen* court feared. As noted in Chapters 8 and 10, *the purpose of the anticloning law is to prevent the birth of George and others like him.* Enforcement of the law may have been ineffective in this particu-lar case, but that does not change the fact that George was born in a country or state that specifically targeted him for nonexistence before his birth, and it does not eliminate the extraordinary legal stigma that George now faces as a result. His successful birth is no thanks to the government and should not be used to insulate anticloning laws from constitutional scrutiny via the standing doctrine.

Support for this conclusion can be gleaned from the history and rea-soning of cases dealing with racial segregation. In the nineteenth cen-tury, the Supreme Court interpreted the equal protection guarantee to permit state laws that treated blacks as "separate but equal." The Court rejected the argument that racial segregation stamped blacks with a badge of inferiority[26] and invalidated only those laws that completely denied blacks access to equivalent services, programs, or facilities.[27]

Slowly, the Court's attitude changed. By 1950, it began to invalidate segregation laws that created not just tangible, but also intangible, disparities in the treatment of whites and blacks.[28] For example, a state could not force blacks to attend a segregated law school that was less influential and prestigious than its white counterpart.[29]

Just 4 years later, the Court reached a critical turning point. In *Brown v. Board of Education*,[30] the plaintiffs challenged a public school system that was racially segregated. The white and black schools were equal, or in the process of being equalized, with respect to tangible factors like buildings, curricula, and teacher qualifications and salaries. Thus, the Court had to base its decision on the intangible effects of segregation on public education.[31] Holding that the segregation violated the equal protection guarantee, the Court reasoned that "to separate [children] from others of similar age and qualifications solely because of their race generates a feeling of inferiority as to their status in the community that may affect their hearts and minds in a way unlikely ever to be undone."[32]

What this brief history of the Civil Rights Era cases reveals is that dignity lies at the very heart of the equal protection guarantee. When it comes to laws that mandate physical segregation, the intangible injury of stigma is the crux of the equal protection violation.

If this is true, George's stigmatic injury is a significant one that deserves to be taken very seriously. Unless the courts are willing to ignore this injury entirely, they must find some way of dealing effectively with existential segregation. If the courts do not want to recognize the fundamental right of parents to procreate through cloning, in the alternative they must adapt principles of standing to the realities of existential segregation so that those principles do not stand as a barrier to the equal protection challenges that George and other victims bring.

I suggest the courts adopt the following rule of standing, which would allow them to address the stigmatic harm that lies at the heart of existential segregation without embroiling themselves in disputes that are unreasonably abstract or theoretical.

Even when no "person" in the Fourteenth Amendment sense has been excluded from life, if a plaintiff can show that the law targeted him or her for nonexistence before birth, he or she should be granted standing to assert the targeting and associated legal stigma as cognizable injuries.

Turning to George, we find that his parents had to commit a crime to have him. Thus, the anticloning law targeted him specifically for nonexistence before birth. He bears the legal stigma associated with that targeting. This is far from the "abstract stigmatic injury" that the *Allen* court rejected as a basis for standing; it is real and specific to George. The courts can recognize his serious injury as a basis for standing without becoming a vehicle for the vindication of the value interests of concerned bystanders.[33]

George's injuries are fairly traceable to the actions of Congress or the state legislature that enacted the relevant anticloning law. However, there may be a problem with redressing at least a part of the injury. Even if the anticloning law is invalidated, it is not possible to turn back the clock and have George conceived and born again in a country or state free of existential segregation. However, a court decision invalidating the discriminatory anticloning law would at least eliminate the stigma that George otherwise is condemned to suffer for the rest of his life. Standing should be granted.

To illustrate how my proposed standing rule can accommodate the holding and spirit of *Allen v. Wright*, I offer a variation on the fourth hypothetical example. Now, let us assume that there is no national ban on cloning but that many states on the mainland do ban the technology. George is born to parents who live in Hawaii – a state that does *not* ban cloning. As explained in the discussion of a similar hypothetical case in Chapter 9, the anticloning laws of the other states do stigmatize George, marking him as unworthy of existence in the eyes of many mainland residents. This spillover stigma could harm George's self-esteem. Also, if George travels to the mainland for vacation, education, or employment, the anticloning laws could inspire others to exclude and discriminate against him. Because Hawaii has no anticloning law, however, it is not possible to claim George was targeted for nonexistence. The stigma that he suffers is real, but it is not linked to a direct attempt to segregate him before birth. If George brings a constitutional challenge to the laws of those other states based on the holding and reasoning of *Allen v. Wright*, a federal court could hold that the spillover stigma is not enough, in and of itself, to confer standing upon George. Otherwise, any human clone residing in any state would have standing to challenge the anticloning laws in any other state, which is the sort of result that the *Allen* court wanted to avoid.

6. Plaintiffs May Find It Easier to Establish Standing to Challenge Anticloning Laws in State Courts

Everything presented about standing so far applies when a plaintiff sues in a federal court that is subject to Article III limitations on its jurisdiction.

At present, the only laws that prohibit cloning specifically are state laws. Until and unless Congress can break the deadlock over the propriety of research cloning, state laws will remain the primary form of discrimination against human clones. A challenge to a state law under the U.S. Constitution can be brought in a federal court, but it need not be; plaintiffs can also bring the challenge in state courts.

State courts are not subject to Article III limitations – even when interpreting the federal Constitution.[34] They are not bound by Supreme Court cases that require the plaintiff to prove that the defendant caused an injury that the courts can redress. Their powers are determined by state and not federal law.

Some state constitutions do not limit state court jurisdiction at all. Other state constitutions grant the courts broad jurisdiction to hear cases without imposing any requirement that the plaintiff have suffered an injury. Still other state constitutions even grant courts the authority to issue advisory opinions.[35]

It is beyond the scope of this book to examine the specific standing rules of all 50 states. Undoubtedly there are many variations, and some state courts grant standing more readily than others. Here, it is enough to note that humans born through cloning often will find it easier to establish standing in state than federal court.

Thus, consider one last time the hypothetical case of George. The laws of his state targeted him for nonexistence, but he managed to achieve birth anyway. In the previous section, it was argued that the targeting of George for nonexistence should be enough to grant him standing once he is born and becomes a "person" with Fourteenth Amendment rights. If the federal courts reject my analysis, they might reason that George's remaining injury is stigmatic and refuse to hear his case.

Even then, however, George may not be out of luck. The courts of his home state are not limited by Article III of the U.S. Constitution, and they do not have to follow the standing rules that the U.S. Supreme Court has enunciated. These state courts might be more willing to recognize his stigmatic injury as a basis for standing and grant him the forum he needs to litigate his equal protection challenge to the state anticloning laws.

7. Summary

This chapter, has examined limitations on standing and advanced the argument that, under a variety of scenarios, human clones will have the standing to bring an equal protection challenge to anticloning laws in federal court. In borderline cases in which federal standing cannot be established, state courts may serve as an alternative forum for the challenge.

An irony arises out of the standing analysis. Anticloning laws will be most effective if they include a prohibition on importing the "product" of cloning. Otherwise, prospective parents will simply flock to offshore cloning clinics and bring contraband pregnancies and babies home along with a nice Caribbean tan. That sort of prohibition, however, which could exclude some babies at the national border, has the greatest chance of triggering the application of existing case precedents that grant standing to the victims of physical segregation. Similarly, to put a stop to cloning, police and prosecutors must enforce anticloning laws vigorously. This includes getting tough with parents. If the authorities bring some high-profile cases and prosecute couples who clone, cloning will be deterred. By taking such strong action, however, the authorities will also inflict substantial injuries that provide a solid basis for standing.

To put it more succinctly, the more tightly anticloning laws are drafted, and the more vigorously they are enforced, the greater the likelihood that human clones will be able to satisfy the basic elements of standing, gain access to federal and state courts, and litigate the laws themselves out of existence.

CHAPTER TWELVE

Anticloning Laws Violate the Equal Protection Guarantee

Chapter 10 established that laws against human reproductive cloning discriminate against human clones, a suspect class. That human clones will experience injuries substantial enough to give them the standing to bring an equal protection challenge to such anticloning laws was explained in Chapter 11.

This chapter presents the final link in the chain of analysis. Even if anticloning laws discriminate against a suspect class, it does not automatically follow that the laws are invalid because no constitutional right is absolute. Given that a suspect class is involved, however, the courts must subject the anticloning laws to the most rigorous level of judicial review, which is known as strict scrutiny.[1] If the laws cannot survive strict scrutiny, they are unconstitutional and invalid as written or applied.[2]

Strict scrutiny has two prongs. First, the law must serve a *compelling* governmental interest; second, the law must be *narrowly tailored* to serve that interest.[3] In other words, the government must advance its compelling interest by the *least restrictive means* available.[4]

This chapter considers whether any of the five objections present a compelling reason to ban human reproductive cloning. Also addressed is whether anticloning laws advance governmental interests by the least restrictive means available, as strict scrutiny requires.

In the interest of clarity, the constitutional analysis is organized consistently with Parts 1 and 2 of this book. Each of the five objections is considered in the same order as before: (1) cloning offends God and nature; (2) cloning threatens to reduce human beings to the level of manmade objects; (3) human clones are equivalents or copies of their DNA donors; (4) human clones threaten the survival of humanity; and (5) cloning is unsafe for participants and produces human clones who are physically flawed. Because many of the counterarguments to these objections have already been presented at length in Parts 1 and 2, the analysis here builds upon and references that prior discussion.

1. The Government Cannot Prove that Cloning Offends God and Nature; Moreover, Religious and Moral Objections Are Not Considered Compelling Interests

The first objection, to wit, that human reproductive cloning is a form of hubris that offends God and nature, is a religious and moral argument. Presumably, the objection would have to be accurate to qualify as a "compelling" ground for discriminating against a suspect class. The nature of the objection, however, is such that the government can never carry its burden of proving that the objection is accurate.

As discussed in Chapter 1, there is no scientific proof that God exists, let alone that cloning offends God. Similarly, there is no way to prove that cloning is "unnatural" in the sense of being an *improper* extension of what humans can and cannot do.

Recent case authority, moreover, indicates that a majority of the members of the Supreme Court recognize that religious and moral arguments do not carry much weight in constitutional analysis *even when enough voters believe in those arguments to succeed in enacting punitive legislation.*

In *Lawrence v. Texas,* the U.S. Supreme Court considered the constitutionality of a Texas law that criminalized homosexual sodomy.[5] The Court reasoned that consensual homosexual relationships are protected under the right to privacy established by the Due Process Clause of the Fourteenth Amendment.[6] Against this liberty interest, the Court weighed the fact that homosexual conduct frequently had been condemned as immoral:

> The condemnation has been shaped by religious beliefs, conceptions of right and acceptable behavior, and respect for the traditional family. For many persons these are not trivial concerns but profound and deep convictions accepted as ethical and moral principles to which they aspire and which thus determine the course of these lives. These considerations do not answer the question before us, however. The issue is whether the majority may use the power of the State to enforce these views on the whole society through operation of the criminal law. "Our obligation is to define the liberty of all, not to mandate our own moral code."[7]

The Court struck down the Texas statute, reasoning that it "furthers no *legitimate* state interest which can justify its intrusion into the personal and private life of the individual."[8] In other words, the Court held that religious and moral objections to homosexual conduct did not rise even to the level of a legitimate interest, let alone the compelling interest that is required when laws infringe on privacy rights.

Reasoning by analogy, we can see that the Supreme Court is not likely to uphold anticloning laws against an equal protection challenge on the ground that human reproductive cloning offends God and nature. No doubt many people fervently believe that cloning is a form of playing God; no doubt many others believe that cloning defiles nature. The fact remains that any such judgment is religious or moral in character. In the wake of *Lawrence,* the Supreme Court is not likely to hold that such a judgment is sufficiently compelling to justify the criminalization of human reproductive cloning.[9]

2. The Government Cannot Prove that Cloning Treats Humans as Products; Moreover, Anticloning Laws Are Not Narrowly Tailored to Protect Human Dignity

The second objection is that human reproductive cloning treats human beings as manufactured products.

As explained in Chapter 2, this objection also finds its roots in religious dogma and moral argument; it cannot be proven as an objective truth. Moreover, if *Lawrence* means what it says, this objection cannot rise to the level of a legitimate state interest, let alone a compelling one.

Even if this objection should be interpreted and evaluated as a warning against bad consequences, it does not pass constitutional muster. Under the strict scrutiny standard, the government must prove that the law it defends serves a compelling interest. To do this, the government must show that the law eliminates harms that are real and substantial and not just speculative.[10] Arguments that parents *might* view cloned children as products, or that cloning *might* degrade the value of human life, are speculative. Worse, they are directly contrary to experience and scientific fact.

As explained in Chapter 2, the same objections have been raised against IVF and other assisted reproductive technologies. Yet, there is no evidence that infertile men and women who use IVF, donor gametes, and surrogacy view their children as manufactured goods or commodities. According to recent psychological studies of children conceived through sperm donation or IVF, the children are normal and their families are stable and loving. Nor is there any evidence that the use of assisted reproductive technologies has degraded the preciousness or humanity of children.

Human reproductive cloning does not present any greater risk that children will be viewed as manufactured products, for it does not involve any greater degree of manufacture. Despite the imaginings of those who cling to the identity fallacy, genes are not destiny; it is not possible for cloning to deliver a specific final "product."[11] Thus, the speculation that cloning would encourage society to view human babies as products in the marketplace runs contrary to scientific fact. An asserted need to

guard against such imaginary evils cannot rise to the level of a compelling interest.

Moreover, even if cloning threatens human dignity because the public does not understand what the technology can and cannot produce,
and even if the government has a compelling interest in protecting human dignity, the anticloning laws cannot survive strict scrutiny given
that they are not narrowly tailored to achieve that compelling interest. Instead, the laws take the most aggressive stance possible, seeking
to prevent the very existence of an entire category of human beings.
This strategy is sweeping rather than narrow; it is likely to produce
the very result it seeks to prevent because the ban strongly implies
that there is something subhuman about human clones.[12] A more effective, yet narrower, strategy is available: public education. The government could work vigorously to debunk scientific fallacies about
cloning and affirm the innate value and human dignity of every individual despite race, color, creed, sexual orientation, or sexual or asexual
origination.

3. The Government Cannot Prove that Human Clones Are Copies; Moreover, Anticloning Laws Are Not Narrowly Tailored to Protect Individuality

The third objection is that human cloning produces humans who are
not individuals but rather equivalents, or copies, of an existing person.
Several arguments flow from this objection. I will consider each in turn.

As explained in Chapter 3, the idea that cloning makes it possible to
copy or extend the life of an existing person is scientifically false. Thus,
the fear that Hitler or other individuals could be duplicated is not rational. Nor can immortality be achieved through cloning. These nightmare
scenarios might have inspired some influential science fiction, but they
do not provide compelling reasons to outlaw cloning.

Softer versions of the identity fallacy are equally inaccurate. Even if
a person shares a genome with his or her DNA donor, that person will
retain his or her individuality just as identical twins born at the same
time do. Also, that individual's autonomy and ability to build his or her
own life will be retained even if the DNA donor has already been alive
for many years. The government cannot assert a legitimate, let alone a

compelling, interest in preventing the birth of certain individuals based on demonstrably false beliefs about their innate characteristics.

Likewise, family concerns are overblown. Because children born through cloning will not be copies of their DNA donors, their parents will have no logical reason to raise them with that false expectation. For the same reason, there is no good reason to think that cloning will damage family structure or blur generational boundaries even if a child's nuclear DNA is drawn from one of the parents. In particular, in as much as that child will not be the same person as the DNA donor, the risk of child abuse will be no greater than in "normal" families. These concerns, which lack a scientific basis, do not provide compelling reasons for banning cloning.

Similarly, the need to combat identity theft does not rise to the level of a compelling interest. Science fiction aside, it is not possible for a human clone to take away the identity or individuality of an existing person. Moreover, because cloning does not compromise individuality or autonomy, it does not threaten democratic institutions based on those values.

What the government might assert with a straight face is that *misperceptions* about human clones could lead to harm. Human clones (incorrectly) may believe they lack individuality or autonomy. Others might treat them as if they were copies, leading to psychological suffering. Humans born through sexual reproduction might be afraid that human clones could steal their identities. Most speculatively, some people might observe cloning in progress, wrongly assume that individuality and autonomy are gone, and lose their faith in democratic institutions.

Even if it is assumed, for the sake of argument, that the government could prove that these psychological and social harms are real and significant, anticloning laws should not be sustained. The root of the harms is the identity fallacy, and anticloning laws are not narrowly tailored to eliminate the fallacy. Indeed, far from it. By seeking to prevent human births, the laws strongly imply that there *is* something wrong with human clones, thereby reinforcing the fallacy and increasing the harms. Again, a more effective, yet narrower, strategy is available: public education. The government could mount a campaign to debunk the identity fallacy and affirm the individuality and autonomy of every human being, no matter how he or she was conceived. Also, as Professor Elizabeth Price Foley has suggested, the government could offer free psychological counseling to human clones and their families.[13]

Lastly, the argument that human clones must not exist because others might be prejudiced against them is worthy of one final refutation. As the *Perez* court stated when it struck down California's antimiscegenation laws, the fact that a class of persons might experience prejudice at the hands of others does not justify governmental discrimination against the class.[14]

4. The Government Cannot Prove Human Clones Threaten the Survival of Humanity; Moreover, Anticloning Laws Are Not Narrowly Tailored to Protect Humanity

The fourth objection is that human clones will be so numerous, homogenous, or superior that their existence threatens the survival of our species. Part 1 explained at some length why these nightmare scenarios are untrue. Here, that discussion is reframed in terms of constitutional analysis.

Under the strict scrutiny standard, the government must carry the burden of establishing a compelling interest. Speculative harms do not qualify.[15] This rule is the determining factor here, for each and every one of the three doomsday scenarios lacks a factual basis and is highly improbable.

As we have seen, there is no reason to believe that cloning would be such a popular technology that it would result in overpopulation. Sexual reproduction is inherently more attractive than asexual reproduction. Certain subgroups, including infertile men and women, gays and lesbians, and carriers of heritable diseases, may find that asexual reproduction suits their needs. There simply will not be enough human clones, however, to increase population pressures significantly. For the same reason, human clones do not present a meaningful threat to genetic diversity.

When it comes to eugenics, anticloning arguments are even wilder. First, opponents incorrectly assume that cloning is a reliable means of copying a "superior" person. Then they leap to the conclusion that the government will coerce people into reproducing asexually rather than sexually so that superior genomes will predominate. As if this were not enough, opponents postulate that cloning, in combination with genetic engineering techniques that are not yet possible, will be used to create a new, superior version of humanity to supplant the old. This chain of events is too improbable to justify discriminating against human clones on the basis of their genomes.[16]

If it is assumed for the sake of argument that human clones would contribute to overpopulation, diminish genetic diversity, or overwhelm others with their superiority, less restrictive means of dealing with these threats are available. If overpopulation became such a dire problem that births had to be restricted, the government could enact laws limiting the number of children that an individual could conceive through sexual *or* asexual reproduction. (The government would have to prove that the threat of overpopulation was compelling, of course, or such laws would violate the constitutional right to procreate sexually and asexually when necessary.) If genetic diversity were a compelling concern, the government could enact laws limiting the number of children conceived from a particular genome.[17] If eugenic cloning were a problem, the government could enact laws limiting the source of the nuclear DNA involved to relatives or other loved ones. Preservation of humanity is a worthy goal, but it can be accomplished without the criminalization of all reproductive cloning under all circumstances.

5. The Government Cannot Prove that Cloning Is Unsafe or that Human Clones Are Physically Flawed; Moreover, Anticloning Laws Are Not Narrowly Tailored to Meet Safety Concerns Today and in the Future

Finally, I come to the fifth objection – that is, human reproductive cloning is unsafe. According to this objection, the technology would endanger the health of egg donors and gestational mothers. Many embryos and fetuses would be lost in the process. Children who made it to birth would suffer from serious birth defects.

Government may have a general interest in protecting the health and safety of its citizens.[18] However, under a strict scrutiny standard, the government must show far more than this. The question is not whether some legislator, regulator, scientist, or ethicist can *hypothesize* that human reproductive cloning *might* involve physical dangers for prospective children, mothers, or other participants. The question is whether the government can *prove* that human reproductive cloning involves physical dangers.[19] Moreover, to establish a *compelling* interest in prohibiting cloning, the government must also prove that these physical dangers are substantial. They must be significantly different in kind and degree from the physical dangers of the sexual reproduction that the government freely permits.

Without such proof, laws that seek to ban cloning on safety grounds cannot withstand constitutional challenge. This is as it should be; otherwise, the government could impose existential segregation indefinitely and without justification.

Thus, for example, when the Food and Drug Administration (FDA) asserts that it will not let human reproductive cloning proceed until and unless researchers prove that the technology is safe to use, it gets the constitutional analysis exactly backward. As explained in Chapter 6, the FDA probably does not have the statutory authority under the Federal Food, Drug, and Cosmetic Act, or the Public Health Service Act, to regulate human reproductive cloning.[20] However, even if it did, the FDA is the one with the burden of proving that human reproductive cloning is unsafe. If the FDA cannot meet that burden, its regulatory program (public statements of authority, warning letters to researchers in general and certain mavericks in particular, laboratory and grand jury investigations) violates the equal protection guarantee.

One immediate obstacle that the government faces in carrying its burden of proof is the lack of data on the safety of cloning in humans. There has been no documented attempt to clone human beings beyond the embryonic stage. The best the government can do is point to data on the safety of animal cloning and argue that the data justify certain conclusions about the safety of human cloning. This is a flawed strategy.

Chapter 5 discussed the science of the safety objection at length, and Chapter 9 explained why safety concerns are not weighty enough to justify a public policy of existential segregation. Those analyses will not be replicated here. Rather, the task is to rework those analyses in light of constitutional law.

a) Protecting Participants from Harm

The first issue to consider is whether the government's interest in protecting egg donors, embryos and fetuses, and gestational mothers is compelling enough to justify a ban on human reproductive cloning.

Egg Donors: Egg donation requires the use of fertility drugs. As explained at greater length in Chapter 9, the risks currently associated with use of fertility drugs are minimal. Cases of severe ovarian hyperstimulation syndrome are few, and deaths are rare. Recent scientific studies have failed to establish any link between fertility drugs and ovarian cancer.

Fertility drugs are legal in the United States. Many thousands of women take them every year with the benefit of informed consent. These facts indicate that the government does not have a compelling reason to ban the drugs despite their known risks.

Moreover, this conclusion holds true even in the context of human reproductive cloning. The risks of the drugs are inherent to the drugs and do not depend on the purpose for which the drugs are used. Even if cloning increases the demand for eggs and donors, the minimal risks associated with fertility drugs do not increase for each individual woman simply because more women choose to take the drugs.

Embryos and Fetuses: As discussed in Chapter 5, most attempts to clone animals do not succeed. In terms of healthy births to embryos transferred, success rates in animal experiments range from less than 1 percent to 11 percent, meaning that anywhere from 89 to 99 percent of embryos never make it to birth.[21]

Most of these failures happen early, before a pregnancy takes hold, or even before an embryo is transferred.[22] However, some cloned fetuses do miscarry – often owing to innate physical flaws (genetic, epigenetic, and developmental). These fetuses are "nonviable" in the sense that they are not capable of developing to a point at which they can survive outside the womb.

Let us assume, for the sake of argument, that human reproductive cloning, if attempted today, would involve similar failure rates. Can the government ban reproductive cloning on the ground that it has a compelling interest in preventing the loss of embryos and fetuses? To find an answer to this question, I reason by analogy to the abortion decisions of the Supreme Court.

In 1973, the Supreme Court issued its decision in Roe v. Wade, holding that a woman's right of privacy includes the decision to terminate her unwanted pregnancy through abortion.[23] Because the privacy right qualified as fundamental, strict scrutiny applied.[24] The Roe court recognized that the government had a legitimate interest in protecting potential life[25] but did not consider this interest compelling until a fetus became "viable," that is, able to live outside the womb.[26] Thus, the *Roe* court reasoned, during the first trimester of a pregnancy, the abortion decision was up to a woman and her doctor. After the first trimester, the government could regulate abortion as necessary to preserve the health of the mother. Once a fetus became viable, the government could regulate or even prohibit abortion except when necessary to save the life or health of the mother.[27] Because a fetus could survive outside the womb at 28 weeks of gestation with the benefit of medical care available in 1973,[28] this amounted to a holding that abortion could be banned during the third trimester of pregnancy.

Nearly 20 years later, in *Planned Parenthood v. Casey*, five members of the Supreme Court affirmed that a woman has a constitutional right to terminate a fetus that is not yet viable.[29] Before viability, the government's interest in protecting fetal life is not strong enough to justify banning abortion or imposing substantial obstacles to the procedure.[30] After viability (which, owing to medical advances, can now occur as early as 23 to 24 weeks of gestation),[31] however, the government can regulate and even prohibit abortion except where necessary to preserve the life or health of the mother.[32]

Although the *Casey* majority upheld the core of *Roe*, three of its five members rejected its rigid trimester framework. In a plurality opinion, these three justices reasoned that the trimester framework undervalued the government's interest in potential life throughout the pregnancy.[33] The justices argued that the proper test is whether a law places an "undue burden" on the woman's decision to terminate her pregnancy.[34] For example, a state could take measures to ensure that a woman's decision to abort was an informed one and could attempt to persuade a woman to choose childbirth instead so long as the woman was granted the ultimate decision.[35]

The relevance of these cases to human reproductive cloning lies in the similarity of the tests used to determine whether the government has overstepped its constitutional boundaries. If humans born through cloning qualify as a suspect class, then laws that discriminate against that class must be subjected to strict scrutiny: that is, the courts must identify a compelling interest that justifies the discrimination and the laws must be narrowly drawn to vindicate that interest. Similarly,

Supreme Court cases, including *Roe*, have identified the right to privacy as a fundamental right,[36] and laws that infringe on fundamental
rights are, as a general rule, also subject to strict scrutiny.[37] Admittedly,
the plurality opinion in *Casey* did not rely on the strict scrutiny test and
did not articulate its analysis in terms of whether and when the government has a compelling interest in protecting potential life. Presumably,
the plurality avoided this formulation because it wanted the flexibility
to permit some regulation of abortion throughout pregnancy – even in
early stages. The *Casey* court, however, did affirm the basic holding of
Roe. The decision to do so necessarily reflected a judgment that the
government's interest in protecting potential life, however it might be
characterized, simply is not compelling enough to overcome a woman's
right to privacy even when perfectly healthy embryos and fetuses face
certain and deliberate destruction.

If this is so, how can the government's interest in protecting potential
life be compelling enough to justify a policy of existential discrimination
against the members of a suspect class? Many embryos and fetuses incapable of surviving to birth (and, thus, nonviable) may die in the course
of asexual reproduction, as they do in the course of sexual reproduction. However, the abortion cases signal that the desire to prevent such
losses is likely to count for very little when weighed against other, more
dominant values pursuant to rigorous constitutional analysis (however
the Supreme Court may label or characterize the test involved).

Gestational Mothers: Animal cloning is inefficient at present, but
most failures (83 to 99 percent) occur before animal mothers become
pregnant[38] and are not relevant here.

As explained in Chapter 5, animal clones do sometimes miscarry late
in the pregnancy. In a handful of experiments, some gestational mothers have died during or shortly after they gave birth. However, for the
following two reasons the government cannot use these data to prove
that human mothers face the same risks.

First, these late miscarriages and maternal deaths may be attributable
to large offspring syndrome, or LOS. This is because it is not easy to
gestate or give birth to oversized offspring. However, the data we have
indicate that LOS does not occur in human IVF and is unlikely to occur in human reproductive cloning for genetic reasons.[39] The National
Academies complained that LOS could not be ruled out in human

reproductive cloning attempts.[40] This is not the appropriate standard, however. Under the strict scrutiny standard, the government must prove that LOS *would* occur. This it cannot do.

Second, as explained in Chapter 9, experimental animals can be forced to continue with a pregnancy no matter what the risks. By contrast, a human mother has a wide range of medical options when faced with a risky pregnancy, including abortion. If a mother wishes to continue, despite the risk, her options include fetal monitoring, medical treatments to prevent miscarriage, drugs that accelerate the development of fetuses that must be born early, induction of labor, and cesarean delivery. Given this crucial distinction between animal and human mothers, bad outcomes for mothers in animal experiments do not provide a compelling reason to ban human reproductive cloning.

The government's failure to regulate sexual reproduction is relevant to this analysis. As explained in Chapter 5, sexual reproduction is hazardous for gestational mothers in general. Late-term miscarriage and maternal death are risks of participation in the process. Despite this, millions of women, including women with a history of repeated miscarriages or serious health problems that would make carrying a pregnancy particularly dangerous for them, continue to reproduce sexually, and the government does not lift a finger to stop them.

From this inaction, it is fair to conclude that the government does not consider medical risks to gestational mothers compelling enough to justify regulation of sexual reproduction.[41] This is true even in cases in which gestational mothers face an unusually high risk of injury or death. This makes sense given that such mothers have chosen (1) to conceive, or, at least, to have sex under conditions in which pregnancy is possible; and (2) to maintain the pregnancy despite the availability of safe, legalized abortion.

The government's laissez faire attitude toward sexual reproduction undercuts its assertion that medical risks to gestational mothers provide a compelling justification for a ban on human reproductive cloning. If anything, the government's case for regulation of asexual reproduction is weaker because the degree of maternal consent is greater. No mother is likely to become pregnant through cloning by accident or force; she must first consent to participation in what is known to be a novel and unpredictable medical procedure. That the government has left sexual reproduction alone, even when it is unsafe for gestational mothers, strongly indicates that its frantic efforts to ban human reproductive cloning rest not on concern for gestational mothers but rather on one or more of the other four objections.

b) Preventing the Birth of Humans with Physical Defects

Thus, it boils down to this: To sustain a legal ban on cloning, the government must show that it has a compelling interest in preventing the birth of humans with physical defects.

As a first step, the government must prove that human clones would be likely to suffer from significant birth defects. This is a nearly impossible task. No data are available on human reproductive cloning, and the animal data are favorable, inapposite, or ambiguous.

As Chapter 5 explained, cloning does not produce prematurely aged animals with shortened telomeres.[42] Human babies, moreover, do not suffer from LOS when conceived through IVF, and there are genetic reasons to believe that they will not suffer from LOS when conceived through cloning.[43] Again, it is not enough to say that LOS cannot be ruled out as a factor in human cloning;[44] the government carries the burden of proving that LOS *is* a factor in human cloning.

The remaining safety concerns are still unproven. Some scientists claim that animal clones suffer from epigenetic abnormalities and that these abnormalities seriously impair the health of the animals. Other scientists claim that animal clones are healthy and normal.[45] As a matter of constitutional analysis, doubt tips the balance against the government, which carries the burden of proof.[46]

As a second step, the government must account for its failure to regulate sexual reproduction. If it does not, even when certain parents are very likely to conceive and give birth to children with significant birth defects, its inaction tends to show that those defects, though deplorable, are not considered to be a compelling reason to regulate sexual reproduction.

As discussed in Chapter 5, sexual reproduction often places children at terrible risk. The rate of birth defects in the offspring of older mothers (who are at risk for having babies with Down's syndrome and other chromosomal abnormalities) ranges as high as 12 percent. The rate of birth defects in the offspring of parents who carry heritable diseases, like cystic fibrosis or Huntington's disease, ranges as high as 25 or even 50 percent.[47] Such birth defects and diseases severely compromise the health and happiness of affected children and are often fatal. Nevertheless, the law permits older women, carriers of genetic diseases, and others at high risk of producing disabled offspring to reproduce.[48] This tolerance of sexual reproduction, even when birth defects are likely and severe, impeaches the government's argument that the risk of birth defects provides a compelling justification for a ban on human reproductive cloning.

Some readers might protest that this analysis is incorrect, for the government has, at least in the past, taken a strong interest in the health of children who are born through sexual reproduction. To respond to that anticipated protest, I must discuss the American eugenics movement once again.

c) The Legacy of *Buck v. Bell*
In the early years of the twentieth century, many states enthusiastically passed laws mandating the sterilization of individuals who were convicted of certain crimes or who suffered from specified mental or physical disabilities.[49] The purpose of such eugenics legislation was to prevent the birth of children who would grow up to be criminals or who would inherit their parents' mental or physical disabilities. This, in turn, would relieve the financial burden on prisons, asylums, and other state institutions.[50]

When these laws were first enacted, they immediately attracted constitutional challenges. Many laws were struck down on the ground that the statutes did not provide due process (in the purely procedural sense of notice, hearing, opportunity to give testimony or confront witnesses, appeal, and the like) to the unfortunate targets of the sterilization orders.[51]

Advocates of eugenic sterilization worked vigorously to rewrite the procedural aspects of the laws so that they could withstand constitutional challenge.[52] In 1927, they were rewarded for their efforts when the U.S. Supreme Court upheld the constitutionality of a eugenics statute in the infamous decision of *Buck v. Bell*.[53]

In that case, Virginia courts issued and affirmed an order to sterilize a woman named Carrie Buck who had been committed to a state institution. The order was issued pursuant to a state eugenics law that provided for the sterilization of people with mental disabilities. According to the facts as presented in the decision, Ms. Buck was the feeble-minded offspring of a feeble-minded mother. Moreover, she herself had given birth to an illegitimate feeble-minded child.[54]

Ms. Buck appealed, contending that the eugenics statute was void under the Fourteenth Amendment because it denied her due process of law and violated the Equal Protection Clause. The Supreme Court rejected the challenge and affirmed the sterilization order. It held that the statutory procedures were adequate to protect Ms. Buck's due process rights[55] and that sterilization only of individuals in mental institutions did not violate the Equal Protection Clause.[56]

Sensing that the thrust of Ms. Buck's challenge went not to procedure, or even to equal protection, but rather to the very substance of the law, the Court reasoned:

> We have seen more than once that the public welfare may call upon the best citizens for their lives. It would be strange if it could not call upon those who already sap the strength of the State for these lesser sacrifices, often not felt to be such by those concerned, in order to prevent our being swamped with incompetence. It is better for all the world, if instead of waiting to execute degenerate offspring for crime, or to let them starve for their imbecility, society can prevent those who are manifestly unfit from continuing their kind. The principle that sustains compulsory vaccination is broad enough to cover cutting the Fallopian tubes. Three generations of imbeciles are enough.[57]

With the *Buck* decision in hand, eugenicists and their companions in state legislatures could write sterilization laws with confidence. The decision sparked an upsurge in enactments, and the pace of sterilizations accelerated with the advent of the Great Depression and a drop in public revenues.[58]

The Supreme Court has never overruled the *Buck* decision.[59] Since 1927, however, the Court has steadily built a jurisprudence of substantive due process that embraces the right to make sensitive reproductive decisions.

Interestingly, the Supreme Court's first foray into that arena also involved a eugenics statute. In *Skinner v. Oklahoma*,[60] Oklahoma courts issued and affirmed an order for the sterilization of a man who had been convicted of stealing chickens once and committing robbery with firearms twice. The Supreme Court held that the eugenics law violated the Equal Protection Clause, reasoning that there was no meaningful distinction between thieves and robbers, who were subject to the law, and embezzlers, who were not.[61]

If this were all the Supreme Court had had to say, the *Skinner* decision would be of little interest today. The lasting significance of the case lies in the following passage:

> We are dealing here with legislation which involves one of the basic civil rights of man. Marriage and procreation are fundamental to the very existence and survival of the race. The power to sterilize, if exercised, may have subtle, farreaching and devastating effects. In evil or reckless hands it can cause races or types which are inimical to the dominant group to wither and disappear. There is no redemption for the individual whom the law touches. Any experiment which the State conducts is to his irreparable injury. He is forever deprived of a basic liberty. We mention these matters not to reexamine the scope of the police power of the States. We advert to them merely in emphasis of our view that strict scrutiny of the classification which a State makes in a sterilization law is essential, lest unwittingly or otherwise invidious discriminations are made against groups or types of individuals in violation of the constitutional guaranty of just and equal laws.[62]

As constitutional scholars John Nowak and Ronald Rotunda have noted, *Skinner* made two key points. First, certain rights are so important that they deserve a heightened level of judicial protection against legislative infringement. This insight led to the development of "fundamental rights" analysis under the Due Process and Equal Protection Clauses. Second, the case identified marital and procreative rights as belonging to that core group of rights with special constitutional significance.[63]

Thus, *Skinner* is properly understood as the ancestor of other, better known decisions in the modern reproductive rights pantheon, from *Griswold v. Connecticut*,[64] which recognized that the right to privacy includes the right of married couples to use contraception, to *Roe v. Wade*[65] and its progeny,[66] which recognized the right of a woman to have an abortion up to the point of fetal viability.

The development of a strong jurisprudence defining reproductive rights as fundamental undermines the authority of *Buck v. Bell* and casts doubt on the constitutionality of those eugenics laws that continue to blot the codes of our states.[67] Since 1927, genetics has advanced. We now know that many of the conditions listed in the eugenics statutes as grounds for sterilization are not heritable; we also know that sterilization is not an effective means of eliminating genes from a large population.[68] It seems unlikely that the Supreme Court would find that the government had an interest in improving the species or protecting society from being "swamped with incompetence" that was compelling enough to justify the severe infringement of reproductive privacy that sterilization represents.[69] This is particularly true given the horrific practices of Nazi Germany, which have made "eugenics" a political dirty word.

What are the implications of *Buck* for my analysis of the constitutionality of anticloning laws? First, the safety objection has not been articulated in terms of the need to eliminate certain physical types in order to improve the species or to save the taxpayer from the expense of caring for them. Instead, the objection appeals to modern political sensibilities by asserting that human clones will suffer. The objection, however, does not seek to "protect" existing persons but rather asserts that certain humans are so deformed and pitiable that they should not be allowed to come into existence. To the extent the objection weighs the prospective lives of disabled persons and finds them wanting, it seems similar to prenatal counseling and testing for Down's syndrome and other chromosomal abnormalities coupled with abortion – a "private" choice that has often been identified as eugenic in character.[70]

Even if one assumes, however, that the safety objection is eugenic and that the anticloning laws can fairly be characterized as eugenics laws,[71] it seems unlikely that *Buck* could provide the government with the precedent necessary to uphold the laws. Because *Buck* did not apply the strict scrutiny standard, its holding that eugenics laws are constitutionally valid is not controlling when a suspect class challenges the laws on equal protection grounds. Further analysis is required to establish that the laws serve a *compelling* interest.

d) Proving the Superiority of Nonexistence

This brings me to a question that is bound to prove nettlesome for any government intent on enforcing anticloning laws.

For the sake of argument, assume that human clones face a significant risk of being born with birth defects. As Professor John Robertson has

noted, those who oppose human cloning on this ground face a philosophical problem. Anticloning laws can protect human clones against
suffering only at the cost of their own existence. Thus, cloning opponents implicitly argue that nonexistence is preferable to existence for
human clones. This is a radical claim. Birth defects can be painful and
even terminal, but few are so awful that those who suffer from them
would elect nonexistence over existence.[72]

Let us return to our constitutional analysis. Suppose that the government seeks to justify anticloning laws on the ground that the laws are
necessary to protect children who otherwise might be conceived and
born through cloning. In essence, this is a claim that the life of a human
clone is so blighted that even the void is preferable.

Imagine the government's attempt to prove this claim. It would need
to do more than put on evidence about birth defects in human clones. It
would also need to prove the philosophical premise that nonexistence is
preferable to existence. This would be very difficult to do – particularly
because advocates of cloning would have the opportunity to put human
clones on the stand to testify that they prefer life to nothingness.

If the government cannot prove that nonexistence is preferable to
existence, it cannot establish a compelling interest in preventing the
birth of human clones, and its laws must be invalidated.

e) Safety in the Future

Everything written here about safety so far is based on the *current* state
of cloning technology. This chapter, however, is about what might happen if an equal protection challenge were brought against anticloning
laws. Such a challenge is unlikely to be brought until a significant number of human clones have been born. At that point, the efficiency and
safety of cloning technology must, by definition, have been significantly
improved; otherwise, prospective parents would not be attracted to the
technology, and the plaintiff class would not exist.

Such improvement is a realistic possibility. Science is not static. As
the years pass, mainstream scientists will continue experiments in animal cloning. Also, unless Congress enacts a complete ban on human
cloning, mainstream scientists will continue to clone human embryos
for research and medical purposes, searching zealously for stem cell
cures to various maladies. If such research becomes illegal in the United

States, it is likely to continue in other countries such as Britain.[73] Lastly, maverick scientists are likely to continue their experiments on human embryos that they have cloned for reproductive purposes. All of this work will improve our understanding of both the theoretical and technical aspects of cloning. This makes it likely that human reproductive cloning, like other new medical technologies, will become more efficient and safer as time passes.

By the time human reproductive cloning has become efficient and safe enough that prospective parents are attracted to the technology in significant numbers, it will be extraordinarily difficult for the government to prove that cloning involves risks above and beyond the risks that the government permits many adults and offspring to run freely in the course of sexual reproduction. The only safety argument left would be that human clones *might* suffer from invisible epigenetic defects that *might* prove harmful to their health at some point. As we have seen, however, the government has the burden of establishing a compelling interest and cannot carry that burden by asserting speculative harms such as this.[74] Therefore, as time passes and technology improves, it will become harder, and ultimately impossible, for the government to prove that it has a compelling interest in protecting participants and preventing the birth of children with birth defects.

Advances in cloning technology, moreover, will undermine the government's legal position in another more political sense. Today, few would care to argue that children with Down's syndrome, cystic fibrosis, dwarfism, or any number of other nonconforming conditions would be better off nonexistent – so much better off that laws should be passed against reproduction that could lead to their existence. The reason for this reluctance is that such an argument is fundamentally antiegalitarian; it assumes that the lives of some children are valuable and worthwhile, whereas the lives of other children are not. And yet, this is precisely what opponents of cloning are implying about the lives of cloned children. The implication may be politically tenable now, when there are no children around to complain, or even in the short term, so long as the children remain safely closeted. A few government lawyers, some expert witnesses, and many judges, however, may be reluctant to advocate, justify, or uphold anticloning laws once those children have come out of the closet – even if they do have some birth defects. In this way, future developments may sap the political will necessary to defend anticloning laws.

f) Narrowly Tailored Means

Finally, the realistic prospect that technological advances could make human reproductive cloning safe and efficient has strong implications – not only for the constitutionality of anticloning laws in the future but also for the constitutionality of anticloning laws today.

Even if the government presently has a compelling interest in protecting the safety of participants, and preventing the birth of children with serious birth defects, anticloning laws cannot survive strict scrutiny unless they are narrowly tailored to achieve that interest. Just the opposite is true. As explained in Chapter 6, all of the federal bills and state laws against cloning impose a flat ban on human reproductive cloning. Most of the laws impose substantial prison sentences as the penalty for their violation. The laws have no expiration dates and do not require lawmakers to review or repeal them if and when human reproductive cloning becomes safe.

Less restrictive strategies are available. The federal and state governments could permit human reproductive cloning to go forward but regulate it in the same way that other medical treatments are regulated to ensure the health and safety of participants and prospective children. For example, the FDA could regulate drugs and medical devices that are marketed in this country to be used in cloning procedures (but only for the purpose of ensuring that such drugs and devices are safe and not for the purpose of covertly blocking their use and making cloning impossible). State governments, which have the authority to license doctors and regulate the practice of medicine, could regulate the qualifications of the doctors and laboratory technicians who participate in human reproductive cloning.[75] Licensing boards could revoke the professional licenses of doctors or other medical personnel who provided reproductive cloning in an irresponsible or unethical manner. (By this, I do not mean to sanction the California anticloning law, which brands any foray into reproductive cloning as unprofessional conduct and revokes the business license of any practitioner who dares to provide reproductive cloning to his or her patients, whether the practitioner is qualified or not, and whether the technology is safe or not.[76]) Tort law also provides an important safeguard against dangerous technologies. Doctors who commit malpractice while cloning could be sued for very large sums of money. The threat of such lawsuits alone is probably enough to ensure that legitimate practitioners would not provide reproductive cloning to their patients until it was reasonably safe. If the government believes that charlatans are offering bogus cloning services to desperate people, its best strategy might be to subject these practitioners to financial penalties pursuant to federal and state laws against unfair and deceptive business practices.

Perhaps most importantly, if federal and state governments are truly concerned about the safety of human reproductive cloning, they could fund research to improve the efficiency and safety of the technology just as they fund research into other novel but promising medical treatments.[77] Instead, President Bill Clinton cut off federal funds for human cloning experiments shortly after Dolly was born, thereby crippling the research necessary to make the technology safe.[78]

Worse, Congress and state legislatures have insisted on proposing and enacting flat bans that carry draconian penalties. Given how difficult it would be to repeal a law against cloning, these efforts are the equivalent of a permanent ban.[79] The laws violate the equal protection guarantee because they go further than necessary to protect participants and prevent the birth of children with birth defects.

This discussion would not be complete without a critique of the FDA. As explained in Chapter 6, the FDA probably does not have the statutory authority to regulate human reproductive cloning. Perhaps for this reason, the FDA has never issued any regulation or substantive rule that explains the statutory basis and extent of its authority to regulate cloning. As Professor Richard Merrill and Bryan Rose have pointed out, "[n]one of the Agency's statements say whether its requirements apply only to experiments whose immediate aim is to produce a human clone or encompass any research where results might facilitate the eventual cloning of a human being."[80] As a result, scientists have been left in the dark as to which of their cloning-related experiments might be subject to FDA control and prohibition. Furthermore, the FDA has not specified which safety concerns inspired it to act or how investigators could assuage those concerns.[81]

Instead, the FDA has proclaimed loudly and repeatedly that it has jurisdiction over cloning. It has sent letters to researchers across the country warning them not to clone a human being without its permission and then informing them that its permission cannot be obtained. It has threatened enforcement action against mavericks, has investigated at least one laboratory, and has initiated one grand jury investigation. The result has been to chill the very research that could make cloning safe.[82] Such actions do not qualify as responsible regulation; rather, the FDA has adopted a program of intimidation designed to prevent all human births. Because this program goes farther than necessary to protect participants and prevent the birth of children with serious birth defects, the Federal Food, Drug, and Cosmetic Act and Public Health Service Act are unconstitutional as the FDA has applied them.

6. Summary

If anticloning laws are challenged under the equal protection guarantee, the appropriate standard of review is strict scrutiny. Federal and state anticloning laws cannot satisfy this standard. None of the five objections provides a compelling reason for preventing the use of cloning technology or for preventing the birth of human clones. Anticloning laws, moreover, are not narrowly tailored to achieve the few interests that the government has to assert. For these reasons, anticloning laws violate the equal protection guarantee and are constitutionally invalid – both as written and as applied.

Conclusion

Much has been written about human reproductive cloning, both pro and con. Comparatively little has been written about laws against human reproductive cloning. This book is my attempt to make three contributions to the literature on cloning and anticloning laws.

Part 1 explained why five common objections to cloning are false. The analysis revealed that the objections reflect, reinforce, and inspire a host of unfair stereotypes regarding human clones. Those stereotypes were then listed and discussed.

Part 2 showed how the five objections have inspired the proposal, application, and enactment of anticloning laws. Reasoning by analogy to antimiscegenation laws, I identified the anticloning laws as a form of existential segregation. This was followed by a systematic analysis of the costs of existential segregation and an explanation of how the segregation stigmatizes human clones. I weighed those costs against the putative benefits of the anticloning laws. This analysis led me to conclude that anticloning laws are bad public policy.

Part 3 staked out my most ambitious claim: anticloning laws are an unconstitutional violation of the equal protection guarantee. Someday, if human clones are born, I hope my analysis will provide them with a strategy for bringing a constitutional challenge to the laws that oppress them.

In addition, it is my hope that this book will make a contribution above and beyond the intertwined topics of cloning and anticloning laws. Existential segregation is not new; it has been injuring its victims since the dawn of our Republic. In the past, racists enacted antimiscegenation laws – in part to deny existence to mixed-race children. Eugenicists enacted sterilization laws – in part to deny existence to children who were believed to harbor criminal tendencies or carry physical and mental disabilities. Of course, these laws did not achieve their goal of eliminating "undesirables," but they did unfairly stigmatize the innocents who were born in defiance of them.

To date, however, challenges to existential segregation have focused on the injuries to adults whose marital and procreative liberties were violated. This is a practical approach in many cases, but it tends to conceal the harm that existential segregation works upon the children who are its targets.

By identifying existential segregation as such, I hope to encourage others to think about legal discrimination in new ways. This is important, not only because past victims deserve to have their injuries recognized and redressed to the greatest extent possible but also because we should strive to protect others from suffering from the effects of existential segregation in the future.

For example, as mentioned in Part 3, legislatures are busily enacting statutes and constitutional amendments that define marriage as a union between a man and a woman. This effort seems to be designed to stop gay and lesbian marriages. Such efforts, however, also could be intended, in part, to discourage gay and lesbian couples from bearing and raising children who (heterosexuals assume) are at risk for deviation from sexual norms.

Also, cloning is not the only assisted reproductive technology that has been, or could be, attacked based on the undesirable characteristics of resulting children. The FDA has already halted variations on IVF that produce two genetic mothers. In the future, if genetic engineering becomes technologically feasible, lawmakers might ban the technology to protect the public against "super-babies."

Finally, if our increasing knowledge of human genetics is coupled with genetic determinism, it might be used to justify the enactment of new eugenics laws. Today, we hear that adults must be sent to prison if they conceive human clones because those children would be physically and psychologically damaged. Tomorrow, we may hear that certain categories of adults with "flawed" genes must be sent to prison if they reproduce because the government thinks it has a compelling interest in preventing the birth of dwarves, children with autism, or others whose genes are unpopular and outside the mainstream.

These examples may sound farfetched, but so was human reproductive cloning a few years ago. In 1997, we learned that cloning adult mammals is scientifically possible. Almost immediately, anticloning bills and laws began to replicate themselves in Congress and state legislatures.

As long as laboratories are active, legislatures will be, too. New laws can do as much, or more, damage to society as new science. It is time to give those laws the critical scrutiny they deserve and to reserve nonexistence only for them.

Notes

Introduction

1   *See* I. Wilmut et al., *Viable Offspring Derived from Fetal and Adult Mammalian Cells*, 385 NATURE 810 (1997).

2   *See id.; see generally* GINA KOLATA, CLONE: THE ROAD TO DOLLY AND THE PATH AHEAD 27 (1998) [hereinafter KOLATA, CLONE].
    Cloning is sometimes referred to as "somatic cell nuclear transfer" (SCNT) because the process involves the transfer of a nucleus from a somatic cell (i.e., any cell other than a reproductive cell) into an egg from which the chromosomes have been removed. *See, e.g.,* THE NATIONAL ACADEMIES, SCIENTIFIC AND MEDICAL ASPECTS OF HUMAN REPRODUCTIVE CLONING 270 (2002).

3   *See* KOLATA, CLONE, *supra* note 2, at 146.

4   For an interesting account of how scientists learned to clone mammals from embryo cells, see *id.* at 157–87.

5   *See* Vittorio Sgaramella & Norton D. Zinder, *Letter*, 279 SCI. 635 (1998).

6   *See, e.g.,* Yoko Kato et al., *Eight Calves Cloned from Somatic Cells of a Single Adult*, 282 SCI. 2095 (December 11, 1998). This early experiment began with 249 eggs. Following nuclear transplantation, 112 eggs were cultured, growing into 108 two-celled embryos. Of these embryos, 38 developed into blastocysts, and 10 of those were selected for implantation into 5 surrogate cows. All of the cows became pregnant, and eight calves were born. Four of the calves died from environmental reasons that the researchers believed were unrelated to cloning (one from heatstroke, two others from breathing in excess amniotic fluid, and the fourth from dystocia and delayed delivery).

7   *See* Irina A. Polejaeva et al., *Cloned Pigs Produced by Nuclear Transfer from Adult Somatic Cells*, 407 NATURE 86 (2000).

8   *See* Alexander Baguisi et al., *Production of Goats by Somatic Cell Nuclear Transfer*, 17 NATURE BIOTECHNOLOGY 456 (1999).

217

9   *See* Tae Young Shin et al., *A Cat Cloned by Nuclear Transplantation*, 415 NATURE 859
    (2002).

10 Patrick Chesne et al., *Cloned Rabbits Produced by Nuclear Transfer from Adult Somatic
    Cells*, 20 NATURE BIOTECHNOLOGY 366 (2002).

11 *See* T. Wakayama et al., *Full-term Development of Mice from Enucleated Oocytes Injected
    with Cumulus Cell Nuclei*, 394 NATURE 369 (1998).

12 *See* Qi Zhou et al., *Generation of Fertile Cloned Rats by Regulating Oocyte Activation*,
    302 SCI. 117 (2003).

13 *See* Cesare Galli et al., *Pregnancy: A Cloned Horse Born to its Dam Twin*, 424 NATURE
    635 (2003).

14 *See* College of Veterinary Medicine, Texas A & M University, *CVM Researchers First
    to Clone White-tailed Deer, at* <http://www.cvm.tamu.edu/news/releases/deer_clone.
    shtml> (Dec. 22, 2003).

15 Cloning has attracted some attention as a technology that could help to preserve
    endangered species. One such species is the Asian gaur. A cloned gaur was born
    in January 2001, but it died shortly afterwards. *See* Rick Weiss, *Clone of Endan-
    gered Species Succeeds*, S. F. CHRON., Apr. 8, 2003, at A3. Another such species
    is the banteng, an animal similar to cattle and native to Asian jungles. In 2003,
    scientists announced the birth of two cloned banteng calves. The calves were
    cloned from skin cells that had been harvested from a captive banteng before it
    died in 1980. One calf was healthy; the other was born abnormally large, and
    was euthanized. *See id.*; Maggie Fox, *Scientists Euthanize Cloned Baby Banteng, at*
    <http://www.planetark.org/dailynewsstory.cfm/newsid/20445/story.htm> (Apr. 11,
    2003).

16 *See* Andrew Pollack, *Researchers Add Mule to Family of the Cloned*, S. F. CHRON., May
    30, 2003, at A2.

17 *See* THE PRESIDENT'S COUNCIL ON BIOETHICS, HUMAN CLONING AND HU-
    MAN DIGNITY: AN ETHICAL INQUIRY 130–33 (July 2002) [hereinafter COUNCIL
    REPORT].

18 Other scientists have cloned human embryos. Though not quite as successful, their
    experiments demonstrate a steady progress toward the goal of creating healthy em-
    bryos from which stem cells can be harvested. In chronological order, *see* Jose B.
    Cibelli et al., *The First Human Cloned Embryo*, 286 SCI. AM. 44 (2002) (reporting
    the first creation of a cloned human embryo that grew to six cells); Rick Weiss,
    Rabbit-human Embryos Reported, S. F. CHRON., Aug. 14, 2002, at A3 (Chinese re-
    searchers combined rabbit eggs with human DNA to create hybrid embryos from
    which embryonic stem cells could be harvested); Wendy Goldman Rohm, *Seven Days
    of Creation: The Inside Story of a Human Cloning Experiment*, WIRED MAGAZINE, Jan.
    2004, at 123 (reporting the successful cloning of an entirely human embryo with at
    least 16 cells).

19 *See* Woo Suk Hwang et al., *Evidence of a Pluripotent Human Embryonic Stem Cell Line
    Derived from a Cloned Blastocyst*, 303 SCI. 1669 (2004).

20 In human sexual reproduction, it takes about 5 or 6 days for a fertilized egg to grow
    to the blastocyst stage. A day or so afterward, the embryo implants in the uterus.
    See SHERMAN J. SILBER, HOW TO GET PREGNANT WITH THE NEW TECHNOLOGY
    80–81 (1991).

21 *See* COUNCIL REPORT, *supra* note 17, at 144.

22 Panayiotis Zavos, *Human Reproductive Cloning: The Time Is Near*, 6 REPROD. BIOMEDICINE ONLINE 397 (2003), *at* <http://www.rbmonline.com>.

23 *See Doctor Says He Has Implanted Cloned Human Embryo, at* <http://www.nytimes.com/reuters/news/news-science-clone.html?ex=1075362431&ei=1&en=25> (Jan. 17, 2004).

24 *See Human Cloning Attempt Has Failed, at* <http://news.bbc.co.uk/1/hi/health/3459009.stm> (Feb. 4, 2004).

25 *See, e.g.,* Mark D. Eibert, *Human Cloning: Myths, Medical Benefits and Constitutional Rights*, 53 HASTINGS L. J. 1097, 1101 (2002); John A. Robertson, *Liberty, Identity, and Human Cloning*, 76 TEX. L. REV. 1371, 1379 (1998).

26 *See, e.g.,* Robertson, *supra* note 25, at 1379.

27 *See id.* at 1380.

28 Some people may think that they can use cloning to resurrect children or other loved ones who have died. *See, e.g.,* CALIFORNIA ADVISORY COMMITTEE ON HUMAN CLONING, CLONING CALIFORNIANS?, REPORT OF THE CALIFORNIA ADVISORY COMMITTEE ON HUMAN CLONING 22 (2002). However, cloning cannot bring back the dead. Any baby conceived through cloning would share the genome of the person who died but nothing more. *See id.; see also* Chapter 3, *infra* (explaining that humans born through cloning are not copies of their DNA donors). As soon as the public realizes this sad truth, this particular market for cloning services should dwindle.

29 *See* Chapter 6, *infra.*

30 *See* ROBIN BAKER & ELIZABETH ORAM, BABY WARS: THE DYNAMICS OF FAMILY CONFLICTS 35 (1998).

31 *See* Eibert, *supra* note 25, at 1113.

32 Laurence Tribe, *On Not Banning Cloning for the Wrong Reasons*, in CLONES AND CLONES: FACTS AND FANTASIES ABOUT HUMAN CLONING 221, 229–30 (Martha C. Nussbaum & Cass R. Sunstein eds. 1998).

33 *Id.* at 230.

34 To write this book, I had to find a concise but respectful way of describing a person conceived with the aid of cloning technology. I have chosen to employ the term "human clone," which is accurate and concise, but conveys the essential humanity of the individual involved.

    Unfortunately, when the word "clone" is used by itself, it has many negative and dehumanizing associations. *See* GREGORY PENCE, WHO'S AFRAID OF HUMAN CLONING? 49 (1998). Therefore, as a general rule, I have eschewed the use of that single word when writing about humans. However, I occasionally use it (within quotation marks) when describing the beliefs of cloning opponents because it accurately reflects their prejudice toward humans conceived with the aid of cloning technology.

Part One: Five Common Objections to Human Reproductive Cloning Reflect, Reinforce, and Inspire Stereotypes About Human Clones

1 See Exec. Order No. 12,975, 60 Fed. Reg. 52,063-64 (October 5, 1995).

2 *See* NATIONAL BIOETHICS ADVISORY COMMISSION, CLONING HUMAN BEINGS, REPORT AND RECOMMENDATIONS OF THE NATIONAL BIOETHICS ADVISORY COMMISSION, Letter from the President (1997).

3 *See id.* at 108–09.
4 *See* Cal. Bus. & Prof. Code §§ 2260.5, 16004, 16105 (West 1998) and Cal. Health & Safety Code §§ 24185, 24187, 24189 (West 1998).
5 *See* S. Con. Res. 39, 1997–1998 Reg. Sess. (Cal. Sept. 12, 1997); 1997 Bill Text Cal. S.C.R. 39 (LEXIS through 2004 Sess., Sept. 12, 1997).
6 *See* California Advisory Committee on Human Cloning, Cloning Californians?, Report of the California Advisory Committee on Human Cloning 37 (2002).
7 The National Academies consist of the National Academy of Sciences (NAS), the National Academy of Engineering (NAE), the Institute of Medicine (IOM), and the National Research Council (NRC). The NAS Report was the result of work done by the Panel on Scientific and Medical Aspects of Human Cloning, which itself was a joint panel of the Committee on Science, Engineering, and Public Policy (a joint committee of NAS, NAE and IOM), and the Board on Life Sciences (a unit under the Division on Earth and Life Studies of the NRC).
8 *See* The National Academies, Scientific and Medical Aspects of Human Reproductive Cloning 2 (2002).
9 *See* Exec. Order No. 13,237, 66 Fed. Reg. 59,851 (November 30, 2001).
10 *See* The President's Council on Bioethics, Human Cloning and Human Dignity: An Ethical Inquiry 200 (2002).

Chapter One: Does Human Reproductive Cloning Offend God and Nature?

1 *See, e.g.,* California Advisory Committee on Human Cloning, Cloning Californians?, Report of the California Advisory Committee on Human Cloning 31 (2002) [hereinafter California Report]; *see also* National Bioethics Advisory Commission, Cloning Human Beings, Report and Recommendations of the National Bioethics Advisory Commission 44–45 (1997) [hereinafter NBAC Report].
2 Patrick D. Hopkins, *Bad Copies: How Popular Media Represent Cloning as an Ethical Problem,* 28 Hastings Center Rep. 6, 11–12 (March–April 1998).
3 Aldous Huxley, Brave New World (Harper & Row, Publishers, Inc. 1969).
4 Mary Shelley, Frankenstein; or, The Modern Prometheus (Washington Square Press 1995) (1818).
5 *See* Hopkins, *supra* note 2, at 11–12.
6 *See* Alan Petersen, *Biofantasies: Genetics and Medicine in the Print News Media,* 52 Soc. Sci. & Med. 1255, 1265–66 (2001).
7 *See* NBAC Report, *supra* note 1, at 54–57. For example, Rabbi Tendler testified that it would be appropriate to clone an otherwise sterile man who was the only one of his family to survive the Holocaust. *See id.* at 55.
8 These people are called "nones," after their response to a common question in public opinion polls: "What is your religion, if any?" *See* Mark O'Keefe, *Number of 'Nones,' Those Who Claim No Religion, Swells in U.S., at* <http://www.startribune.com/stories/389/4235279.html> (November 30, 2003).
9 Lee Silver, *Public Policy Crafted in Response to Public Ignorance is Bad Public Policy,* 53 Hastings L.J. 1037, 1045 (2002).
10 *See generally* Sherman J. Silber, How to Get Pregnant with the New Technology 288–319 (1991).

11 *See* THE NATIONAL ACADEMIES, SCIENTIFIC AND MEDICAL ASPECTS OF HUMAN CLONING 63 (2002).
12 *See* Mark D. Eibert, *Human Cloning: Myths, Medical Benefits and Constitutional Rights*, 53 HASTINGS L.J. 1097, 1102 (2002).
13 *See* GREGORY E. PENCE, WHO'S AFRAID OF HUMAN CLONING? 26–27 (1998).
14 SILBER, *supra* note 10, at 268.
15 *See* Eibert, *supra* note 12, at 1103.
16 *See Test Tube Babies, 25 Years Later, at* <http://www.cnn.com/2003/HEALTH/parenting/07/25/ivf.anniversary/index.html> (July 25, 2003); Patricia Reaney, *Test Tube Babies Celebrate 25 Years of IVF, at* <http://uk.news.yahoo.com/030725/80/e4wm8.html> (July 25, 2003).
17 *See* NBAC REPORT, *supra* note 1, at 51–52.
18 CALIFORNIA REPORT, *supra* note 1, at 31 (emphasis added).
19 *See* STANLEY N. SALTHE, EVOLUTIONARY BIOLOGY 57 (1972).
20 *See* Silver, *supra* note 9, at 1039.
21 *See* THE COLUMBIA ENCYCLOPEDIA 112–13 (Paul Lagasse ed., 6th ed. 2000).
22 Dale L. Bartos, *Landscape Dynamics of Aspen and Conifer Forests*, USDA FOREST SERVICE PROC. RMRS-P18 at 5 (2001).
23 *See* WEBSTER'S NEW WORLD DICTIONARY OF THE AMERICAN LANGUAGE 1594 (college ed. 1968).
24 Erasmus Darwin, the grandfather of Charles Darwin, was one of the first to assert this point of view. *See* ANNE K. MELLOR, MARY SHELLEY, HER LIFE, HER FICTION, HER MONSTERS 97–98 (1989 ed.). Professor Mellor has argued that the novel *Frankenstein* draws upon this view in portraying the creation of life through scientific means as a violation of the canons of nature. *See id.* at 101.
25 *See* Eibert, *supra* note 12, at 1103.
26 For a fuller development of the argument that anticloning laws could perpetuate stereotypes by restricting information about human clones, see Chapter 9, *infra*.
27 *See* Hopkins, *supra* note 2, at 12.
28 *See, e.g.,* Liza Porteus, *Human Cloning Ban Debate* Resurfaces, *at* <http://www.foxnews.com/story/0,2933,75014,00.html> (Jan. 9, 2003) (explaining that sponsors of the 2003 Weldon bill want to avoid "Franken-babies").
29 *See* SHELLEY, *supra* note 4, at 47.
30 *See id.* at 49–50.
31 *Id.* at 52.
32 *See id.* at 143.
33 *See id.* at 69, 74 , 150.
34 *See id.* at 79–88, 151.
35 *See id.* at 152–56.
36 *See id.* at 178–79.
37 *See id.* at 188–90.
38 *See id.* at 211–12.
39 *See id.* at 219–26, 235–37.
40 *See id.* at 237–43.
41 Some people mistakenly believe that human reproductive cloning can cheat death by producing copies of people who die. However, this belief is incorrect; the most cloning can do is produce a new individual who shares the nuclear DNA of the person who died. For more on the identity fallacy, see Chapter 3, *infra*.

42 For more on physical flaws and why they might be expected, even if not immediately visible, see Chapter 5, *infra*.

Chapter Two: Should Children Be Begotten and Not Made?

1 *See* THE PRESIDENT'S COUNCIL ON BIOETHICS, HUMAN CLONING AND HUMAN DIGNITY: AN ETHICAL INQUIRY 8–10, 104–07, (2002) [hereinafter COUNCIL REPORT]; *accord*, NATIONAL BIOETHICS ADVISORY COMMISSION, CLONING HUMAN BEINGS, REPORT AND RECOMMENDATIONS OF THE NATIONAL BIOETHICS ADVISORY COMMISSION 49, 50, 52, and 69, (1997) [hereinafter NBAC REPORT].

2 NBAC REPORT, *supra* note 1, at 49 (citations omitted).

3 *See* CALIFORNIA ADVISORY COMMITTEE ON HUMAN CLONING, CLONING CALIFORNIANS?, REPORT OF THE CALIFORNIA ADVISORY COMMITTEE ON HUMAN CLONING 29 (2002); COUNCIL REPORT, *supra* note 1, at 107; NBAC REPORT, *supra* note 1, at 51, 73.

4 *See* Ashutosh Bhagwat, *Cloning and Federalism*, 53 HASTINGS L.J. 1133, 1134 (2002)

5 *See* JOHN A. ROBERTSON, CHILDREN OF CHOICE 140 (1994). One recent article reported that sperm donors typically are paid $50 per ejaculation; recipients pay $140 to $175 per vial because of the medical testing involved. *See* Gina Kolata, *Choosing Sperm, Egg Donors – Right Down to the IQ*, S. F. EXAMINER, Jan. 4, 1998, at A8.

   Egg donors receive more money than sperm donors because it is harder and more painful to grow and harvest a cycle of eggs than it is to ejaculate sperm. *See* Christy Ogelsby, *Egg Donation Long, Hard Process*, at <http://us.cnn.com/2001/HEALTH/parenting/07/13/ egg.donation/> (visited Aug. 19, 2003). A random sampling of Web sites shows that egg donors currently receive fees ranging from $2,000 to $15,000 per cycle of eggs. The cost to recipient couples is much higher. They must pay fees to the agencies that bring them into contact with egg donors. They also must pay for the donor's medical expenses and drugs in addition to their own. *See* <http://www.eggdonor.com/ercost.html> ($3,500 to $12,000); <http://www.eggdonation.com/frees_don.htm> ($5,000); <http://www.reproductivehealthctr.com/eggdonation/fee.htm> ($2,000); <http://www.advancedfertility.com/eggdonationcost.htm> ($5,000); and <http://www.fertilityalternatives.com/new1777267.html> ($5,000 to $15,000) (visited Aug. 19, 2003).

6 *See* Kolata, *supra* note 5.

7 *See id.*

8 *See* NBAC REPORT, *supra* note 1, at 52.

9 *See, e.g.*, Margaret Radin, *Market-Inalienability*, 100 HARV. L. REV. 1849 (1987).

10 Just over 10 years ago, the California Supreme Court refused to hold that gestational surrogacy violated public policy, reasoning in part that "we are likewise unpersuaded by the claim that surrogacy will foster the attitude that children are mere commodities; no evidence is offered to support it. The limited data available seem to reflect an absence of significant adverse effects of surrogacy on all participants." *See* Johnson v. Calvert, 5 Cal. 4th 84, 97, 851 P.2d 776, 785, 19 Cal. Rptr. 2d 494, 503 (1993).

11 *See* S. Golombok et al., *The European Study of Assisted Reproduction Families: The Transition to Adolescence*, 17 HUM. REPROD. 830 (2002).

12 *See* ROBERTSON, *supra* note 5, at 141.
13 COUNCIL REPORT, *supra* note 1, at 106.
14 *See* Lee Silver, *Public Policy Crafted in Response to Public Ignorance Is Bad Public Policy*, 53 HASTINGS L. J. 1037, 1041 (2002).
15 *See* NBAC REPORT, *supra* note 1, at 50.
16 *See* Chapter 3, *infra*.

Chapter Three: Do Human Clones Lack Individuality?

1 *See* Patrick D. Hopkins, *Bad Copies: How Popular Media Represent Cloning as an Ethical Problem*, 28 HASTINGS CENTER REP. 7 (March–April 1998).
2 *See id.* at 8.
3 *See, e.g.*, LEE M. SILVER, REMAKING EDEN: CLONING AND BEYOND IN A BRAVE NEW WORLD 107 (1997).
4 *See* GREGORY PENCE, WHO'S AFRAID OF HUMAN CLONING? 13–23 (1998).
5 *See, e.g.*, Mark D. Eibert, *Human Cloning: Myths, Medical Benefits and Constitutional Rights*, 53 HASTINGS L. J. 1097, 1100 (2002); John A. Robertson, *Liberty, Identity, and Human Cloning*, 76 TEX. L. REV. 1371, 1413 (1998).
6 Nancy L. Segal, *Human Cloning: Insights from Twins and Twin Research*, 53 HASTINGS L. J. 1073, 1076 (2002). For example, despite their common rearing, unrelated infants who are adopted and raised by the same family at the same time are less alike in mental abilities than identical twins who are raised apart until adulthood.
7 *Id.*
8 *See* Eibert, *supra* note 5, at 1100.
9 *See, e.g.*, JOHN CHARLES KUNICH, THE NAKED CLONE: HOW CLONING BANS THREATEN OUR PERSONAL RIGHTS 124 (2003); DAVID S. MOORE, THE DEPENDENT GENE: THE FALLACY OF "NATURE VS. NURTURE" 237–39 (2001); THE NATIONAL ACADEMIES, SCIENTIFIC AND MEDICAL ASPECTS OF HUMAN CLONING 26 (2002) [hereinafter NAS REPORT]; Eibert, *supra* note 5, at 1098–99; Robertson, *supra* note 5, at 1413.
10 BRUCE ALBERTS et al., MOLECULAR BIOLOGY OF THE CELL 30 (4th ed. 2002).
11 *See* KUNICH, *supra* note 9, at 121.
12 In theory, it would be possible for a woman to clone herself using her own nuclear DNA and eggs. This would produce a female child with the same nuclear and mitochondrial DNA as the mother. Of course, men cannot accomplish the same feat. Moreover, most women who could benefit from cloning are unlikely to benefit from such a procedure. If a woman has eggs that are healthy enough to use in cloning, she should be able to reproduce sexually. If sexual reproduction is not possible for her because she is in a lesbian relationship, she can conceive a child together with her partner by merging her nuclear DNA with the partner's eggs, or vice versa. Perhaps some women with heritable disorders might choose to use their own eggs for cloning if those eggs are healthy.
13 *See* NAS REPORT, *supra* note 9, at 26.
14 Most identical twins share a single placenta. About one-third of twin pairs, however, result when an egg splits only a few days after fertilization. In such cases, each twin develops its own placenta. This accentuates differences in the nature and quantity of nutrients flowing to each twin. Studies show that identical twins are more likely

to differ from each other in both physical and psychological traits when they have their own placentas. See MOORE, *supra* note 9, at 57.

15   See *id.* at 117–28.
16   See LAURA GOULD, CATS ARE NOT PEAS: A CALICO HISTORY OF GENETICS 132–33 (1996).
17   See NANCY L. SEGAL, ENTWINED LIVES: TWINS AND WHAT THEY TELL US ABOUT HUMAN BEHAVIOR 31–32 (1999).
18   See *id.* at 32.
19   See NAS REPORT, *supra* note 9, at 49.
20   See Eibert, *supra* note 5, at 1099.
21   See Jonathan Leake, *Human Cloning Hits a Natural Barrier, at* <http://www.sunday-times.co.uk/news/pages/sti/1999/12/26/stinwenws03022.html?99> (Dec. 26, 1999).
22   See Gregory S. Archer et al., *Behavioral Variation among Cloned Pigs*, 82 APPLIED ANIMAL BEHAV. SCI. 151, 152 (2003).
23   "Time budget" refers to how much time the pigs chose to spend in various activities such as lying in a bedded area, lying on concrete, standing up, feeding, and playing or fighting. See *id.* at 154.
24   See *id.* at 151.
25   *Id.* at 160.
26   See Tae Young Shin et al., *A Cat Cloned by Nuclear Transplantation*, 415 NATURE 859 (2002); *Copied Cat Hardly Resembles Original, at* <http://www.cnn.com/2003/TECH/science/01/21/cloned.cat.ap/index.html> (Jan. 21, 2003).
27   One expert on cloning had predicted this outcome. In lectures around the country, he used his own calico cat, "Tribble," as an example of how random X inactivation could produce a diverse assortment of cloned calico kittens. See Eibert, *supra* note 5, at 1099.
28   See NAS REPORT, *supra* note 9, at 26; NATIONAL BIOETHICS ADVISORY COMMISSION, CLONING HUMAN BEINGS, REPORT AND RECOMMENDATIONS OF THE NATIONAL BIOETHICS ADVISORY COMMISSION 32 (1997) [hereinafter NBAC REPORT]; THE PRESIDENT'S COUNCIL ON BIOETHICS, HUMAN CLONING AND HUMAN DIGNITY: AN ETHICAL INQUIRY 102 (2002) [hereinafter COUNCIL REPORT].
29   See NBAC REPORT, *supra* note 28, at 69.
30   For more on science fiction as the inspiration of such fears, see, *e.g.*, PENCE, *supra* note 4, at 39–43 and Robertson, *supra* note 5, at 1384–85.
31   THE BOYS FROM BRAZIL (Fox 1978).
32   STAR WARS, EPISODE II, ATTACK OF THE CLONES (20th Century Fox 2002).
33   See NBAC REPORT, *supra* note 28, at 69.
34   *Id.* at 33.
35   See, *e.g.*, Jeffrey Kluger, *Will We Follow the Sheep?* 149 TIME, March 10, 1997, at 67, 71 (suggesting that a despot may want to clone himself so that his leadership will go on forever); Wray Herbert et al., *The World after Cloning*, U.S. NEWS & WORLD REP., March 10, 1997, at 59, 60–61 (suggesting a megalomaniac might clone an heir in a quest to achieve immortality).
36   THE SIXTH DAY (Columbia Pictures 2000).
37   See CALIFORNIA ADVISORY COMMITTEE ON HUMAN CLONING, CLONING CALIFORNIANS?, REPORT OF THE CALIFORNIA ADVISORY COMMITTEE ON HUMAN

CLONING 24 (2002) [hereinafter CALIFORNIA REPORT]; COUNCIL REPORT, *supra* note 28, at 102; NBAC REPORT, *supra* note 28, at 66.

38   *See* Segal, *supra* note 6, at 1081.

39   *See id.*

40   *See id.* at 1078, 1081–82; SEGAL, *supra* note 17, at 205.

41   *See, e.g.,* CALIFORNIA REPORT, *supra* note 37, at 25; NBAC REPORT, *supra* note 28, at 67.

42   COUNCIL REPORT, *supra* note 28, at 104.

43   *See id.; accord,* CALIFORNIA REPORT, *supra* note 37, at 25.

44   *See* PENCE, *supra* note 4, at 46.

45   COUNCIL REPORT, *supra* note 28, at 103; *accord* CALIFORNIA REPORT, *supra* note 37, at 25.

46   *See* CALIFORNIA REPORT, *supra* note 37, at 27–28; COUNCIL REPORT, *supra* note 28, at 110; NBAC REPORT, supra note 28, at 70.

47   *See* CALIFORNIA REPORT, *supra* note 37, at 28; NBAC REPORT, *supra* note 28, at 70.

48   *See* COUNCIL REPORT, *supra* note 28, at 111.

49   *Id.; see also* FRANCIS FUKUYAMA, OUR POSTHUMAN FUTURE: CONSEQUENCES OF THE BIOTECHNOLOGY REVOLUTION 207 (2002) (insinuating that the unrelated parent will be attracted to the clone when he or she becomes sexually mature).

50   If (as the hypothetical insinuates) the father goes so far as to have sex with the daughter, would he also be guilty of incest? This is a trickier question than it may seem at first glance.

State criminal laws define the crime of incest. For example, in California, it is a crime for a "parent" to marry or have sex with his or her "child." *See* CAL. PENAL CODE § 285 (West 1999) and CAL. FAMILY CODE § 2200 (West 1994).

In the case of the hypothetical, however, it is not clear whether the father would qualify as a "parent" of the daughter within the meaning of these statutes. He did not sire the girl, but he is married to her gestational mother, who also is related to the girl in a genetic sense.

Many states do have laws defining the parentage of children, but these laws have not yet been updated to take the possibility of cloning into account. In California, moreover, one statute provides that child of a wife cohabiting with a husband who is not impotent or sterile is conclusively presumed to be a child of the marriage. See CAL. FAMILY CODE § 7540 (West 1994). This presumption of legitimacy applies to incest prosecutions. *See* People v. Russell, 22 Cal. App. 3d 330, 335, 99 Cal. Rptr. 277, 280 (1971).

Thus, it seems that California law would presume the hypothetical father to be a "parent," thereby subjecting him to prosecution for incest, unless he was infertile. Blood tests could be used to rebut the "conclusive presumption," but only if a motion for testing was filed within 2 years of the child's birth. *See* CAL. FAMILY CODE § 7541 (West 2004); *see also* June Carbone & Naomi Cahn, *Which Ties Bind? Redefining the Parent–Child Relationship in an Age of Genetic Certainty,* 11 WM. & MARY BILL RTS. J. 1011, 1051–56 (2003) (examining the case law interpreting the California statutes).

51   *See* STEPHEN PINKER, HOW THE MIND WORKS 117 (1997).

52   *See id.* at 456.

53 *Id.*

54 *Id.* at 458–59; PAUL H. RUBIN, DARWINIAN POLITICS: THE EVOLUTIONARY ORIGIN OF FREEDOM 9 (2002).

55 Pinker theorizes that men may feel a weaker taboo because the costs of reproduction are lower for them in general. Unlike a woman, who must invest many months of gestation, nursing, and care in order to reproduce, a man need only have sex. Thus, a child with genetic defects represents a greater reproductive loss to a mother than to a father. PINKER, *supra* note, 52, at 457–58.

56 *See* CALIFORNIA REPORT, *supra* note 37, at 26; *see also* PENCE, *supra* note 4, at 33 (noting the false belief that clones lessen the worth of the original).

57 *See* PENCE, *supra* note 4, at 33. Just as the appropriate response to rape is to ban rape, and not sex, the appropriate response to unauthorized cloning is to ban unauthorized cloning, and not cloning per se.

58 CALIFORNIA REPORT, *supra* note 37, at 30 (emphasis added); *see* Francis C. Pizzulli, Note, *Asexual Reproduction and Genetic Engineering: A Constitutional Assessment of the Technology of Cloning*, 47 S. CAL. L. REV. 476, 583 (1974).

59 *See* Hopkins, *supra* note 1, at 8.

60 There is another inflammatory argument against cloning that reasons by analogy to incest. If the right to reproduce through incest is not constitutionally protected, so the argument goes, then neither should be the right to reproduce asexually. *See, e.g.*, Lori Andrews, *Is There a Right to Clone? Constitutional Challenges to Bans on Human Cloning*, 11 HARV. J. L. & TECH. 643, 669 (1998); *see also* COUNCIL REPORT, *supra* note 28, at 84 (suggesting that the reproductive freedom of adults must sometimes be limited for the sake of children, and citing incest as an example).

    American courts once upheld the constitutionality of antimiscegenation laws, which prohibited interracial marriages, by analogizing them to laws that barred incestuous marriages. *See, e.g.*, Harvey M. Applebaum, *Miscegenation Statutes: A Constitutional and Social Problem*, 53 GEO. L. J. 49, 58 (1964). More recently, Senator Rick Santorum generated a storm of controversy when he argued that if the U.S. Supreme Court recognized a privacy right to engage in consensual gay sex, then there must also be a constitutional right to commit bigamy, polygamy, incest, and adultery. *See* Associated Press, *Excerpt from Santorum Interview, at* <http://www.usatoday.com/news/washington/2003-04-23-santorum-excerpt_x.htm> (Apr. 23, 2003). Shortly thereafter, the Supreme Court did strike down a Texas law that criminalized homosexual sodomy, reasoning that consensual gay sex is protected under the right to privacy established by the Due Process Clause of the Fourteenth Amendment. *See* Lawrence v. Texas, 539 U.S. 558 (2003).

    Although such arguments ostensibly focus on the constitutionality of certain laws, their subtext is that the disfavored sexual, reproductive, or marital practice is as despicable and repugnant as incest. This is the reason Senator Santorum's comments generated so much justifiable anger in the gay and lesbian community.

    For the record, human reproductive cloning does not involve sexual intercourse between a parent and child, or between any other blood relatives, and therefore is not incest. Persistent comparisons of cloning with incest are themselves repugnant; they serve only to incite disgust and hatred toward the men, women, and children who may use the technology or be born through it.

Chapter Four: Could Human Clones Destroy Humanity?

1 MARY SHELLEY, FRANKENSTEIN; OR, THE MODERN PROMETHEUS 178 (Washington Square Press 1995) (1818).

2 See CALIFORNIA ADVISORY COMMITTEE ON HUMAN CLONING, CLONING CALIFORNIANS?, REPORT OF THE CALIFORNIA ADVISORY COMMITTEE ON HUMAN CLONING 30 (2002) [hereinafter CALIFORNIA REPORT].

3 See id.

4 See CALIFORNIA REPORT, supra note 2, at 28; NATIONAL BIOETHICS ADVISORY COMMISSION, CLONING HUMAN BEINGS, REPORT AND RECOMMENDATIONS OF THE NATIONAL BIOETHICS ADVISORY COMMISSION 74–75 (1997) [hereinafter NBAC REPORT]; THE PRESIDENT'S COUNCIL ON BIOETHICS, HUMAN CLONING AND HUMAN DIGNITY: AN ETHICAL INQUIRY 107–10 (2002) [hereinafter COUNCIL REPORT].

5 THOMAS ROBERT MALTHUS, AN ESSAY ON PRINCIPLE OF POPULATION (Penguin ed. 1983).

6 See CALIFORNIA REPORT, supra note 2, at 30.

7 For example, bdelloid rotifers are microscopic animals. All are female and reproduce asexually. Nevertheless, over the course of millions of years, bdelloids have survived, thrived, and evolved into some 360 described species. This contradicts the biological dogma that if animals do not reproduce sexually, they are doomed to extinction. See Jessica L. Mark Welch et al., Cytogenetic Evidence for Asexual Evolution of Bdelloid Rotifers, 101 PROC. NAT'L ACAD. SCI. 1618 (2004); David Mark Welch & Matthew Meselson, Evidence for the Evolution of Bdelloid Rotifers without Sexual Reproduction or Genetic Exchange, 288 SCI. 1211 (2000).

8 See id.

9 MATT RIDLEY, THE RED QUEEN: SEX AND THE EVOLUTION OF HUMAN NATURE 71–74 (1993).

10 See CALIFORNIA REPORT, supra note 2, at 30.

11 See id.; GREGORY E. PENCE, WHO'S AFRAID OF HUMAN CLONING? 130 (1998).

12 It is possible that human clones could be vulnerable to parasites because their genetic "locks" have not been changed recently. See generally RIDLEY, supra note 9, at 71–74. This, however, is not a danger to humans born through sexual reproduction or to the species more generally.

13 DANIEL J. KEVLES, IN THE NAME OF EUGENICS, GENETICS AND THE USES OF HUMAN HEREDITY 100 (1995 ed.); DIANE B. PAUL, CONTROLLING HUMAN HEREDITY, 1865 TO THE PRESENT 82 (1995).

14 See KEVLES, supra note 13, at 116.

15 See id. at 116–17; STEFAN KUHL, THE NAZI CONNECTION, EUGENICS, AMERICAN RACISM AND GERMAN NATIONAL SOCIALISM 42–43 (1994); Edwin Black, Eugenics and the Nazis – the California Connection, S. F. CHRON., Nov. 9, 2003, at D1.

16 See KEVLES, supra note 13, at 117–18; PAUL, supra note 13, at 90–91.

17 See COUNCIL REPORT, supra note 4, at 107.

18 See NBAC REPORT, supra note 4, at 75.

19 Id. at 74.

20 PENCE, supra note 11, at 130.

21 *See* John A. Robertson, *Liberty, Identity, and Human Cloning,* 76 TEX. L. REV. 1371, 1430–31 (1998).
22 *See* Mark D. Eibert, *Human Cloning: Myths, Medical Benefits and Constitutional Rights,* 53 HASTINGS L. J. 1097, 1106–07 (2002) (arguing that anticloning laws are eugenics laws intended to weed out unpopular human clones).
23 For a discussion of the technology involved in genetic engineering, see THE PRES-IDENT'S COUNCIL ON BIOETHICS, REPRODUCTION & RESPONSIBILITY: THE REG-ULATION OF NEW BIOTECHNOLOGIES, 107–10 (2004) [hereinafter REPRODUCTION AND RESPONSIBILITY]; LEE M. SILVER, REMAKING EDEN: CLONING AND BEYOND IN A BRAVE NEW WORLD 230–33 (1997).
24 *See* CALIFORNIA REPORT, *supra* note 2, at 28.
25 *See* COUNCIL REPORT, *supra* note 4, at 108.
26 *See* GREGORY STOCK, REDESIGNING HUMANS: OUR INEVITABLE GENETIC FUTURE (2002).
27 *See* FRANCIS FUKUYAMA, OUR POSTHUMAN FUTURE: CONSEQUENCES OF THE BIOTECHNOLOGY REVOLUTION (2002); BILL MCKIBBEN, ENOUGH: STAYING HUMAN IN AN ENGINEERED AGE (2003).
28 *See* Steven Pinker, *The Designer Baby Myth,* at <http://www.guardian.co.uk/life/ opinion/story/0,12981,970318,00.html> (June 5, 2003).
29 *See* REPRODUCTION & RESPONSIBILITY, *supra* note 23, at 112.
30 *Id.* at 110–11.

Chapter Five: Does Human Reproductive Cloning Harm Participants and Produce Children with Birth Defects?

1 *See* Chapter 7, *infra.*
2 *See* CALIFORNIA ADVISORY COMMITTEE ON HUMAN CLONING, CLONING CAL-IFORNIANS?, REPORT OF THE CALIFORNIA ADVISORY COMMITTEE ON HUMAN CLONING (2002) [hereinafter CALIFORNIA REPORT]; NATIONAL BIOETHICS ADVI-SORY COMMISSION, CLONING HUMAN BEINGS, REPORT AND RECOMMENDATIONS OF THE NATIONAL BIOETHICS ADVISORY COMMISSION (1997) [hereinafter NBAC REPORT]; THE PRESIDENT'S COUNCIL ON BIOETHICS, HUMAN CLONING AND HUMAN DIGNITY: AN ETHICAL INQUIRY (2002) [hereinafter COUNCIL REPORT].
3 *See* John A. Robertson, *Liberty, Identity, and Human Cloning,* 76 TEX. L. REV. 1371 (1998).
4 *See* NBAC REPORT, *supra* note 2, at 108–09.
5 *See* THE NATIONAL ACADEMIES, SCIENTIFIC AND MEDICAL ASPECTS OF HUMAN CLONING 2 (2002) [hereinafter NAS REPORT].
6 *See* CALIFORNIA REPORT, *supra* note 2, at 37.
7 *See id.* The California Advisory Committee on Human Cloning rationalized that the California State Legislature could permit human reproductive cloning in the future but that cloning proponents should be the ones with the burden of convinc-ing the state to make such a change. As noted in Chapter 9, inertia makes it hard to repeal even uncontroversial laws. Repeal is even harder when a law is targeted against an unpopular practice or group, as anticloning laws are. Thus, it seems likely that California's flat ban will serve as a permanent ban until some plaintiff

brings a constitutional challenge. As explained in Chapter 12, California, and *not* cloning proponents, will be the one with the burden of proving that its flat ban is justifiable.

8   See COUNCIL REPORT, *supra* note 2, at 91–94; 96–99. This sort of reasoning is not new. A philosopher named Daniel Callahan once argued that the first successful IVF cycle, which produced Louise Brown, was unethical because there could be no guarantee that she would be normal. *See* GREGORY E. PENCE, WHO'S AFRAID OF HUMAN CLONING? 27 (1998).

9   *See* Woo Suk Hwang et al., *Evidence of a Pluripotent Human Embryonic Stem Cell Line Derived from a Cloned Blastocyst*, 303 SCI. 1669 (2004).

10 *See id.* at 1671.

11 *See id.* at 1670.

12 *See id.*

13 *See* SHERMAN J. SILBER, HOW TO GET PREGNANT WITH THE NEW TECHNOLOGY 80–81 (1991).

14 *See* NAS REPORT, *supra* note 5, at 51.

15 *See* Calvin Simerly et al., *Molecular Correlates of Primate Nuclear Transfer Failures*, 300 SCI. 297 (2003).

16 *See* Rosie Mestel, *Primate Cloning Could Be Blocked at Molecular Level*, S. F. CHRON., Apr. 11, 2003, at A6.

17 *See* Wendy Goldman Rohm, *Seven Days of Creation: The Inside Story of a Human Cloning Experiment*, WIRED MAGAZINE, Jan. 2004, at 123, 129 (reporting that American researchers had succeeded in cloning human embryos with 16 cells).

18 *See* Calvin Simerly et al., *Embryogenesis and Blastocyst Development After Somatic Cell Nuclear Transfer in Nonhuman Primates: Overcoming Defects Caused by Meiotic Spindle Extraction*, 276 DEVELOPMENTAL BIOL. 237 (2004).

19 *See* NAS REPORT, *supra* note 5, at 39–42.

20 See I. Wilmut et al., *Viable Offspring Derived from Fetal and Adult Mammalian Cells*, 385 NATURE 810 (1997).

21 H.R. Rep. No. 107–170, at 4 (2001).

22 *See* LEE M. SILVER, REMAKING EDEN: CLONING AND BEYOND IN A BRAVE NEW WORLD 103 (1997).

23 *See* GINA KOLATA, CLONE: THE ROAD TO DOLLY AND THE PATH AHEAD 217–19 (1998) [hereinafter KOLATA, CLONE].

24 *See* STEVEN PINKER, THE BLANK SLATE 225 (2002); SILVER, REMAKING EDEN, *supra* note 22, at 43.

25 Robert P. Lanza et al., *Cloned Cattle Can Be Healthy and Normal*, 294 SCI. 1893 (2001) [hereinafter Lanza, *Cloned Cattle*]. This work was a follow-up on two experiments that Advanced Cell Technology had conducted earlier. *See* Robert P. Lanza et al., *Extension of Cell Life-Span and Telomere Length in Animals Cloned from Senescent Somatic Cells*, 288 SCI. 665 (2000) [hereinafter Lanza, *Telomere Length*]; Jose B. Cibelli et al., *Cloned Transgenic Calves Produced from Nonquiescent Fetal Fibroblasts*, 280 SCI. 1256 (1998).

26 *See* Lanza, *Cloned Cattle, supra* note 25, at 1893.

27 *Id.*

28 *Id.*

29 *See* Kimiko Inoue et al., *Faithful Expression of Imprinted Genes in Cloned Mice*, 295 SCI. 297 (2002).

A recent experiment involving cats hints that better success rates are possible. First, researchers made 188 attempts to transfer the nuclei of adult fibroblast cells from oral mucosa into eggs. This resulted in 82 cloned embryos, all of which were transferred into 7 surrogate mother cats. There was one pregnancy, but the fetus stopped developing and was surgically removed. *See* Tae Young Shin et al., *A Cat Cloned by Nuclear Transplantation*, 415 NATURE 859 (2002). Despite this discouraging early failure, the researchers did not give up. They transferred three embryos cloned from cumulus cells and two embryos derived from fibroblast cells into a surrogate queen. One of the three cumulus cell embryos developed to term and was born as a healthy, normal kitten. *See id.* Thus, in terms of live births to embryos transferred, the second stage of the experiment had a 20-percent success rate.

30 *See* NAS REPORT, *supra* note 5, at Table 1, 114–19.

31 For adult cell experiments, the yield of fetuses from embryos produced ranged from 0.36 to 16.7 percent; that lowest percentage is from the Dolly experiment. *See id.* (comparing Table 1, column 3 [number of embryos produced] to Table 1, column five [number of fetuses after embryo transfer]).

32 *See id.* at Table 1, column 6.

33 The NAS REPORT provides the percentage of offspring alive or healthy at the time of its publication. This percentage ranged from 100 percent (the Dolly experiment and several others) to 0 percent (a lone experiment in which the only calf died). *See id.* at Table 1, column 10. The mouse data likely understate success because mice have short life spans and may have died from natural causes before publication.

34 *See* Jose B. Cibelli et al., *The Health Profile of Cloned Animals*, 20 NATURE BIOTECHNOLOGY 13 (2002) [hereinafter Cibelli, *Health Profile*].

35 *See id.*

36 *See* H. Niemann et al., *Gene Expression Patterns in Bovine in vitro – Produced and Nuclear Transfer-Derived Embryos and Their Implications for Early Development*, 4 CLONING AND STEM CELLS 29, 30 (2002); Lorraine E. Young et al., *Large Offspring Syndrome in Cattle and Sheep*, 3 REV. REPROD. 155 (1998) [hereinafter Young, *Large Offspring Syndrome*].

37 *See* Young, *Large Offspring Syndrome*, *supra* note 36.

38 *See* NAS REPORT, *supra* note 5, at 41.

39 *See id.*; Niemann, *supra* note 36, at 31.

40 *See* Niemann, *supra* note 36, at 30.

41 *See* COUNCIL REPORT, *supra* note 2, at 90; CALIFORNIA REPORT, *supra* note 2, at 11, 23.

42 *See* Mark D. Eibert, *Human Cloning: Myths, Medical Benefits and Constitutional Rights*, 53 HASTINGS L. J. 1097, 1110 (2002).

Current research has raised some questions about the safety of IVF and related technologies such as intracytoplasmic sperm injection (ICSI). Although most studies have not shown an increased risk of major birth defects, recent data from Australia suggest that the rate of such defects is doubled (from 4 to 8–9 percent) in children conceived through IVF or ICSI. *See* Michele Hansen et al., *The Risk of Major Birth Defects after Intracytoplasmic Sperm Injection and In Vitro Fertilization*, 346 NEW ENG.

J. MED. 725 (2002). Similarly, in a Swedish study, researchers found an increased rate of defects (2.4 percent in a control group, 4.1 percent in IVF children, and 6.2 percent in ICSI children) but admitted selection bias towards healthier control children might have skewed their results. See ICSI Kids Have More Malformations, at <http://www.newscientist.com/news/news.jsp?id=ns99993902> (July 2, 2003).

Of the birth defects reported in IVF and ICSI children, the only one that seems analogous to LOS is Beckwith–Wiedemann syndrome (BWS), a congenital disorder that involves overgrowth of the fetus. Recently, researchers found that, even though children conceived through IVF and ICSI constituted only 0.76 percent of live births, 4.6 percent of the children listed in a BWS registry had been conceived through IVF and ICSI. See Michael R. DeBaun et al., Association of In Vitro Fertilization with Beckwith–Wiedemann Syndrome and Epigenetic Alterations of LIT1 and H19, 72 AM. J. HUM. GENETICS 156 (2003). This study suggested that IVF and ICSI were associated with a sixfold increase in the risk of BWS. The researchers speculated that the causes of this association might include culture media, culture duration, sperm differentiation, and ICSI itself because some of the children with BWS had been conceived with the aid of that technology. See id. at 159.

Although a sixfold increase sounds significant, BWS is very rare, normally occurring in only 1 of 15,000 births. See In-Vitro Babies May Be at Risk for Rare Disorder, S. F. CHRON., Nov. 16, 2002, at A5. Thus, even if further research validates the association between IVF and BWS, the actual number of children who suffer from BWS remains tiny.

Strangely, another recent study found that IVF children were more likely to have low birth weights, even when born at term as singletons. See Laura A. Schieve et al., Low and Very Low Birth Weight in Infants Conceived with Use of Assisted Reproductive Technology, 346 NEW ENG. J. MED. 731 (2002).

43   See RICHARD M. TWYMAN, ADVANCED MOLECULAR BIOLOGY: A CONCISE REFERENCE 93 (reprinted ed. 1999).

44   See id.

45   See WEBSTER'S NEW WORLD DICTIONARY OF THE AMERICAN LANGUAGE 1098 (college ed. 1968).

46   So, for example, a typical human being inherits 23 chromosomes from his or her mother (the egg) and 23 from his or her father (the sperm), making a total of 23 chromosome pairs, or 46 chromosomes. See LAURALEE SHERWOOD, HUMAN PHYSIOLOGY: FROM CELLS TO SYSTEMS 714 (1989).

47   See TWYMAN, supra note 43, at 97.

48   See id.

49   See id.

50   See J. Keith Killian et al., Divergent Evolution in M6P/IGF2R Imprinting from the Jurassic to the Quaternary, 10 HUM. MOLECULAR GENETICS 1721 (2001).

51   The scientists cited a different experiment in which a team of researchers from the Roslin Institute fertilized sheep eggs in vivo and then cultured the eggs in vitro for 5 days before implanting them in surrogate mothers. Approximately 25 percent of them grew into fetuses that qualified as large offspring. The scientists found that expression of IGF2R was reduced in those fetuses and that this often corresponded to a loss of methylation. The scientists concluded that laboratory manipulation, culture

of embryos, or both could lead to epigenetic alterations in imprinted genes such as IGF2R. *See* Lorraine E. Young et al., *Epigenetic Change in IGF2R is Associated with Fetal Overgrowth after Sheep Embryo Culture*, 27 NATURE GENETICS 153 (2001).

52 *See id.* at 1726.

53 *See* NAS REPORT, *supra* note 5, at 41–42. Similarly, the California Advisory Committee on Human Cloning noted that cloned cattle suffered from LOS but did not comment on the current research suggesting that humans would not suffer from LOS given their divergent genetic evolution. *See* CALIFORNIA REPORT, *supra* note 2, at 11, 23.

54 *See* NAS REPORT, *supra* note 5, at 14.

55 *Genesis* 1:26 (King James): "And God said, Let us make man in our image, after our likeness: and let them have dominion over the fish of the sea, and over the fowl of the air, and over the cattle, and over all the earth, and over every creeping thing that creepeth upon the earth."

56 *See* CALIFORNIA REPORT, *supra* note 2, at 31.

57 *See* NAS REPORT, supra note 5, at 41–42.

58 *See id.* at 44, 46.

59 *See generally id.* at 43; KOLATA, CLONE, *supra* note 23, at 24–25.

60 Alex Bortvin et al., *Incomplete Reactivation of Oct4-related Genes in Mouse Embryos Cloned from Somatic Nuclei*, 130 DEVELOPMENT 1673 (2003).

61 *See id.* at 1673, 1676.

62 *See id.* at 1678–79 (citations omitted).

63 The article was first published online in SCIENCE EXPRESS, <http://www.sciencemag.org/scienceexpress> *at* 10.1126/science.1060463, on March 28, 2001. Citations in this book are to the subsequently published hardcopy: Rudolf Jaenisch and Ian Wilmut, *Don't Clone Humans!* 291 SCI. 2552 (2001).

64 *See id.*

65 *See id.*

66 *See id.*

67 *Issues Raised by Human Cloning Research: Hearing before the Subcomm. on Oversight and Investigations of the Comm. on Energy and Commerce, House of Representatives*, 107th Cong., Serial No. 107-5, 44–46 (2001) (statement of Dr. Rudolf Jaenisch, Professor of Biology, Massachusetts Institute of Technology).

68 *See* David Humpherys et al., *Epigenetic Instability in ES Cells and Cloned Mice*, 293 SCI. 95 (2001).

69 *See id.* at 97.

70 *See id.*

71 *See* William M. Rideout III et al., *Nuclear Cloning and Epigenetic Reprogramming of the Genome*, 293 SCI. 1092 (2001) [hereinafter "Rideout III"].

72 *See id.* at 1095. Interestingly, Dr. Jaenisch distinguished epigenetic changes that occur before formation of the zygote from two changes that occur after formation of the zygote: X chromosome inactivation and readjustment of telomere length. He conceded that the processes of X inactivation and telomere length adjustment were faithfully accomplished following nuclear transfer and would not be expected to impair survival of cloned animals. *See id.* at 1095. *But see* C. Wrenzycki et al., *In Vitro Production and Nuclear Transfer Affect Dosage Compensation of the X-linked*

Gene Transcripts G6PD, PGK, and Xist in Preimplantation Bovine Embryos, 66 BIOL. REPROD. 127, 133 (2002) (higher levels of X-inactive specific transcript found in cloned bovine embryos may be due to aberrant reactivation of silent X chromosome in adult cells used for nuclear transfer).

73   *See* Rideout III, *supra* note 71, at 1096.
74   *See id.* at 1097.
75   *See id.*
76   *See, e.g.,* Gina Kolata, *Researchers Find Big Risk of Defect in Cloning Animals*, N.Y. TIMES, March 25, 2001, at A1 [hereinafter Kolata, *Big Risk*]; Rick Weiss, *Scientists Testify on Human Cloning Plans*, WASH. POST, March 29, 2001, at A10.
77   *See* Kolata, *Big Risk, supra* note 76. A subsequently published study reported that mice cloned from cumulus cells became obese when they reached adulthood. Interestingly, embryos produced through normal mating but cultured in the same lab setting also got fat, suggesting that culture media or laboratory manipulation could have been to blame. The problem was not likely to have been caused by genetic factors, for when the cloned mice reproduced naturally, their offspring were not obese. Kellie L. K. Tamashiro et al., *Cloned Mice Have an Obese Phenotype Not Transmitted to Their Offspring*, 8 NATURE MED. 262 (2002).
78   *See* Lanza, *Cloned Cattle, supra* note 25.
79   *See id.*
80   *See* Inoue, *supra* note 29.
81   *See id.* These findings contrast sharply with those of a different group of scientists that testified before the National Academy of Sciences in 2002. This group, which included Dr. Jaenisch, reported that mice cloned from uncultured cumulus cells with normal imprints also had aberrant expression of imprinted genes. David Humpherys et al., *Abnormal Gene Expression in Cloned Mice Derived from Embryonic Stem Cell and Cumulus Cell Nuclei*, 99 PROC. NAT'L ACAD. SCI. 12889 (2002).
82   *See* Inoue, *supra* note 29.
83   *See id.* Dr. Jaenisch had raised this same possibility (*see* Rideout III, *supra*, note 71, at 1097), but his statements about faulty reprogramming were more dramatic and received much more public attention.
84   A recent study reinforces the conclusion that some types of donor cells produce better results in cloning than others. When researchers cloned cow embryos from fetal fibroblast cells, they found epigenetic abnormalities much more frequently than when they cloned cow embryos from granulosa cells. Further, embryos cloned from granulosa cells developed into blastocysts, fetuses, and newborns more often than did embryos cloned from fetal fibroblast cells. The researchers took this correlation as an indication that there was a link between the epigenotype of cloned embryos and developmental success. Fatima Santos et al., *Epigenetic Marking Correlates with Developmental Potential in Cloned Bovine Preimplantation Embryos*, 19 CURR. BIOL. 1118, 1120 (2003).
85   *See* Lee Silver, *Public Policy Crafted in Response to Public Ignorance is Bad Public Policy*, 53 HASTINGS L. J. 1037, 1042–43 (2002).
86   Cibelli, *Health Profile, supra* note 34, at 13.
87   *Id.* at 14, Table 1.
88   *Id.* at 13.

89 *See* COUNCIL REPORT, *supra* note 2, at 62–64.

90 *See id.* at 62.

91 *See* CALIFORNIA REPORT, *supra* note 2, at 10, 23. Unfortunately, it is not possible to assess the Committee's treatment of the article *Faithful Expression of Imprinted Genes in Cloned Mice* because it was not published until January 11, 2002, which is also the date of the report.

92 *See* Susan M. Rhind et al., *Human Cloning: Can It Be Made Safe?*, 4 NATURE REVIEWS GENETICS 855, 862 (2003).

93 *See id.*

94 *See id.* at 859–61.

95 *See* KOLATA, CLONE, *supra* note 23, at 240; NBAC REPORT, *supra* note 2, at 24. Interestingly, the National Bioethics Advisory Commission speculated that the process of cloning would reset telomere length, which is a speculation that later turned out to be correct. *See* discussion *infra*.

96 *See* KOLATA, CLONE, *supra* note 23, at 240.

97 *See id.*

98 *See id.*

99 Paul G. Shiels et al., *Analysis of Telomere Lengths in Cloned Sheep*, 399 NATURE 316, 317 (1999). The paper also documented the telomere length of two other cloned sheep. One had been cloned from an embryo cell, and another had been cloned from a fetal cell. These sheep showed telomere shortening of approximately 9 to 15 percent.

100 *See id.*

101 Gina Kolata, *Cloned Sheep Showing Signs of Old Cells, Report Says*, N.Y. TIMES, May 27, 1999, at A19 [hereinafter Kolata, *Old Cells*].

102 *See* Shiels, *supra* note 99, at 317.

103 *See id.*

104 *See* Rick Weiss, *Dolly: "A Sheep in Lamb's Clothing,"* WASH. POST, May 27, 1999, at A01.

105 *See, e.g., id; but see* Kolata, *Old Cells, supra* note 101 (explaining that the measured difference in telomere length could be within the range of natural variation among sheep.)

106 *See, e.g.*, Lanza, *Telomere Length, supra* note 25.

107 Teruhiko Wakayama et al., *Cloning of Mice to Six Generations*, 407 NATURE 318 (2000).

108 *See* Rideout III, *supra* note 71, at 1095 (2001).

109 *See* NAS REPORT, *supra* note 5, at 48.

110 *See* CALIFORNIA REPORT, *supra* note 2, at 10.

111 *See* Lanza, *Telomere Length, supra* note 25.

112 *See* Rick Weiss, *Middle-Aged Dolly Develops Arthritis, Questions on Clone's Aging Raised*, WASH. POST, Jan. 5, 2002, at A03.

113 *See id.*

114 *See id.*; Gina Kolata, *First Mammal Clone Dies; Dolly Made Science History*, N.Y. TIMES, Feb. 15, 2003, at A4 [hereinafter Kolata, *Clone Dies*].

115 *See* Ulysses Torassa, *Dolly Euthanized for Lung Disease*, S.F. CHRON., Feb. 15, 2003, at A2.

116 *See* Kolata, *Clone Dies, supra* note 114.

117 *See, e.g., First Cloned Sheep Dolly Dies at 6, at* <http://www.cnn.com/ 2003/WORLD/europe/ 02/14/cloned.dolly.dies/index.html> (Feb. 14, 2003).

118 Chikara Kubota et al., *Serial Bull Cloning by Somatic Cell Nuclear Transfer,* NATURE BIOTECHNOLOGY advance online publication, May 23, 2004 (doi:10.1038/nbt975), *at* <http://www.crb.uconn.edu/webupdate_files/reclone-nt-final0604.pdf.>

119 Those who oppose anticloning laws have sometimes emphasized the hazards of sexual reproduction. Dr. Silver has used statistics on sexual reproduction to demand that the law treat all forms of reproduction equally. *See* Silver, *supra* note 85, at 1043. Mark Eibert has used the statistics to assert that safety arguments against cloning are pretextual. *See* Eibert, *supra* note 42, at 1110–12.

   My purpose here is different. I am using the statistics to show that exaggerating the dangers of cloning may inspire damaging stereotypes about human clones.

120 *See* CALIFORNIA REPORT, *supra* note 2, at 24; NAS REPORT, *supra* note 5, at 61–62 (emphasizing that most miscarriages occur during the first trimester).

121 *See* text accompanying note 24, *supra.*

122 *See Infant Mortality Rates, Fetal Mortality Rates, and Perinatal Mortality Rates, According to Race: United States 1950–2000, at* <http://www.cdc.gov/nchs/data/ hus/tables/2002/02hus023.pdf> (visited Sept. 6, 2003).

123 *See* CENTERS FOR DISEASE CONTROL AND PREVENTION, FROM DATA TO ACTION: CDC's PUBLIC HEALTH SURVEILLANCE FOR WOMEN, INFANTS, AND CHILDREN, CDC's MATERNAL & CHILD HEALTH MONOGRAPH 171 (1994).

124 *See id.*

125 *See* Silver, *supra* note 85, at 1043.

126 *See* CALIFORNIA REPORT, *supra* note 2, at 24.

127 *Achievements in Public Health, 1900–1999: Healthier Mothers and Babies,* 48 MMWR WEEKLY 849 (1999).

128 *Id.* at 851–52.

129 *See id.*

130 *See* ANNE K. MELLOR, MARY SHELLEY, HER LIFE, HER FICTION, HER MONSTERS 31–32 (1989 ed.).

131 *See id.* at 40.

132 *Id.* at 41.

133 Social psychologists have found that certain medical conditions, such as cancer or physical disabilities, elicit a fear of contamination or contagion, even though the conditions are not transmissible. *See* EDWARD E. JONES et al., SOCIAL STIGMA: THE PSYCHOLOGY OF MARKED RELATIONSHIPS 69 (1984).

134 *See* Steven L. Neuberg et al., *Why People Stigmatize: Toward a Biocultural Framework, in* THE SOCIAL PSYCHOLOGY OF STIGMA 47 (Todd F. Heatherton et al. eds. 2003).

135 *See* Cibelli, *Health Profile, supra* note 34; Kolata, *Clone Dies, supra* note 114 (noting that Dolly gave birth to six healthy lambs conceived through sexual reproduction).

136 *See* JONES, *supra* note 133, at 71.

Chapter Six: What Anticloning Laws Say and Do

 1 When I use the term "anticloning laws," I refer to pending bills and enacted laws that directly ban human reproductive cloning as well as more general laws that have

been construed to give government agencies the authority to regulate human reproductive cloning.

2   In this book, the term "parent" is used to describe any person who uses cloning to
produce a child so long as he or she plans to raise the child as his or her own. This
broad usage is appropriate for two reasons. First, a person who decides to have and
raise a child is playing the social role of parent. Second, most social parents of human clones will also qualify as biological or legal parents, or both.

Infertile men and women, individuals who carry heritable diseases, and gays and
lesbians all face the same problem: they do not have the gametes necessary to conceive via sexual reproduction – at least not safely and within their own partnerships.
If they are indifferent about having a genetic link to their children, they can use
donated gametes from strangers. If they do care or do not want to introduce the
gametes of strangers, they can clone from their own nuclear DNA or the nuclear
DNA of their partners. Thus, many social parents will also have donated the nuclear
DNA for the cloning procedure or will be partnered with someone who did. Also,
if the partnership includes at least one woman, she may be the one to donate eggs,
gestate the child in her uterus, or both.

From a biological point of view, what relationship does a DNA donor have to
the cloned child? Some biologists argue that the genetic parents of a cloned child
must be the *grandparents* of the DNA donor because they were the last to reproduce
sexually and create a new genome. This would make the DNA donor the sibling of
the cloned child. However, inasmuch as cloning involves *asexual* reproduction, it is
equally valid to describe the DNA donor as the single genetic parent of the child.

Also, from a biological point of view, a woman partner who donates eggs, or gestates the child and gives birth, qualifies as a biological mother of that child regardless
of whether her nuclear DNA was used in the cloning procedure.

From a legal point of view, what relationship would the DNA donor, egg donor,
and gestational mother have to the cloned child? For the most part, this will be a
matter for individual states to determine. Courts working with traditional parentage
statutes will find creative ways to apply them to cloning as they have already done
with other reproductive technologies. *Compare* Johnson v. Calvert, 5 Cal. 4th 84,
851 P.2d 776, 19 Cal. Rptr. 2d 494 (1993) (holding that a woman who provided the
egg for an IVF procedure but then hired a surrogate to gestate the child was the
"natural mother" under the Uniform Parentage Act because the parties to the surrogacy contract intended that outcome; also, noting in *dictum* that, if the situation had
been reversed, and a woman had donated an egg with no intention of parenting the
resulting child, the gestational mother would be the intended and "natural mother").
If faced with enough cloned children, legislatures might get into the act and enact
new statutes defining their legal parentage.

3   *See id.*

4   *See* Sheryl Gay Stolberg, *Legislation to Ban Cloning Stalls in Senate*, S. F. CHRON.,
June 14, 2002, at A3.

5   *See* H.R. 534, 108th Cong. § 2 (2003).

6   *See* H.R. 2505, 107th Cong. (2001).

7   H.R. Rep. No. 107-170, at 67 (2001).

8   *Id.* at 68.

9   *Id.*

10   Such language may be unconstitutionally vague because the term "embryo" is not adequately defined. Some researchers claim that zygotes are just "preembryos" and that "embryos" come into being only after 14 days. *See* Jonathan S. Swartz, *The Human Cloning Prohibition Act of 2001: Vagueness and Federalism*, 43 JURIMETRICS J. 79, 85 (2002).
11   *See* H.R. 534, 108th Cong. § 2 (2003).
12   The turgid language of the 2003 Weldon bill lent itself to some additional interpretations that were quite bizarre. I think it is worthwhile to comment on those interpretations here. Even though the 2003 Weldon bill has expired, Congress soon will consider a reintroduced version of it. Some states, moreover, have adopted laws that use similar language, and more states may unwittingly stumble down the same path in the future.
     The 2003 Weldon bill made it unlawful for any person knowingly "to ship or receive for any purpose an embryo produced by human cloning or any product derived from such embryo." *Id.*; *see also* N.D. CENT. CODE § 12.1-39-02 (2003) (prohibiting transfer or receipt of the product of human cloning); 2004 S.D. Laws 227 (same). Most likely, this provision was designed to clamp down on research cloning. The sponsors of the 2003 Weldon bill wanted to stop trade in cloned embryos and therapies generated from cloned embryos. However, the word "product" is broad. Is the provision violated if United Airlines knowingly transports (that is, "ships") a human clone as a passenger on one of its jets? What if the Hyatt Regency rents a hotel room to a human clone? Has it "received for any purpose" a product derived from a cloned embryo?
     Similarly, the 2003 Weldon bill prohibited importing any product derived from a cloned embryo. If such language were interpreted as broadly as possible, it could erect a kind of "Clone Wall" at the national border. If an American who is a human clone goes abroad for business or pleasure and comes back home, has that person "imported" himself or herself? What about foreign tourists or students – are they banned from entering the United States if they were born abroad through cloning?
     Optimistically, one might hope that the courts would be intelligent enough to reject such bizarre statutory interpretations. The 2003 Weldon bill and laws that incorporate similar language are designed to prevent the birth of humans through cloning. Interpretations that prohibit Americans from going abroad and coming home with cloned pregnancies or babies may be consistent with that purpose, but interpretations that prevent existing human clones from engaging in interstate or international travel are not.
     Let us assume, however, for the sake of argument that some wayward court might construe a federal or state law as prohibiting the transportation and hospitality industries from providing services to human clones. This would significantly restrict the right of human clones to travel interstate based on their genetic status. American citizens have a fundamental right to travel freely within the country. *See, e.g.*, Mem'l Hospital v. Maricopa County, 415 U.S. 250, 254 (1974); JOHN E. NOWAK & RONALD D. ROTUNDA, CONSTITUTIONAL LAW § 14.38 (5th ed. 1995) [hereinafter NOWAK & ROTUNDA]. When a law classifies people in a way that restricts their right of travel, the law is invalid unless necessary to further a compelling interest. *See Mem'l Hospital*, 415 U.S. at 254; NOWAK & ROTUNDA, *supra*, at 929–30. Restricting the travel of human clones within the United States would not serve

a legitimate purpose, let alone a compelling one. Therefore, the laws would be unconstitutional to the extent they were so construed and applied.

Similarly, international travel is also a fundamental freedom, though more qualified than the right to travel interstate. Restrictions are tolerated if tailored to serve a government interest that the cases describe variously as "reasonable," see Haig v. Agee, 453 U.S. 280, 306–07 (1980) or "legitimate and substantial." See Aptheker v. Sec'y of State, 378 U.S. 500, 507–09 (1964); In re Aircrash in Bali, Indonesia on April 22, 1974, 684 F.2d 1301, 1309 (9th Cir. 1982). There is nothing to be gained by preventing American citizens from traveling abroad for business or pleasure simply because they are human clones. Thus, federal or state laws would be unconstitutional to the extent they were so construed and applied.

13   See H.R. 534, 108th Cong. § 2 (2003).
14   See Edward Epstein, House Passes Bill to Prohibit Human Cloning, S. F. CHRON., Feb. 28, 2003, at A3.
15   S. 245, 108th Cong. § 2 (2003).
16   See 18 U.S.C. § 2 (2003).
17   See id. at § 371.
18   See S. 303, 108th Cong. § 101 (2003).
19   See id.
20   See Edward Epstein, Bush Tries to Sway Senators against Cloning, S. F. CHRON., Apr. 11, 2002, at A3.
21   See, e.g., Lori B. Andrews, Is There a Right to Clone? Constitutional Challenges to Bans on Human Cloning, 11 HARV. J. L. & TECH. 643, 671–75 (1998).
22   529 U.S. 598 (2000).
23   See id. at 611; accord United States v. Lopez, 514 U.S. 549 (1995) (federal law that made it a crime to possess a gun knowingly in a school zone had nothing to do with commerce or any economic enterprise; therefore, the law exceeded Congress's authority under the Commerce Clause).
24   See Morrison, 529 U.S. at 617.
25   See id. at 613 (quoting Lopez, 514 U.S. at 564).
26   See, e.g., Andrews, supra note 21, at 671–72.
27   See Ashutosh Bhagwat, Cloning and Federalism, 53 HASTINGS L. J. 1133, 1137 (2002).
28   See H.R. 534, 108th Cong. § 2 (2003).
29   See Chapter 7, infra.
30   See Bhagwat, supra note 27.
31   See Andrews, supra note 21, at 673–74.
32   See Chapter 9, part 1, infra.
33   See Bhagwat, supra note 27, at 1139.
34   See H.R. 534, 108th Cong. § 2 (2003). The 2003 Hatch bill did not include such an express jurisdictional element.
35   See United States v. Lopez, 514 U.S. 549, 562 (1995) (law did not include a jurisdictional element limiting its application to cases that had an explicit connection with, or effect on, interstate commerce); United States v. Morrison, 529 U.S. 598, 613 (2000) (same).
36   See Scientist Says He Plans to Clone Human, S. F. CHRON., Jan. 7, 1998, at A2.

37   *See* Dirk Johnson, *Did Media Turn a Nonentity into a Monster?*, *at* <http://www. nytimes.com/library/national/012498clone-seed-media.html> (Jan. 24, 1998).

38   *See* Rick Weiss, *FDA Says Human Cloning Needs Its OK*, S. F. CHRON., Jan. 20, 1998, at A3.

39   *See id.*

40   *See* Dr. Stuart Nightingale, *Dear Colleague Letter about Human Cloning*, *at* <http:// www.fda.gov/oc/ohrt/irbs/irbletr.html> (Oct. 26, 1998).

41   *See id.*

42   *See id.*

43   *Id.*

44   *See* Richard A. Merrill & Bryan J. Rose, *FDA Regulation of Human Cloning: Usurpation or Statesmanship?* 15 HARV. J. L. & TECH. 85, 101 (2001)

45   *See Issues Raised by Human Cloning Research: Hearing before the Subcomm. on Oversight and Investigations of the House Comm. on Energy and Commerce*, 107th Cong., Serial No. 107-5, 78, 80 (2001) (statement of Dr. Kathryn C. Zoon, Director, Center for Biologics Evaluation and Research, FDA) [hereinafter Zoon testimony].

46   *Id.* at 81.

47   *See* Kathryn C. Zoon, *Letter to Associations – Cloning Technology*, *at* <http://www.fda. gov/cber/ltr/aaclone.htm> (March 28, 2001).

48   *See* Rick Weiss, *Politech: Legal Barriers to Human Cloning May Be Few*, WASH. POST, May 23, 2001, at A01.

49   Nell Boyce & David E. Kaplan, *The God Game No More: The Feds Crack Down on a Human Cloning Lab*, U.S. NEWS & WORLD REP., July 9, 2001, at 20.

50   Dr. Panayiotis Zavos is the Director of the Andrology Institute of America and Associate Director of the Kentucky Centre for Reproductive Medicine and IVF, both located in Lexington, Kentucky. However, he is not conducting his cloning research at these institutions but rather at an undisclosed location abroad. *See* Panayiotis Zavos, *Human Reproductive Cloning: The Time Is Near*, 6 REPROD. BIOMEDICINE ONLINE 397, 398 (2003), *available at* <http://www.rbmonline.com>. Interestingly, Dr. Zavos seems to operate a company called "The Reprogen Organization" in Cyprus. Its mission is to conduct scientific research into reproductive cloning and bring about human births. The Web site is careful to state that all testing and procedures will be conducted outside the United States and that no human cloning will be conducted in the United States. *See* <http://www.reprogen.org/mission.htm> (visited Jan. 21, 2004).

51   For example, the Federal Food, Drug, and Cosmetic Act states that no person shall introduce new drugs into interstate commerce without FDA approval. *See* 21 U.S.C. § 355(a) (2003). First-time violations are punishable by up to 1 year in prison and fines of up to $1,000; second offenses draw prison sentences for up to 3 years and fines of up to $10,000. *See id.* § 331 (d) and § 333(a). The act also imposes various requirements relating to medical devices; for most of those requirements, a person faces a civil fine of up to $15,000 for each violation. *See id.* § 333(f).
     The Public Health Service Act regulates biological products. A violation of the act is a misdemeanor punishable by a fine of up to $500 and a prison sentence of up to 1 year. *See* 42 U.S.C. § 262(f) (2003).

52   *See* Merrill & Rose, *supra* note 44, at 102.

53   *See* 18 U.S.C. § 2 (2003); 42 U.S.C. § 262(f) (2003) (those who aid and abet a violation of the law regulating biological products commit a misdemeanor).
54   18 U.S.C. § 371 (2003).
55   *See* Elizabeth C. Price, *Does the FDA Have Authority to Regulate Human Cloning?* 11 HARV. J. L. & TECH. 619, 628 (1998).
56   *See, e.g., id.* at 629–41; *Issues Raised by Human Cloning Research: Hearing before the Subcomm. on Oversight and Investigations of the House Comm. on Energy and Commerce,* 107th Cong., Serial No. 107-5, 107, 108, 143–44 (2001) (statement and answers of Mark Donald Eibert, Attorney); *see also* Merrill & Rose, *supra* note 44, at 117–24 (arguing that the FDA's assertion of authority might be upheld if challenged but expressing some doubts).
57   *See* Price, *supra* note 55, at 630–31.
58   *See* Merrill & Rose, *supra* note 44, at 125.
59   *See id.* at 124–29.
60   *See id.* at 106. Such a lawsuit could face procedural obstacles. The FDA has not issued any new regulation that can be reviewed pursuant to provisions in the Federal Food, Drug, and Cosmetic Act permitting pre-enforcement review. A scientist could challenge the FDA's claim that its existing IND regulations apply to cloning experiments, but the FDA might argue that there is no final action that the courts can review. *See id.* at 106, n.106. However, the courts should not accept this argument.
     For agency action to be final, it must mark the consummation of the agency's decision-making process and not be tentative. The action must also be one by which rights or obligations have been determined or from which legal consequences will flow. *See* Appalachian Power Co. v. Envtl. Prot. Agency, 208 F.3d 1015, 1022 (D.C. Cir. 2000).
     The FDA's regulatory actions satisfy these two criteria. First, its decision-making process is complete. The FDA eschewed formal rulemaking in the area of cloning; thus, there is no pending effort to issue a new regulation or rule, nor will there ever be. Instead, the FDA has released documents from headquarters that represent its final position. In 1998, the FDA first issued a "Dear Colleague" letter that asserted its authority to regulate human cloning experiments. In the six years that have followed, the agency has never deviated from this position. Instead, it has continued on the same course, issuing a nearly identical letter in 2001.
     Second, the two letters informed researchers of their rights and obligations in conducting human cloning experiments. Failure to comply with the procedures set forth in the letters can have legal consequences; the FDA has investigated those mavericks who have claimed to be cloning without permission.
     Thus, the FDA's regulatory actions against cloning are sufficiently final to support judicial review. To rule otherwise would reward the FDA for its deplorable failure to engage in formal rulemaking and immunize its regulatory actions from judicial review.
61   *See* Merrill & Rose, *supra* note 44, at 138.
62   *See* Zoon testimony, *supra* note 45, at 90.
63   Louisiana had a law against cloning, but it expired in 2003 and was not renewed. *See* LA. REV. STAT. ANN. §§ 40:1299.36 to .36.6 (West 1997).
64   *See* ARK. CODE ANN. § 20-16-1001 to -1004 (Michie 2003).
65   *See* IOWA CODE § 707B.1 to B.4 (2003).

66 *See* MICH. COMP. LAWS §§ 333.16274, 333.16275, 333.20197 750.430a (2003).
67 N.D. CENT. CODE § 12.1-39-02 (2003).
68 2004 S.D. LAWS 227.
69 *See* MICH. COMP. LAWS § 750.430a(1) (2003).
70 *See id.* § 333.16274(5)(a).
71 *See id.* § 750.430a(3).
72 *See id.* §§ 333.16221, 333.16226, 333.16274(3).
73 *See id.* §§ 333.16274(3), 333.16275.
74 *See* ARK. CODE ANN. § 20-16-1002(a) (Michie 2003).
75 The statute uses the term "oocyte" and defines it as the "*human* female germ cell, the egg." *See id.* § 20-16-1001(5) (emphasis added). This raises the somewhat disturbing possibility that, in Arkansas, reproductive cloning is permitted but only as long as scientists employ an animal egg rather than a human one.
76 *See id.* § 20-16-1001(4).
77 *See id.* § 20–16–1002(b), -1002(d).
78 *See* CAL. BUS. & PROF. CODE § 2260.5 (West 2003) and §§ 16004, 16105 (West 2004); CAL. HEALTH & SAFETY CODE §§ 24185, 24186, 24187 (West 2004).
79 *See* N.J. STAT. ANN. § 2C:11A-1 (West 2004).
80 *See* R.I. GEN. LAWS §§ 23-16.4 to 23-16.4-4 (2003).
81 VA. CODE ANN. §§ 32.1–162.21, 32.1–162.22 (Michie 2003). Virginia's law is a bit vague because it prohibits the use of cloning to create human beings but does not define "human being." If "human being" includes an embryo, then the statute would prohibit research cloning; but at least one commentator believes that was not the intent of the state legislature. *See* JOHN CHARLES KUNICH, THE NAKED CLONE 33 (2003).
82 *See* CAL. BUS. & PROF. CODE §§ 2260.5, 16004, 16105 (1998); CAL. HEALTH & SAFETY CODE §§ 24185, 24187, 24189 (1998).
83 *See* CAL. HEALTH & SAFETY CODE § 125115 (West 2002) repealed and reenacted with minor changes in 2003 as § 125300 (West 2004).
84 *See* S. Bill 1230, § 6, 2001–2002 Reg. Sess. (Cal. 2002).
85 *See* CAL. HEALTH & SAFETY CODE § 24185 (West 2004).
86 *See id.* § 24185(c)(1).
87 *See id.* § 24185(c)(3).
88 *See id.* § 24187(a) and (b).
89 *See id.* § 24187(c).
90 *See* CAL. BUS. & PROF. CODE § 2260.5 (West 2003).
91 *See* CAL. BUS. & PROF. CODE §§ 16004 (city licenses), 16105 (county licenses) (West 2004).
92 *See* N.J. STAT. ANN. §§ 26:2Z-1 to 26:2Z-2 (West 2004).
93 *See* N.J. STAT. ANN. § 2C:11A-1 (West 2004).
94 *See id.*
95 *See id.*
96 *See* MICH. COMP. LAWS §§ 333.16274, 750.430a (2003).
97 As a general rule, Congress has the power to regulate foreign commerce, *see* U.S. CONST. art. I, § 8. The Executive Branch has the right to place restrictions on international travel. State legislatures are unlikely to assert authority in these areas. In fact, none of the existing state laws against human cloning include a prohibition

on importing the "product" of cloning from abroad. *But cf.* N.D. CENT. CODE §
12.1-39-02 (2003) and 2004 S.D. LAWS 227 (prohibiting a person from transferring
or receiving the product of human cloning).

Chapter Seven: The Five Objections Have Inspired Anticloning Laws

1 *See Issues Raised by Human Cloning Research: Hearing before the Subcomm. on Oversight
   and Investigations of the House Comm. on Energy and Commerce*, 107th Cong., Serial
   No. 107-5, 78, 80 (2001) (statement of Dr. Kathryn C. Zoon, Director, Center for
   Biologics Evaluation and Research, FDA) [hereinafter Zoon testimony].
2 *See, e.g.*, Representative Howard Coble, R-N.C.: "H.R. 534 would prevent experimental procedures that the National Bioethics Advisory Commission, the NBAC,
   called scientifically and ethically objectionable." 149 CONG. REC. H. 1397, 1408
   (2003); Representative Lamar Smith, R-Tex.: "The National Bioethics Advisory
   Commission unanimously concluded that 'Any attempt to clone a child is uncertain in its outcome, is unacceptably dangerous to the fetus and, therefore morally
   unacceptable.'" 147 CONG. REC. H. 4916, 4919 (2001); Representative Bob Barr,
   R-Georgia: "[T]he National Bioethics Commission has quite clearly stated the creation of a human being by somatic cell nuclear transfer is both scientifically and
   ethically objectionable." *See id.* at 4928; Senator Edward Kennedy, D-Mass.: "The
   legislation that Senator Feinstein and I have introduced will assure the American
   public that reproducing human beings by cloning will be prohibited. It follows…
   the recommendations of the Commission [NBAC]." 144 CONG. REC. S. 434
   (1998).
3 Representative David Price, D-N.C., relied on the recommendations of the National
   Academies and the President's Council on Bioethics in urging that Congress ban reproductive cloning, but not research cloning. *See* 149 CONG. REC. H. 1397, 1430
   (2003). Similarly, Senator Dianne Feinstein, D-Cal., stated: "The National Bioethics
   Advisory Commission, the National Academies' Panel on Scientific and Medical
   Aspects on Human Cloning, and the California Advisory Committee on Human
   Cloning all concluded that we should ban human reproductive cloning, but not interfere with important areas of scientific research, including nuclear transplantation."
   148 CONG. REC. S. 3627, 3633 (2002).
4 *See* NATIONAL BIOETHICS ADVISORY COMMISSION, CLONING HUMAN BEINGS,
   REPORT AND RECOMMENDATIONS OF THE NATIONAL BIOETHICS ADVISORY COM-
   MISSION 108 (1997).
5 *See id.* at 44.
6 *See id.* at 72–74.
7 *See id.* at 66–68.
8 *See id.* at 74.
9 *See* THE NATIONAL ACADEMIES, SCIENTIFIC AND MEDICAL ASPECTS OF HUMAN
   REPRODUCTIVE CLONING 2 (2002).
10 *See* THE PRESIDENT'S COUNCIL ON BIOETHICS, HUMAN CLONING AND HUMAN
   DIGNITY: AN ETHICAL INQUIRY 200 (2002).
11 *See id.* at 96–99.
12 *See id.* at 98–99.
13 *See id.* at 104–07.

14   *See id.* at 102–04.

15   *See id.* at 107–10.

16   *See* 149 CONG. REC. H. 1397, 1413 (2003).

17   *Id.* at 1399.

18   *Id.* at 1433.

19   Remarks by the president on Human Cloning Legislation, *at* <http://www. whitehouse.gov/ news/releases/2002/04/20020410-4.html> (Apr. 10, 2002).

20   149 CONG. REC. H. 1397, 1400 (2003).

21   *Id.* at 1411.

22   *Id.* at 1422.

23   *Id.* at 1403.

24   President Clinton made this comment on March 4, 1997, shortly after the birth of Dolly was announced. *See* Patrick D. Hopkins, *Bad Copies: How Popular Media Represent Cloning as an Ethical Problem*, 28 HASTINGS CENTER REP. 6, 9 (March–April 1998).

25   149 CONG. REC. H. 1397, 1424 (2003).

26   147 CONG. REC. H. 4916, 4935 (2001).

27   *Id.* at 4929.

28   149 CONG. REC. H. 1397, 1414 (2003).

29   *Id.* at 1432.

30   148 CONG. REC. H. 1161 (2002).

31   147 CONG. REC. H. 4916, 4927 (2001).

32   *Id.* at 4940.

33   *Id.* at 4920.

34   *Id.* at 4919.

35   Remarks by the president on Human Cloning Legislation, *supra* note 19.

36   149 CONG. REC. H. 1397, 1399 (2003).

37   *Id.* at 1420.

38   *Id.* at 1422.

39   *Id.* at 1413. For more comments, see, *e.g.,* Representative Donald Manzullo (R-Ill.): "When animals are cloned, 95–98 percent of the attempts end in failure, and those that are successful have genetic abnormalities." *Id.* at 1416; Representative Melissa Hart (R-Penn.): "We have heard the statistic before that between 95 and 98 percent of cloning in animals fails. This could translate into countless children who would be products of cloning who would be born with serious birth defects, debilitating diseases, and shortened, terrible lives." *Id.* at 1412; Representative Phil Gingrey (R-Ga.): "Human cloning for reproduction poses serious risks of producing children who are stillborn, severely malformed or disabled. We can make this assertion because most cloned animals have demonstrated serious genetic defects. The most high-profile example, of course, is Dolly the sheep, with the premature aging situation." *Id.* at 1406; Representative Lee Terry (R-Neb.): "Cloned humans would likely have serious defects such as premature aging which may have led to premature death of Dolly, the cloned sheep." *Id.* at 1403.

40   *See* Zoon testimony, *supra* note 1, at 80.

41   *See* S. Con. Res. 39, 1997–1998 Reg. Sess. (Cal. Sept. 12, 1997); 1997 Bill Text Cal. S.C.R. 39 (LEXIS through 2004 Sess., Sept. 12, 1997).

42   *See id.*

43 *See, e.g.,* Tom Abate, *Quest for an AIDS Vaccine Is a Story of Courage and Determination, at* <http://www.aegis.com/news/sc/2001/SC011204.html> (Dec. 3, 2001).
44 *See* S. Bill 1230, 2001–2002 Reg. Sess. (Cal. 2002).
45 *See* CALIFORNIA ADVISORY COMMITTEE ON HUMAN CLONING, CLONING CALI-FORNIANS?, REPORT OF THE CALIFORNIA ADVISORY COMMITTEE ON HUMAN CLONING 37 (2002).
46 *See id.*
47 *See id.* at 31–32.
48 *See id.* at 29–30.
49 *See id.* at 24–25.
50 *See id.* at 30. The committee admitted this argument was weak. Reproductive cloning would increase the population only if women had more babies through cloning than sex. Given the cost and risks associated with cloning, this was unlikely. *Id.*
51 *See id.*
52 *See id.* at 28.
53 California State Senate, Senate Daily File, schedule for Tuesday, Jan. 15, 2002 (on file with author).

Chapter Eight: Anticloning Laws Reflect a Policy of Existential Segregation

1   *See* H.R. 534, 108th Cong. § 2 (2003).
2   *See id.*
3   *See* S. 303, 108th Cong. § 101 (2003).
4   *See id.*
5   *See* MICH. COMP. LAWS §§ 333.16274 § 750.430a (2003).
6   *See* ARK. CODE ANN. §§ 20-16-1001, 20-16-1002 (Michie 2003).
7   *See* CAL. HEALTH & SAFETY CODE §§ 24185, 24187 (West 2004).
8   *See* N.J. STAT. ANN. § 2C: 11A-1 (West 2004).
9   *See* Chapter 7, *supra.*
10 *See* Robinson v. State of California, 370 U.S. 660, 666–67 (1962).
11 *See* Lawrence v. Texas, 539 U.S. 558 (2003).
12 *See* Gay Alliance of Students v. Matthews, 544 F.2d 162, 166 (4th Cir. 1976).
13 148 CONG. REC. H. 3760, 3765 (2002). For more comments along the same lines, see, *e.g.,* Representative F. James Sensenbrenner (R-Wis.): "If scientists were permitted to clone embryos, they would eventually be stockpiled and mass marketed." 149 CONG. REC. H. 1397, 1407 (2003); Representative Mark Souder (R-Indiana): "Stockpiles of embryonic human clones could be produced, bought and sold. Implantation of cloned embryos – an easy procedure – could take place out of sight, and not even the most elaborate and intrusive regulations and policing could detect or prevent the initiation of a clonal pregnancy." 148 CONG. REC. E. 1118 (2002); Representative Lamar Smith (R-Tex.): "A partial ban would allow for stockpiles of cloned human embryos to be produced, bought and sold without restrictions. Implantation of cloned embryos, a relatively easy procedure, would inevitably take place. Once cloned embryos are produced and available in laboratories, it is impossible to control what is done with them, so a partial ban is simply unenforceable." 147 CONG. REC. H. 4916, 4919 (2001).
14 *See* ERWIN CHEMERINSKY, CONSTITUTIONAL LAW 557 (1997).

15 The tradition of banning interracial marriage can be traced back to the seventeenth century, when it was invented in this country. *See* Harvey M. Applebaum, *Miscegenation Statutes: A Constitutional and Social Problem*, 53 GEO. L.J. 49, 50 (1964); Walter Wadlington, *The Loving Case: Virginia's antimiscegenation Statute in Historical Perspective*, 52 VA. L. REV. 1189, 1191 (1966).

16 *See* Applebaum, *supra* note 15, at 51–52; 63.

17 *See* RACHEL F. MORAN, INTERRACIAL INTIMACY: THE REGULATION OF RACE AND ROMANCE 18 (2001).

18 *See id.* at 43–44.

19 *Id.* at 19.

20 Some early statutes did make it a crime to have a mixed-race child. *See* Wadlington, *supra* note 15, at 1192.

21 *See* Applebaum, *supra* note 15, at 64.

22 See MORAN, *supra* note 17, at 20, 43.

23 *See id.* at 19.

24 For example, in Pace v. Alabama, 106 U.S. 583 (1883), the U.S. Supreme Court upheld an Alabama statute that punished adultery and fornication more severely when committed by members of different races. Decades later, the Supreme Court invalidated a Florida statute that prohibited interracial cohabitation. *See* McLaughlin v. Florida, 379 U.S. 184 (1964).

25 *See* MORAN, *supra* note 17, at 21.

26 Scott v. State, 39 Ga. 321 (1869). The challenge to the antimiscegenation law was based on a clause in the state constitution that forbade the state legislature from regulating the social status of its citizens. The court rejected the challenge, reasoning that the clause was not intended to stop the regulation of marriage. Rather, the clause was designed to prevent the legislature from enacting laws that sought to enforce social equality between races. Thus, for example, this "antiequal protection" clause forbade the legislature from enacting laws requiring railroads to place persons of different races in the same cars.

27 *Id.* at 324 (emphasis added).

28 State v. Brown, 236 La. 562, 108 So. 2d 233 (1959). Although the court upheld the law against the constitutional challenge, it reversed the convictions of appellants, a black man and white woman, on the ground that the trial judge had failed to explain to the jury properly that the law's prohibition against "habitual cohabitation" was a prohibition on repeated acts of sexual intercourse. *Id.* at 570, 108 So. 2d at 235.

29 347 U.S. 483 (1954).

30 *Brown*, 236 La. at 567, 108 So. 2d at 234 (emphasis added).

31 *See* Wadlington, *supra* note 15, at 1213–15.

32 *See* Perez v. Sharp, 32 Cal.2d 711, 712, 198 P.2d 17, 18 (1948).

33 CA. CIV. CODE § 69 (1948).

34 *Id.* § 60.

35 *See Perez*, 32 Cal. 2d at 713, 198 P.2d at 18.

36 *See id.* at 713–14, 198 P.2d at 18.

37 *See id.* at 720, 198 P.2d at 21.

38 *See id.* at 722, 198 P.2d at 23.

39 *See id.* at 724, 198 P.2d at 25.

40 *See id.* at 720–21, 198 P.2d at 22.

41 *See id.* at 722 and 723, 198 P.2d at 23–24 and 26.

42 *Id.* at 727, 198 P.2d at 26 (emphasis added).

43 *Id.* at 727, 198 P.2d at 27. In the alternative, the Court held that the antimiscegenation laws were too vague and uncertain to be upheld as a valid regulation of the right to marry because their application to persons of mixed ancestry was not clear. *See id.* at 728–31, 198 P.2d at 27–29.

44 *See id.* at 731–32, 198 P.2d at 29.

45 *See* Loving v. Virginia, 388 U.S. 1, 2–3 (1967).

46 *See* VA. CODE ANN. § 20–58 (1960).

47 *See Loving,* 388 U.S. at 3.

48 *Id.*

49 *Id.*

50 206 Va. 924, 147 S.E.2d 78 (1966). Although the Supreme Court of Appeals of Virginia upheld the convictions against Mr. and Mrs. Loving, it declared their suspended sentences void. By suspending the sentences on the condition that Mr. and Mrs. Loving not return to Virginia together or at the same time, the trial court had gone further than necessary to achieve the purpose of the antimiscegenation statute, which prohibited their cohabitation as man and wife. The court vacated the sentences and remanded the case to the trial court so that it could resentence Mr. and Mrs. Loving consistent with its decision. *See id.* at 930–31, 147 S.E.2d at 82–83.

51 197 Va. 80, 89–90, 87 S.E.2d 749, 756 (1955) (emphasis added), *vacated by* Naim v. Naim, 350 U.S. 891 (1955).

52 388 U.S. 1 (1967).

53 *Id.* at 11–12.

54 *Id.* at 12. Neither *Loving* nor *Perez* addressed the question of whether antimiscegenation laws violated the equal protection rights of mixed-race children, who surely existed in our society, even though mixed marriages were prohibited. *See* Applebaum, *supra* note 15, at 64. Perhaps adults seeking to marry made better plaintiffs for important test cases – particularly in view of the fact that the U.S. Supreme Court already had recognized a fundamental right to marry. *See* Meyer v. Nebraska, 262 U.S. 390, 399 (1923).

55 *See* Wadlington, *supra* note 15, at 1211.

Chapter Nine: The Costs of Anticloning Laws Outweigh Their Benefits

1 *See* Harvey M. Applebaum, *Miscegenation Statutes: A Constitutional and Social Problem,* 53 GEO. L. J. 49, 71–72 (1964).

2 I use the term "parent" to refer to any person who uses cloning to produce a child so long as he or she plans to raise the child as his or her own. As explained in the notes to Chapter 6, such a person may qualify as a biological or legal parent of the cloned child, or both. More importantly, because such a person plays the social role of parent, his or her prosecution and imprisonment would inflict the greatest losses on the cloned child.

3 For example, the Federal Food, Drug, and Cosmetic Act states that no person shall introduce new drugs into interstate commerce without FDA approval. *See* 21 U.S.C. § 355(a) (2003). First-time violations are punishable by up to 1 year in prison and

fines of up to $1,000; second offenses draw prison sentences for up to 3 years and fines of up to $10,000. *See id.* § 331 (d) and § 333(a). The act also imposes various requirements relating to medical devices; for most of those requirements, a person faces a civil fine of up to $15,000 for each violation. *See id.* § 333(f).

The Public Health Service Act regulates biological products. A violation of the act is a misdemeanor punishable by a fine of up to $500 and a prison sentence of up to 1 year. *See* 42 U.S.C. § 262(f) (2003).

4 *See* 18 U.S.C. § 2 (2003) (those who aid or abet a federal offense are punishable as principals); 18 U.S.C. § 371 (2003) (establishing conspiracy to commit a federal offense as a separate crime); 42 U.S.C. § 262(f) (2003) (those who aid and abet a violation of the law regulating biological products commit a misdemeanor).

5 *See* H.R. 534, 108th Cong. § 2 (2003).

6 316 U.S. 535 (1942).

7 *Id.* at 541.

8 JOHN E. NOWAK & RONALD D. ROTUNDA, CONSTITUTIONAL LAW § 14.27, at 797 (5th ed. 1995).

9 Griswold v. Connecticut, 381 U.S. 479 (1965).

10 *See* Roe v. Wade, 410 U.S. 113 (1973); Planned Parenthood v. Casey, 505 U.S. 833, 846 (1992).

11 Lifchez v. Hartigan, 735 F. Supp. 1361, 1377 (N.D. Ill. 1990), *aff'd*, 914 F.2d 260 (1990) (unpublished opinion), *cert. denied sub nom* Scholberg v. Lifchez, 498 U.S. 1069 (1991).

12 *See, e.g.,* JOHN CHARLES KUNICH, THE NAKED CLONE 119–32 (2003); Mark D. Eibert, *Human Cloning: Myths, Medical Benefits and Constitutional Rights*, 53 HASTINGS L. J. 1097 (2002); Elizabeth Price Foley, *The Constitutional Implications of Human Cloning*, 42 ARIZ. L. REV. 647 (2000); John A. Robertson, *Procreative Liberty in the Era of Genomics*, 29 AM. J. L. & MED. 439, 471 (2003); John A. Robertson, *Liberty, Identity, and Human Cloning*, 76 TEX. L. REV. 1371, 1379 (1998) [hereinafter Robertson, *Liberty*]; *but see, e.g.,* Cass R. Sunstein, *Is There a Constitutional Right to Clone?* 53 HASTINGS L. J. 987 (2002) (Supreme Court would not recognize a right to clone).

13 *See, e.g., Roe*, 410 U.S. at 155.

14 *See* KUNICH, *supra* note 12 at 133; Foley, *supra* note 12, at 725–26; *cf.* Eibert, *supra* note 12, at 1112 (arguing that safety is a pretext advanced to hide other motivations for banning cloning).

15 *See* KUNICH, *supra* note 12, at 135–37.

16 *See id.* at 94.

17 *See* John A. Robertson, *The Scientist's Right to Research: A Constitutional Analysis,* 51 S. CAL. L. REV. 1203, 1217–18 (1977) [hereinafter Robertson, *The Scientist's Right*]; *see also* Roy G. Spece Jr. & Jennifer Weinzierl, *First Amendment Protection of Experimentation: A Critical Review and Tentative Synthesis/Reconstruction of the Literature,* 8 S. CAL. INTERDISC. L. J. 185, 213–14 (1998) (First Amendment protects experimentation because it is an essential part of the scientific method).

Critics charge that the Robertson theory has no principled limits. Even eating and sleeping could be protected as preconditions to the scientist's speech. *See* KUNICH, *supra* note 12, at 96 (summarizing this critique). The line, however, may not be so

difficult to draw. Experimentation is different than other, more general preconditions to the creation of scientific knowledge; it is the core of the scientific method.
See Spece & Weinzierl, *supra*, at 218.

18 *See* KUNICH, *supra* note 12, at 97.

19 *See* KUNICH, *supra* note 12, at 98; Robertson, *The Scientist's Right, supra* note 17, at
1210–11.

20 *See* Matthew B. Hsu, *Banning Human Cloning: An Acceptable Limit on Scientific Inquiry or an Unconstitutional Restriction on Symbolic Speech?* 87 GEO. L. J. 2399, 2413–
16 (1999).

21 *See id.* at 2418.

22 *See id.* at 2418–19.

23 *See id.* at 2419.

24 *See* United States v. O'Brien, 391 U.S. 367, 377 (1968).

25 If reproductive cloning protocols turn out to have certain features in common with
IVF protocols involving donor eggs, it seems likely that mothers could leave the care
of their offshore fertility doctors before they began to "show."

In IVF protocols involving donor eggs, the doctor must suppress the gestational
mother's own natural hormones and replace them with carefully timed supplements
of estrogen and progesterone; this is done to synchronize her uterus with the ovula-
tion of the egg donor so that it is ready for implantation once embryos are produced.
Thereafter, the gestational mother must take daily supplements and injections of estrogen and progesterone (both prescription drugs) to support the uterus for roughly
3 months until the placenta is ready to take over the production of hormones on its
own. *See* SHERMAN J. SILBER, HOW TO GET PREGNANT WITH THE NEW TECHNOL-
OGY 378–79 (1991).

Because cloning requires eggs, it often will require the services of egg donors. Recipients frequently may need to be synchronized with the cycles of the donors in the
manner I just described. In the immediate weeks after embryo transfer, a gestational
mother who is nervous about legal complications may feel most comfortable filling
her prescriptions for drugs and syringes offshore. However, because this treatment
ends in only 3 months, many women still should be able to hide their pregnancies
when they return home. Once the mother is back in the United States, she can
receive treatment from any obstetrician, for her pregnancy will be impossible to distinguish from any other pregnancy obtained through sexual reproduction.

26 All persons born or naturalized in the United States are citizens of the United States
and the state in which they reside. U.S. CONST. amend. XIV, § 1.

27 A person who is born outside the United States is a citizen when his or her parents
are both citizens of the United States and at least one parent had a residence in the
United States before he or she was born. *See* 8 U.S.C. § 1401(b) (2003). Other provisions grant citizenship to persons born outside the United States when at least one
parent is a United States citizen under specified circumstances. *See id.* § 1401(d),
(e), (g).

This raises the important question of who qualifies as a "parent." The Immigration
and Nationality Act does not define "parent" in its section on nationality other than
to note that the term can include a deceased parent in the case of a posthumous
child. *See id.* § 1101(c). The act, however, defines "parent" in an earlier section on

immigration. There, the term "parent" applies where the relationship exists because there is a "child," *see id.* § 1101(b)(2); a "child" includes an unmarried person under 21 years of age who is born in wedlock. *See id.* § 1101(b)(1)(A).

On the assumption these definitions apply throughout the act, many parents should be able to confer American citizenship on their cloned children. To understand why, remember that cloning is a good solution for inadequate gametes; however, the need to resort to cloning does not necessarily imply lack of a proper uterine environment. It seems likely that many married couples interested in cloning will choose to have the wife carry the child. This means that many cloned children will be "born in wedlock" to American husbands and wives capable of conferring citizenship upon them. (Unfortunately, this analysis does not help gays and lesbians who live in jurisdictions that do not permit them to marry.)

Cloning opponents are unlikely to stop this outcome by arguing that "parent" means only a genetic parent. As discussed in Chapter 6, note 2, some biologists believe that the genetic parents of a human clone are, in fact, the mother and father of the person who donated the nuclear DNA for the procedure. It seems likely that most parents will choose to clone from their own nuclear DNA; therefore, the genetic parents will be the *grandparents* of the baby. Since the grandparents are likely to be American citizens, this interpretation also confers citizenship on the baby.

28   E. GOFFMAN, STIGMA: NOTES ON THE MANAGEMENT OF SPOILED IDENTITY 4 (1963).

29   Monica Biernat & John F. Dovidio, *Stigma and Stereotypes*, in THE SOCIAL PSYCHOL-OGY OF STIGMA 89 (Todd F. Heatherton et al. eds. 2003).

30   *See* Carol T. Miller & Brenda Major, *Coping with Stigma and Prejudice*, in THE SOCIAL PSYCHOLOGY OF STIGMA 244 (Todd F. Heatherton et al. eds. 2003).

31   *See* Steven L. Neuberg et al., *Why People Stigmatize: Toward a Biocultural Framework*, in THE SOCIAL PSYCHOLOGY OF STIGMA 31 (Todd F. Heatherton et al. eds. 2003).

32   347 U.S. 483 (1954).

33   *Id.* at 494.

34   *Id.*

35   Christopher R. Leslie, *Creating Criminals: The Injuries Inflicted by "Unenforced" Sodomy Laws*," 35 HARV. C.R.–C.L.L. REV. 103, 110–11 (2000). A handful of states have sodomy laws that prohibit only same-sex sodomy. *See id.*

36   *See id.* at 111–12.

37   *See id.* at 116–18.

38   *See id.* at 136, 140–42.

39   *See id.* at 122–25.

40   *See* Lawrence v. Texas, 539 U. S. 558 (2003).

41   *See Human Cloning: Hearings on S. 790 before the Senate Commerce Subcomm. On Science, Technology and Space*, 107th Cong. (2001) (statement of Richard M. Doerflinger, Committee for Pro-Life Activities, National Conference of Catholic Bishops).

42   *See* 18 U.S.C. § 2 (2003); 42 U.S.C. § 262(f) (2003) (those who aid and abet a violation of the law regulating biological products commit a misdemeanor).

43   *See* 18 U.S.C. § 371 (2003).

44   In 2002, the Florida Department of Children and Families found that a 5-year-old
      girl had been missing from her foster home for 15 months. The girl's caseworker re-
      signed in the face of charges that she had falsified visitation reports. Further inves-
      tigation revealed that Florida could not account for nearly 400 children under state
      supervision. See Rebecca Winters, Florida's Little Girl Lost, TIME, May 15, 2002, at
      55. In another Florida case that same year, a state-appointed caregiver beat a 2-year-
      old boy to death and dumped his body alongside a highway. The boy's caseworker
      falsified records to indicate that she had visited him on the day his body was found
      and that he looked happy. See Tim Padgett, Is Florida Bad for Kids?, TIME, July 22,
      2002, at 27.
          A recent study reviewing foster care services in Atlanta, Georgia, found that more
      than 22 percent of all children were abused by their caretakers or had to be removed
      from foster homes because of harmful conditions or treatment. More than two-thirds
      of foster children entitled to monthly visits from a caseworker were not so visited,
      and over 40 percent of foster children under the age of two never received their re-
      quired annual health checkups. See University of South Carolina Institute for Fam-
      ilies in Society, Hess Provides Research Revealing that Foster Children are Unsafe and
      Underserved in Atlanta, Georgia, at <http://ifs.sc.edu/PressReleases/USC Release –
      Hess 11-14-03.pdf> (Nov. 18, 2003).
45   See Robertson, Liberty, supra note 12, at 1379.
46   See DENIS M. DONOVAN & DEBORAH MCINTYRE, HEALING THE HURT CHILD: A
      DEVELOPMENTAL–CONTEXTUAL APPROACH 74 (1990).
47   See 18. U.S.C. § 3282 (2003).
48   See id. § 3290.
49   See, e.g., United States v. Wazney, 529 F.2d 1287, 1289 (9th Cir. 1976).
50   See Frances Kerry, Florida Court Sets Date in Clone Baby Case, at <http://www.
      siliconvalley.com/mld/bayarea/news/4869551.htm> (Jan. 3, 2003).
51   See Catherine Wilson, Judge Bars Suit Seeking Guardian for "Baby Eve," S. F. CHRON.,
      Jan. 30, 2003, at A4.
52   See Leslie, supra note 35, at 148–49.
53   See Laura Smart & Daniel M. Wegner, The Hidden Costs of Hidden Stigma, in THE
      SOCIAL PSYCHOLOGY OF STIGMA 221 (Todd F. Heatherton et al. eds. 2003).
54   See EDWARD E. JONES et al., SOCIAL STIGMA: THE PSCYHOLOGY OF MARKED
      RELATIONSHIPS 205 (1984).
55   See Smart & Wegner, supra note 53.
56   See Miller & Major, supra note 30, at 255–56, 263; Frederick X. Gibbons, Stigma
      and Interpersonal Relationships, in THE DILEMMA OF DIFFERENCE: A MULTIDISCI-
      PLINARY VIEW OF STIGMA 131, 140–42 (Steven C. Ainlay et al. eds. 1986).
57   See RACHEL F. MORAN, INTERRACIAL INTIMACY: THE REGULATION OF RACE AND
      ROMANCE 48 (2001).
58   See JONES, supra note 54, at 205.
59   See Leslie, supra note 35, at 153–61.
60   See David Friedman, A World of Strong Privacy: Promises and Perils of Encryption, 13
      SOC. PHIL. & POL'Y 212 (Summer 1996).
61   See Jennifer Crocker and Neil Lutsky, Stigma and the Dynamics of Social Cognition,
      in THE DILEMMA OF DIFFERENCE: A MULTIDISCIPLINARY VIEW OF STIGMA 118
      (Steven C. Ainlay et al. eds. 1986).

62   *See id.* at 115–16.

63   *Cf.* Leslie, *supra* note 35, at 114 (sodomy laws codify morality, take on lives of their own, and provide their own justification).

64   *Cf. id.* at 110 (sodomy laws brand all gay men and lesbians as criminals whether they live in a state with a sodomy law or not).

65   Of course, these same spillover effects could occur if there were a federal ban on cloning that did not prohibit parents from returning home with the product of offshore cloning. In cases in which parents cloned offshore, they could not be prosecuted; nevertheless, their children would be subject to legal stigma and could also suffer the effects of parental silence, passing, and isolation for the same reasons noted in the text.

66   *See* CALIFORNIA ADVISORY COMMITTEE ON HUMAN CLONING, CLONING CALIFORNIANS?, REPORT OF THE CALIFORNIA ADVISORY COMMITTEE ON HUMAN CLONING 37 (2002).

67   *See* R. Alta Charo, *Cloning: Ethics and Public Policy*, 27 HOFSTRA L. REV. 503, 506 (1999).

68   *See* S. Golombok et al., *The European Study of Assisted Reproduction Families: The Transition to Adolescence*, 17 HUM. REPROD. 830 (2002).

69   *See, e.g.*, THE PRESIDENT'S COUNCIL ON BIOETHICS, HUMAN CLONING AND HUMAN DIGNITY: AN ETHICAL INQUIRY 90 (2002) [hereinafter COUNCIL REPORT].

70   *See* THE NATIONAL ACADEMIES, SCIENTIFIC AND MEDICAL ASPECTS OF HUMAN REPRODUCTIVE CLONING 62 (2002) [hereinafter NAS REPORT]. Moderate or severe OHSS includes the following symptoms: bloating, nausea, enlarged ovaries, accumulation of serous fluid in the peritoneal cavity or hydrothorax, breathing difficulties, a change in blood volume, increased blood viscosity, coagulation abnormalities, and diminished renal function. *See* A. Golan et al., *Ovarian Hyperstimulation Syndrome: An Update Review*, 44 OBSTETRICAL & GYNECOLOGICAL SURV. 430, 432 (1989).

71   *See* NAS REPORT, *supra* note 70, at 62.

72   *See* A. S. Whittemore et al., *Characteristics Relating to Ovarian Cancer Risk – Collaborative Analysis of 12 US Case-control Studies II: Invasive Epithelial Cancers in White Women*, 136 AM. J. EPIDEMIOLOGY 1184 (1992).

73   For example, the article compared the rate of ovarian cancer in infertile women who have been treated with fertility drugs with the rate of ovarian cancer in the general population. This was inappropriate because women who are infertile or childless are known to have a higher rate of ovarian cancer even when no fertility drugs are involved. A more appropriate comparison would have been between infertile women who are treated with fertility drugs and infertile women who are not treated with fertility drugs. Even then, a study should take account of the fact that some women treated with fertility drugs become pregnant. Pregnancy is known to reduce the risk of ovarian cancers. *See* S. Kashyap & O. K. Davis, *Ovarian Cancer and Fertility Medications: A Critical Appraisal*, 21 SEMIN. REPROD. MED. 65 (2003), *available at* <http://www.medscape.com/viewarticle/456560_print>.

74   *See id.*

75   *See* Roberta B. Ness et al., *Infertility, Fertility Drugs, and Ovarian Cancer: A Pooled Analysis of Case Control Studies*, 155 AM. J. EPIDEMIOLOGY 217 (2002).

76   *See* COUNCIL REPORT, *supra* note 69, at 95–96.

77   *See* Chapter 5, part 1, *supra*.
78   *See id.*
79   *See id.*
80   *See* NAS REPORT, *supra* note 70, at 40.
81   *See* Chapter 5, part 2, *supra*.
82   *See* Chapter 5, part 4, *supra*.
83   *See* Chapter 5, part 2, *supra*.
84   *See* Chapter 5, part 5, *supra*.
85   *See* Eibert, *supra* note 12, at 1111.
86   *See* Robertson, *Liberty*, *supra* note 12, at 1371.
87   *See* Eibert, *supra* note 12, at 1113–14.
88   *See* KUNICH, *supra* note 12, at 154.
89   ALA. CONST. art IV, § 102 (1901, repealed 2000).
90   *See id.* amend. 667.
91   *See* Nicole Davis, *Race File*, 4 ColorLines (Spring 2001), *available at* <http://www.arc.org/C_Lines/CLArchive/story 4_1_03.html>.

Part Three: Anticloning Laws Violate the Equal Protection Guarantee and Are Unconstitutional

1   *See* Loving v. Virginia 388 U.S. 1 (1967).
2   Cytoplasm transfer was developed as a fertility treatment for older, infertile women whose embryos were not developing properly. The doctors who pioneered the treatment believed that fresh cytoplasm from young eggs would promote proper embryonic development. *See* Jacques Cohen et al., *Birth of Infant after Transfer of Anucleate Donor Oocyte Cytoplasm into Recipient Eggs*, 350 LANCET 186 (1997).
3   As originally conceived and pioneered in the United States, nuclear transfer involved reconstituting the egg before fertilization. Dr. Jamie Grifo and his colleagues at New York University attempted to achieve pregnancy via this technique twice, with two different patients, without success. See Rick Weiss, *Fertility Experiments Mix Genes of 2 Women*, WASH. POST, Oct. 9, 1998, at A01. After the FDA halted clinical trials in the United States, scientists in China continued the research, but altered the method slightly, fertilizing the egg before removing the new genome from the embryo and inserting it into a donor egg. In 2003, the scientists reported that they had achieved a twin pregnancy in an infertile woman, but the fetuses died owing to premature labor and infection. After that experiment was conducted, China banned the technique. *See* Denise Grady, *Pregnancy Created Using Egg Nucleus of Infertile Woman*, N.Y. TIMES, Oct. 14, 2003, at A1.
4   Mitochondria are tiny organisms that exist within the cytoplasm of eggs and other cells. They have their own DNA and are inherited through the maternal line. They serve a variety of functions, including the processing of energy within cells. CLAUDE A. VILLEE, BIOLOGY 58 (1972).
5   The fertility doctors who pioneered cytoplasm transfer later confirmed that the technique produces children with mitochondrial heteroplasmy – that is, the children carry a mix of mitochondrial DNA from both the infertile patient and the cytoplasm donor. See Jason A. Barritt et al., *Mitochondria in Human Offspring Derived from*

Ooplasmic Transplantation: Brief Communication, 16 HUM. REPROD. 513 (2001). Although the children are healthy, this article created a stir both because it reported the
first cases of germline genetic modification and because patients suffering from certain mitochondrial diseases also exhibit heteroplasmy. However, it does not necessarily follow that heteroplasmy per se causes disease. As the fertility doctors pointed out,
there is an important distinction between benign heteroplasmy that comes about
through the mixing of two normal populations of mitochondria and pathological
heteroplasmy, which may occur as the result of harmful mutations in mitochondrial
DNA. *See id.* at 515.

6   *See* BIOLOGICAL RESPONSE MODIFIERS ADVISORY COMM., CENTER FOR BIOLOG-
    ICS EVALUATION AND RESEARCH, FOOD AND DRUG ADMINISTRATION, DEP'T OF
    HEALTH AND HUMAN SERVICES, OPEN SESSION, MEETING #32, 41–48 (May 9,
    2002).

7   THE PRESIDENT'S COUNCIL ON BIOETHICS, REPRODUCTION & RESPONSIBILITY:
    THE REGULATION OF NEW BIOTECHNOLOGIES, 224–25 (2004) [hereinafter
    REPRODUCTION & RESPONSIBILITY].

8   The council does not mention cytoplasm transfer directly in the section that recom-
    mends a ban on conception by any means other than the union of egg and sperm.
    However, the technique involves the union of two eggs (or parts of two eggs) and
    sperm, and so the proscription would seem to apply. Moreover, in another section,
    the council complains that cytoplasm transfer creates children with three genetic
    parents. *See id.* at 46. "[C]hildren conceived with these technologies [including cy-
    toplasm transfer] might be denied the bi-parental origins that human beings have
    always taken for granted, and that have always been the foundation of familial rela-
    tions and generational connections." *Id.* at 47.

9   *See id.* at 201.

10 In theory, parthenogenesis involves the activation of a human egg through some
    means other than fertilization with sperm. In the council's view, the problem with
    parthenogenesis is that it produces a baby with only one genetic parent. *See id.*

11 *See id.* 224–25. In a recent experiment, researchers harvested stem cells from mouse
    embryos and used them to grow mouse eggs. *See* Karin Hubner et al., *Derivation
    of Oocytes from Mouse Embryonic Stem Cells*, 300 SCI. 1251 (2003). The experiment
    raised the possibility that infertile men and women who lack functional gametes
    could be treated – not by reproductive cloning but by research cloning. Embryos
    cloned from their nuclear DNA could be harvested for stem cells, and the stem cells
    could be grown into sperm or eggs to be employed in sexual reproduction. Through
    this technique, it might even be possible for same-sex couples to reproduce sexually.
    For example, a man could use his sperm to fertilize the artificially constructed eggs
    of his male partner. REPRODUCTION & RESPONSIBILITY, *supra* note 7, at 46.

12 *See* REPRODUCTION & RESPONSIBILITY, *supra* note 7, at 224–25.

13 *Id.* at 224.

14 *See* Goodridge v. Dep't of Pub. Health, 440 Mass. 309, 798 N.E.2d 941 (2003).

15 In 2004, the Massachusetts Legislature approved a state constitutional amendment
    that would ban gay and lesbian marriage but legalize civil unions for same-sex cou-
    ples. The amendment will become law if the legislature passes it again during the
    2005 legislative session and if Massachusetts voters approve it in November 2006.

See Elizabeth Mehren, *New Tactic by Governor to Delay Ruling*, S. F. CHRON., Apr. 16, 2004, at A3.

16 *See* CAL. FAMILY CODE § 300 (West 1994) (defining marriage as a personal relation arising out of a civil contract between a man and a woman); *see also id.* § 308.5 (West 2004) (only marriage between a man and a woman is valid or recognized in California).

17 *See* S.J. Res. 30, 108th Cong. (2004); H.J. Res. 56, 108th Cong. (2003); *President Calls for Constitutional Amendment Protecting Marriage, at* <http://www.whitehouse.gov/news/releases/2004/02/print/20040224-2.html> (Feb. 24, 2004).

18 *See* Goodridge v. Dep't of Pub. Health, 440 Mass. 309, 385, 798 N.E.2d 941, 998 (2003) (Cordy, J., dissenting).

19 *See id.* at 386–89, 798 N.E.2d at 998-1000. Child custody decisions that go against gay and lesbian parents may also be said to reflect existential segregation to the extent they rest on concerns that the parent might "recruit" the child to the homosexual lifestyle or otherwise damage his or her heterosexual identity. *See, e.g.*, S. v. S, 608 S.W.2d 64 (Ky. Ct. App. 1980), *cert. denied sub nom.* Stevenson v. Stevenson, 451 U.S. 911 (1981) (awarding custody of child to heterosexual father based in part on the testimony of a psychologist that the mother's lesbianism could make it hard for the child to achieve a heterosexual identity of her own in the future); N.K.M. v. L.E.M., 606 S.W.2d 179 (Mo. Ct. App. W.D. 1980) (affirming change of custody from lesbian mother to heterosexual father; reasoning that child should not be placed in milieu that would incline her toward homosexuality, and thereby subject her to sexual disorientation, social ostracism, contempt and unhappiness).

20 *See* U.S. CONST. amend. V and amend. XIV, § 1; JOHN E. NOWAK & RONALD D. ROTUNDA, CONSTITUTIONAL LAW § 14.11, at 737–38 (5th ed. 1995).

Chapter Ten: Anticloning Laws Classify Human Clones and Are Subject to Strict Scrutiny

1 U.S. CONST. amend. XIV, § 1.

2 *See* City of Cleburne v. Cleburne Living Ctr., Inc., 473 U.S. 432, 439 (1985); Elizabeth Price Foley, *The Constitutional Implications of Human Cloning*, 42 ARIZ. L. REV. 647, 704 (2000).

3 *See* Bolling v. Sharpe, 347 U.S. 497 (1953).

4 *See* Adarand Constructors v. Pena, 515 U.S. 200, 217 (1995); Buckley v. Valeo, 424 U.S. 1, 93 (1976); JOHN E. NOWAK & RONALD D. ROTUNDA, CONSTITUTIONAL LAW § 14.1, at 595–96 (5th ed. 1995).

5 Because the amendments refer broadly to "persons," they have been interpreted to grant rights to noncitizens as well as citizens. *See* U.S. CONST. Amend. V and Amend. XIV, § 1; NOWAK & ROTUNDA, § 14.11, at 737–38. The federal government retains the power to deport illegal aliens and legal aliens who engage in activities considered to be harmful to the United States. *See id.* at 741.

6 *See* NOWAK & ROTUNDA, *supra* note 4, § 14.4, at 621.

7 *See* H.R. 534, 108th Cong. § 2 (2003).

8 *See id.*

9   *See* S. 303, 108th Cong. § 101 (2003).

10 *See* MICH. COMP. LAWS §§ 333.16274, § 750.430a (2003).

11 *See* ARK. CODE ANN. §§ 20-16-1001, 20-16-1002 (Michie 2003).

12 *See* CAL. HEALTH & SAFETY Code §§ 24185, 24187 (West 2004).

13 *See* N.J. STAT. ANN. § 2C:11A-1 (West 2004).

14 Arlington Heights v. Metro. Housing Corp., 429 U.S. 252, 266 (1977) (citations omitted).

15 *See id.* at 267.

16 *See id.* at 268.

17 Some also might question whether lawmakers intend to cause all of the negative effects of anticloning laws. Certainly, lawmakers intend to bar human clones from life. To make the laws an effective deterrent, they also intend to throw some parents into prison and (under the 2003 Weldon bill and its successors) exclude some cloned babies at the national border. Lawmakers, however, may not intend to stigmatize human clones, deprive them of medical or personal history, inflict the injuries associated with passing, or subject them to isolation.

    This argument is a weak one. What the case precedents require is that lawmakers intend to discriminate against the suspect class and not that lawmakers intend each and every effect of that discrimination. So, for example, a deliberate scheme to segregate blacks in public facilities would be actionable under the equal protection guarantee even if lawmakers cared only about keeping blacks away from whites and did not intend to stigmatize blacks or cause them to pass as white.

18 *See* Hunter v. Underwood, 471 U.S. 222, 228 (1985).

19 *See* Chapter 1, Section 2, *supra.*

20 *See* Chapter 2, Section 1, *supra.*

21 *See* Chapter 5, Section 1, *supra.*

22 *See, e.g.,* McLaughlin v. Florida, 379 U.S. 184, 192 (1964); Bolling v. Sharpe, 347 U.S. 497, 499 (1953).

23 *See, e.g.,* Korematsu v. United States, 323 U.S. 214, 216 (1944).

24 *See, e.g.,* Bernal v. Fainter, 467 U.S. 216, 219 (1984); Graham v. Richardson, 403 U.S. 365, 372 (1971). As constitutional scholars have pointed out, the Supreme Court has not been consistent in its treatment of laws affecting aliens. For example, as a general matter, the Court subjects state laws that classify persons on the basis of U.S. citizenship to strict scrutiny; however, if those state laws relate to the political process (e.g., the right to vote or hold government office), the Court applies only a rational basis standard of review. For more on this confusing area of law, see NOWAK & ROTUNDA, *supra* note 4, § 14.12.

25 *See, e.g., Graham,* 403 U.S. at 372; NOWAK & ROTUNDA, *supra* note 4, § 14.3, at 601–02.

26 *See, e.g.,* Mark Strasser, *Suspect Classes and Suspect Classifications: On Discriminating, Unwittingly or Otherwise,* 64 TEMP. L. REV. 937 (1991).

27 *See* Lawrence v. Texas, 539 U.S. 558 (2003) (plurality opinion strikes down law against homosexual sodomy on substantive due process grounds without reaching question of whether homosexuals are a suspect class for equal protection purposes); Mathews v. Lucas, 427 U.S. 495 (1976) (declining to find that illegitimate children

are a suspect class); Frontiero v. Richardson, 411 U.S. 677 (1973) (plurality opinion states that sex is a suspect class but fails to command a majority).

The Supreme Court subjects gender and legitimacy classifications to an intermediate level of review. Under this standard, the government must show that a legal classification has a substantial relationship to an important governmental interest. *See, e.g.*, Clark v. Jeter, 486 U.S. 456, 461 (1988) (illegitimacy); Mississippi Univ. for Women v. Hogan, 458 U.S. 718, 724–25 (1982) (gender); Orr v. Orr, 440 U.S. 268, 279 (1979) (gender).

28 San Antonio School Dist. v. Rodriguez, 411 U.S. 1, 28 (1973); *accord*, Massachusetts Bd. of Ret. v. Murgia, 427 U.S. 307, 313 (1976); Johnson v. Robison, 415 U.S. 361, 375 n.14 (1974).

29 According to one poll undertaken at that time, 93 percent of Americans opposed human cloning. *See* David Masci, *Scientists Argue Pros-Cons of the Cloning of Humans*, S.F. EXAMINER, May 29, 1997, at A11. Similarly, focus groups and interviews undertaken in Britain in 1998 revealed that the public was afraid of human cloning and upset about its possible applications. *See* Alan Petersen, *Biofantasies: Genetics and Medicine in the Print News Media*, 52 Soc. Sci. & Med. 1255, 1265 (2001).

30 *See* John A. Robertson, *Liberty, Identity, and Human Cloning*, 76 Tex. L. Rev. 1371 (1998).

31 NATIONAL BIOETHICS ADVISORY COMMISSION, CLONING HUMAN BEINGS, REPORT AND RECOMMENDATIONS OF THE NATIONAL BIOETHICS ADVISORY COMMISSION 108–09 (1997).

32 *See Scientist Says He Plans to Clone Human*, S.F. CHRON., Jan. 7, 1998, at A2.

33 Declaring an emergency, Senate Majority Leader Trent Lott bypassed the usual committee process and attempted to bring Republican-sponsored anticloning legislation to a floor vote. Human reproductive cloning escaped this legislative steamroller only because Democrats in the Senate, upset that the proposed legislation would have banned research cloning also, led a filibuster and prevented voting. *See* Elizabeth C. Price, *Does the FDA Have Authority to Regulate Human Cloning?* 11 HARV. J.L. & TECH. 619, 626 (1998).

34 *See* Chapter 6, Section 3, *supra*.

35 *See Anti-Clone Bill Awaits Signature*, at http://www.chicago.tribune.com/news/nationworld/article/0,1051,SAV-9805200105,00.html (May 20, 1998).

36 In a 2002 poll, 84 percent of respondents stated that the government should ban cloning. *See Opinions Split on Reproductive Technology: U.S. Poll*, at http://story.news.yahoo.com/news?tmpl=story&u=/nm/20021211/hl_nm/reproduction_poll_dc_1 (Dec. 11, 2002). Popular culture, as reflected in movies like *The Sixth Day* and *Star Wars, Episode II, Attack of the Clones*, portrayed human reproductive cloning and human clones as evil and dangerous.

37 *See* CALIFORNIA ADVISORY COMMITTEE ON HUMAN CLONING, CLONING CALIFORNIANS?, REPORT OF THE CALIFORNIA ADVISORY COMMITTEE ON HUMAN CLONING 37 (2002); THE NATIONAL ACADEMIES, SCIENTIFIC AND MEDICAL ASPECTS OF HUMAN REPRODUCTIVE CLONING 2 (2002); THE PRESIDENT'S COUNCIL ON BIOETHICS, HUMAN CLONING AND HUMAN DIGNITY: AN ETHICAL INQUIRY 200, (2002).

38 *See* Chapter 6, Section 1 *supra.*
39 *See* Chapter 6, Section 3 *supra.*
40 This distinguishes human clones from illegitimate children (a quasi-suspect class). A society that discriminates against illegitimate children does not object to their inherent characteristics; it objects to the fact that their parents are having sex and children even though they are unmarried.
41 *See* City of Cleburne v. Cleburne Living Ctr., Inc., 473 U.S. 432, 445 (1985).
42 304 U.S. 144 (1938).
43 *See id.* at 153 n.4. *Accord,* Sugarman v. Dougall, 413 U.S. 634, 642 (1973); Graham v. Richardson, 403 U.S. 365, 372 (1971).
44 *See, e.g.,* Lyng v. Castillo, 477 U.S. 635, 638 (1986) (close relatives do not exhibit obvious, immutable, or distinguishing characteristics and are not a suspect class); Frontiero v. Richardson, 411 U.S. 677, 686 (1973) (plurality opinion notes that gender is a highly visible characteristic).
45 *See, e.g., Lyng,* 477 U.S. at 638.
46 *See Frontiero,* 411 U.S. at 686 (arguing that the visibility of gender is relevant because it leads to discrimination).
47 *See, e.g., Lyng,* 477 U.S. at 638; Bowen v. Gilliard, 483 U.S. 587, 602 (1987).
48 *See* City of Cleburne v. Cleburne Living Ctr., Inc., 473 U.S. 432, 472 n.24 (1985) (Marshall, J., dissenting); *see also* U.S. v. Carolene Prod. Co., 304 U.S. 144, 153 n.4 (1938) (prejudice against discrete and insular minorities undermines the political process and calls for a more searching judicial inquiry).
49 This factor distinguishes human clones from illegitimate children. In the recent past, when legal rights often turned on legitimacy, statutes in many states provided that illegitimate children could be legitimated if their parents married after they were born. *See* Annotation, *Legitimation by Marriage to Natural Father of Child Born During Mother's Marriage to Another,* 80 A.L.R. 3d 219, 222–23, 230–33 (1977). Today, of course, legitimacy matters much less than it used to. The Supreme Court has invalidated laws that discriminate against illegitimate children. *See, e.g.,* Trimble v. Gordon, 430 U.S. 761 (1976). The National Conference of Commissioners on Uniform State Laws has also moved to eliminate legal distinctions based on legitimacy; since 1973, its Uniform Parentage Act has provided that a child born to unmarried parents has the same rights under the law as a child born to married parents. *See* UNIFORM PARENTAGE ACT, § 202 (1973 and 2000).
50 *See, e.g., Frontiero,* 411 U.S. at 686 (plurality opinion).
51 *See, e.g., id.* (quoting Weber v. Aetna Casualty & Surety Co., 406 U.S. 164, 175 (1972)).
52 *See* Regents of Univ. of Cal. v. Bakke, 438 U.S. 265, 360 (1978) (plurality opines that state-sponsored advancement should be based on individual merit, or, at least, on factors within the control of an individual); *Developments in the Law – Equal Protection,* 82 HARV. L. REV. 1076, 1126–27 (1969).
53 *See, e.g., Frontiero,* 411 U.S. at 686 (plurality opinion) (citing *Developments in the Law – Equal Protection, supra* note 52, at 1173–74).
54 *See* 473 U.S. at 441–42.
55 *See* Massachusetts Bd. of Ret. v. Murgia, 427 U.S. 307, 313 (1976) (reasoning that the aged have not experienced a history of unequal treatment or been subjected to

unique disabilities on the basis of stereotyped characteristics not truly indicative of their abilities).

56 See City of Cleburne v. Cleburne Living Ctr., Inc., 473 U.S. 432, 445–46 (1985).

57 See Frontiero, 411 U.S. at 686 (plurality opinion).

58 See, e.g., Sail'er Inn, Inc. v. Kirby, 5 Cal. 3d 1, 18, 485 P.2d 529, 540, 95 Cal. Rptr. 329, 340 (1971); Strasser, supra note 26, at 939; Note, The Constitutional Status of Sexual Orientation: Homosexuality as a Suspect Classification, 98 HARV. L. REV. 1285, 1301 (1985); Developments in the Law – Equal Protection, supra note 52, at 1127.

59 See id.

60 See Note, supra note 58, at 1301.

61 See Frontiero, 411 U.S. at 687–88 (plurality opinion).

62 See City of Cleburne v. Cleburne Living Ctr., Inc., 473 U.S. 432, 443 (1985).

63 Alternatively, if the Supreme Court declines to recognize human clones as a suspect class, it should, at the very least, recognize them as a quasi-suspect class based on the analysis in this chapter. Then, under the prevailing intermediate level of review, the government would have to show that anticloning laws bear a substantial relationship to an important governmental interest. Even under this lesser standard, the laws cannot survive challenge; for, as Chapter 12 demonstrates, most of the five objections present only weak or speculative governmental interests. Even if the safety objection qualifies as "important" now, it will be insignificant by the time human clones are born and ready to bring an equal protection challenge.

Chapter Eleven: Anticloning Laws Inflict Judicially Cognizable Injuries that Confer Standing

1 The Eleventh Amendment provides that "[t]he Judicial power of the United States shall not be construed to extend to any suit in law or equity, commenced or prosecuted against one of the United States by Citizens of another State, or by Citizens or Subjects of any Foreign State." U.S. CONST. amend. XI. Essentially, the amendment limits the ability of plaintiffs to subject states, or their agencies and instrumentalities, to suit in federal court. The Supreme Court, however, has carved out an exception allowing federal courts to hear lawsuits that seek to force state officials to conform their conduct to federal law, including the U.S. Constitution. See Ex parte Young, 209 U.S. 123 (1908); JOHN E. NOWAK & RONALD D. ROTUNDA, CONSTITUTIONAL LAW § 2.11, at 48–50 (5th ed. 1995) [hereinafter NOWAK & ROTUNDA]. Thus, plaintiffs can sue state officials charged with the enforcement of state anticloning laws if they seek a declaration that the state laws violate the federal equal protection guarantee or an injunction against enforcement of the laws on the same ground.

2 See, e.g., Bennett v. Spear, 520 U.S. 154, 162 (1997); Valley Forge College v. Americans United, 454 U.S. 464, 472 (1982).

3 See Christopher R. Leslie, Standing in the Way of Equality: How States Use Standing Doctrine to Insulate Sodomy Laws from Constitutional Attack, 2001 WIS. L. REV. 29, 61–62 (2001); Gene R. Nichol, Jr., Standing for Privilege: The Failure of Injury Analysis, 82 B.U.L. REV. 301, 304 n.4 (2002) (listing articles criticizing the Supreme Court's treatment of standing).

4   *See* FED. R. CIV. P. 17(c). A "next friend" must prove his or her suitability for the position according to three general criteria: (1) the friend must explain why the minor cannot sue himself or herself; (2) the friend must have a true dedication to the best interests of the minor; and (3) the friend must have some significant relationship with the minor. 4 JAMES W. MOORE, MOORE'S FEDERAL PRACTICE § 17.25[2] (3rd ed. 2003).

5   *See* FED. R. CIV. P. 17(c).

6   A person who is born outside of the United States is a citizen when his or her parents are both citizens of the United States and at least one parent had a residence in the United States before he or she was born. *See* 8 U.S.C. § 1401(b) (2003). As explained in Chapter 9, note 27, the courts are likely to conclude that Angela is the child of both parents because she was born to her mother and within wedlock. *See id.* § 1101(b)(1)(A), (b)(2) (2003).

7   *See* United States v. Verdugo-Urquidez, 494 U.S. 259 (1990) (declining to extend Fourth Amendment protections against search and seizure to property owned by a nonresident alien and located in Mexico, a foreign country); Johnson v. Eisentrager, 339 U.S. 763 (1950) (holding that nonresident enemy aliens captured and imprisoned abroad have no constitutional right to sue in U.S. courts for a writ of habeas corpus; the protections of the Fifth Amendment do not extend to nonresident enemy aliens).

8   For example, in Reid v. Covert, 354 U.S. 1 (1957), the Supreme Court reversed the convictions of two civilian dependents living abroad during peacetime who had been tried and convicted in courts-martial for the crime of killing their husbands, who were soldiers. A majority of the justices held that, under these circumstances, the women had a constitutional right to grand jury indictment and jury trial pursuant to Article III and the Fifth and Sixth Amendments to the Constitution. In a plurality opinion, four justices spoke expansively of the rights of citizens:

> [W]e reject the idea that when the United States acts against citizens abroad it can do so free of the Bill of Rights. The United States is entirely a creature of the Constitution. Its power and authority have no other source. It can only act in accordance with all the limitations imposed by the Constitution. When the Government reaches out to punish a citizen who is abroad, the shield which the Bill of Rights and other parts of the Constitution provide to protect his life and liberty should not be stripped away just because he happens to be in another land.

Id. at 5–6. Three years later, the Supreme Court extended *Reid*, holding that civilian dependents overseas could not be court-martialed for noncapital offenses (*see* Kinsella v. Singleton, 361 U.S. 234 (1960)) and that civilian employees of the armed services overseas could not be court-martialed for capital or noncapital offenses. *See* McElroy v. Gaugliardo, 361 U.S. 281 (1960); Grisham v. Hagan, 361 U.S. 278 (1960).

9   In this chapter, the terms "legal stigma" or "stigma" refer to the mark of unworthiness that discriminatory laws inflict on their victims. Although originating in law, this stigma can have devastating social consequences for its victims. This usage is consistent with the usage of stigma in Chapter 9, Section 1.

10 *See* Brown v. Bd. of Educ., 347 U.S. 483 (1954).

11 *See* City of New Orleans v. Barthe, 376 U.S. 189 (1964); Watson v. Memphis, 373 U.S. 526 (1963); Wright v. Georgia, 373 U.S. 284 (1963); New Orleans City Park Improvement Ass'n v. Detiege, 358 U.S. 54 (1958).

12 The Supreme Court has held that the government cannot segregate the following facilities: courthouses, *see* Johnson v. Virginia, 373 U.S. 61 (1963); airports, *see* Turner v. City of Memphis, 369 U.S. 350 (1962); parking garages, *see* Burton v. Wilmington Parking Auth., 365 U.S. 715 (1961); golf courses, *see* Holmes v. City of Atlanta, 350 U.S. 879 (1955); beaches, *see* Mayor and City Council of Baltimore City v. Dawson, 350 U.S. 877 (1955); or auditoriums, *see* Muir v. Louisville Park Theatrical Ass'n, 347 U.S. 971 (1954).

13 *See* Allen v. Wright, 468 U.S. 737, 755 (1984); *see also* Heckler v. Mathews, 465 U.S. 728, 738–40 (1984) (granting standing to man claiming gender discrimination; recognizing that discrimination can inflict serious noneconomic injuries, including stigma, on those who are denied equal treatment).

14 Note, however, that Angela may still experience the spillover stigma of being a human clone residing in a country in which reproductive cloning has been made a crime. *See* Chapter 9, Section 2 *supra* (discussing how spillover stigma injures its victims).

15 Under Supreme Court precedent, if a district attorney initiated a prosecution against parents under state anticloning laws, the parents could not obtain an injunction against those ongoing proceedings in federal court, absent allegations of bad faith or harassment. *See* Younger v. Harris, 401 U.S. 37 (1971). Thus, given the facts and circumstances of the second hypothetical, which involves an ongoing prosecution, I do not assume that parents are attempting to challenge a state anticloning law in federal court.

16 In general, when a person is arrested, indicted, or prosecuted, he or she has the standing to challenge a criminal law. *See* Younger, 401 U.S. 37, 41 (1971).

17 *See* Warth v. Seldin, 422 U.S. 490, 505 (1975).

18 *See* Powers v. Ohio, 499 U.S. 400, 411 (1991).

19 *See id.* at 411, 413.

20 *See* Singleton v. Wulff, 428 U.S. 106, 114–15 (1976) (plurality opinion).

21 *See* Powers, 499 U.S. at 411.

22 *See* Roe v. Wade, 410 U.S. 113, 158 (1973).

23 Gays and lesbians are familiar with the problem presented here. In the recent past, sodomy laws existed on the books of many states, but gays and lesbians were seldom prosecuted for engaging in private, consensual sodomy. (By definition, private conduct is unlikely to be observed and punished.) Some federal and state courts reasoned that, absent arrest and prosecution, the laws inflicted no injury that could provide a basis for standing to challenge the laws. *See* Leslie, *supra* note 3, at 45–48. As a result, sodomy laws continued to stigmatize gays and lesbians and encourage discrimination and violence against them. Eventually, an unwary district attorney in Texas prosecuted two gay men for engaging in consensual anal sex within the privacy of an apartment (*see id.* at 55), yielding a constitutional challenge and a Supreme Court holding that sodomy laws violate the right to privacy. Lawrence v. Texas, 539 U.S. 558 (2003).

24   468 U.S. 737 (1984).

25   *See id.* at 755–56 (citation omitted).

26   Plessy v. Ferguson, 163 U.S. 537 (1896).

27   For example, McCabe v. Atchison, T & S.F. Railway Co., 235 U.S. 151 (1914) involved a challenge to Oklahoma's separate coach law, which mandated racial segregation in railway accommodations, including sleeping, dining, and chair cars. *See id.* at 158. Segregated sleeping, dining, and chair cars for blacks were unprofitable (owing to low demand), and railways did not provide them. *See id.* at 161. Five blacks sued five railway companies, seeking an injunction to prevent the companies from making any distinction in service on account of race. *See id.* at 158–59. The Supreme Court opined that the equal protection guarantee had been violated. Market demand could drive the initial decision whether to provide specialized cars, but once the cars were made available to white passengers, they must be made available to black passengers also. *See id.* at 161–62.

     Similarly, in Missouri ex rel. Gaines v. Canada, 305 U.S. 337 (1938), a qualified black student was denied admission to the School of Law of the State University of Missouri solely on account of his race. Because there was no segregated law school for blacks in Missouri, the state offered to send the student to a law school in a neighboring state. *See id.* at 342–43. The Supreme Court rejected this alternative, holding that the student was entitled to be admitted to the School of Law of the State University of Missouri. *See id.* at 352. Equal protection of the laws required Missouri to furnish blacks with facilities for legal education within its borders that were substantially equal to the facilities provided to whites. *See id.* at 351; *accord* Sipuel v. Board of Regents of University of Oklahoma, 332 U.S. 631 (1948) (holding that the only public law school in Oklahoma must admit a qualified black student).

28   *See* NOWAK & ROTUNDA, *supra* note 1, § 14.8 at 652.

29   In Sweatt v. Painter, 339 U.S. 629 (1950), the Supreme Court held that a qualified black student had the right to attend the University of Texas Law School. Although the student could have attended a segregated law school, the education he could have received there would not have been equal to the education available at the University of Texas Law School, which was superior in terms of both tangible assets (*e.g.*, number of faculty, courses, students, books, and activities), and intangible factors (*e.g.*, faculty reputation, administrative experience, alumni influence, community standing, traditions, prestige, and the opportunity to interact with whites). *See id.* at 633–34.

     On the same day it decided *Sweatt*, the Supreme Court also handed down its decision in McLaurin v. Oklahoma State Regents for Higher Education, 339 U.S. 637 (1950). In that case, a black student admitted to the University of Oklahoma's graduate program in education was assigned to segregated rows or tables in the classroom, library, and cafeteria. There was no disadvantage to the assigned seats based on their location. By setting the student apart, however, the university had handicapped his ability to study, exchange views with other students, and learn his profession. *See id.* at 640–41. Therefore, the segregation violated the equal protection guarantee.

30   347 U.S. 483 (1954).

31   *See id.* at 492.

32   *Id.* at 494.
33   *See* Allen v. Wright, 468 U.S. 737, 755–56 (1984).
34   *See, e.g.,* ASARCO Inc. v. Kadish, 490 U.S. 605, 617 (1989); Leslie, *supra* note 3 at 57.
35   *See* Leslie, *supra* note 3, at 57–58.

Chapter Twelve: Anticloning Laws Violate the Equal Protection Guarantee

1   *See* JOHN E. NOWAK & RONALD D. ROTUNDA, CONSTITUTIONAL LAW § 14.3, at 602 (5th ed. 1995) [hereinafter NOWAK & ROTUNDA].
2   The Federal Food, Drug, and Cosmetic Act and the Public Health Service Act do not expressly address cloning; however, the Food and Drug Administration (FDA) has applied them to stop cloning in the United States. In this chapter, the question is whether the FDA has applied these general regulatory laws in a manner that violates the constitutional rights of human clones.
3   *See, e.g.,* Graham v. Richardson, 403 U.S. 365, 372 (1971); NOWAK & ROTUNDA, *supra* note 1, § 14.3, at 601–02.
4   *See* Bernal v. Fainter, 467 U.S. 216, 219 (1984). In reciting the test of strict scrutiny in this way, I am hewing to a traditional formulation that provides the strongest protection possible for the vulnerable members of suspect classes.

  In the recent case of Grutter v. Bollinger, 539 U.S. 306 (2003), the Supreme Court seemed to retreat from this traditional formulation. Straining to uphold the constitutionality of the University of Michigan Law School's affirmative action program in student admissions, a bare majority opined that narrow tailoring only requires "serious, good faith consideration of workable race-neutral alternatives." *See id.* at 339. As authority for this watered-down version of strict scrutiny, the majority could cite only a footnote in one case and a plurality opinion in another. *See id.* Dissenters vigorously asserted that the majority had failed to apply strict scrutiny; *see id.* at 387 (Kennedy, J., dissenting).

  Grutter, however, should not be taken as a sign that the Court has articulated a new standard that applies in all equal protection cases. Rather, the majority claimed that it was adapting strict scrutiny to the context of affirmative action, which helps, rather than hurts, racial minorities. "Since *Bakke,* we have had no occasion to define the contours of the narrow-tailoring inquiry with respect to race-conscious university admissions programs. That inquiry must be calibrated to fit the distinct issues raised by the use of race to achieve student body diversity in public higher education." *See id.* 333–34. By "adapting" the standard in this way, the majority retreated from the Court's tradition of applying the strictest of scrutiny, regardless of the government's reason for making decisions based on race. *See id.* at 379–80 (Rehnquist, J., dissenting); Adarand Constructors v. Pena, 515 U.S. 200, 226 (1995) (refusing to subject "benign" racial classifications to a lower standard of scrutiny under the Fifth Amendment); Richmond v. J. A. Croson, 488 U.S. 469, 493–94 (1989) (plurality opinion) (same, under Fourteenth Amendment). In any event, anticloning laws do not help the members of a suspect class. Rather, they *hurt* human clones. Therefore, even if a weakened standard of *Grutter* endures the test of time in affirmative action cases, the Supreme Court should not apply it when assessing the constitutionality of anticloning laws under the equal protection guarantee.

5   *See* Lawrence v. Texas, 539 U.S. 558 (2003).
6   *See id.* at 567.
7   *Id.* at 571 (citation omitted).
8   *Id.* at 578 (emphasis added).
9   *See* R. Alta Charo, *The Politics of Bioethics*, paper presented at Santa Clara University (August 21, 2003).
10 Cf. United States v. National Treasury Employees Union, 513 U.S. 454, 475 (1995) (speculative harms do not justify burdens on free speech).
11 *See* Lee Silver, *Public Policy Crafted in Response to Public Ignorance is Bad Public Policy*, 53 Hastings L. J. 1037, 1041 (2002).
12 *See* Chapter 9, part 3, *supra*.
13 *See* Elizabeth Price Foley, *The Constitutional Implications of Human Cloning*, 42 Ariz. L. Rev. 647, 719 (2000).
14 Perez v. Sharp, 32 Cal.2d 711, 727, 198 P.2d 17, 26 (1948).
15 *See* text accompanying note 10, *supra*.
16 *See also* John A. Robertson, *Liberty, Identity, and Human Cloning*, 76 Tex. L. Rev. 1371, 1431–32 (1998) (arguing that the possibility of public eugenics programs or private efforts at genetic engineering are too speculative a basis to justify infringing reproductive freedom).
17 *Cf. id.* at 1451 (arguing for a limit on the number of children born with the same nuclear DNA as a means of protecting the individuality of those children).
18 *See* Foley, *supra* note 13, at 721.
19 *See id.* at 725.
20 *See* Chapter 6, Section 2, *supra*.
21 *See* Chapter 5, Section 1, *supra*.
22 *See id.*
23 410 U.S. 113 (1973).
24 *See id.* at 155.
25 *See id.* at 162.
26 *See id.* at 163.
27 *See id.* at 164–65.
28 *See id.* at 160.
29 *See* Planned Parenthood v. Casey, 505 U.S. 833, 846 (1992).
30 *See id.*
31 *See id.* at 860.
32 *See id.* at 846.
33 *See id.* at 874.
34 *See id.* at 876.
35 *See id.* at 878–79.
36 *See, e.g.*, Griswold v. Connecticut, 381 U.S. 479 (1965).
37 *See* Roe v. Wade, 410 U.S. 113, 155 (1973).
38 *See* Chapter 5, Section 1, *supra*.
39 *See* Chapter 5, Section 2, *supra*.
40 *See* The National Academies, Scientific and Medical Aspects of Human Cloning 41–42 (2002) [hereinafter NAS Report].
41 Some might think I am reading too much into the government's failure to regulate sexual reproduction. They might argue that the government has abandoned the field

because it has no other choice; a long line of Supreme Court decisions recognizes a fundamental right to procreate and make other reproductive decisions.

Laws that impinge on the exercise of a fundamental right, however, are not per se invalid if they are supported by a compelling governmental interest. *See* Nowak & Rotunda, *supra* note 1, § 14.27, at 797–98. Legislators know this. When they believe there is a compelling interest in regulating reproduction, they have not hesitated to make the attempt despite Supreme Court decisions that limit their authority. For example, since 1973, when Roe v. Wade was decided, Congress and state legislatures have repeatedly sought to impose restrictions upon legalized abortion.

Thus, it is significant that the government has not even tried to ban sexual reproduction for women who face serious medical risks if they become pregnant and give birth. Apparently, the government does not think these risks are a big enough problem to justify interfering with the exercise of a fundamental right.

42 *See* Chapter 5, Section 4, *supra*.

43 *See* Chapter 5, Section 2, *supra*.

44 *See* NAS Report, *supra* note 40, at 42.

45 *See* Chapter 5, Section 3, *supra*.

46 *See* Foley, *supra* note 13, at 725.

47 *See* Chapter 5, Section 5, *supra*.

48 *See* California Advisory Committee on Human Cloning, Cloning Californians?, Report of the California Advisory Committee on Human Cloning 24 (2002).

49 Daniel J. Kevles, In the Name of Eugenics, Genetics and the Uses of Human Heredity 100 (1995 ed.); Diane B. Paul, Controlling Human Heredity, 1865 to the Present 82 (1995).

50 *See* Paul, *supra* note 49, at 78–82.

51 *See* Kevles, *supra* note 49, at 109–110; Annotation, *Validity of Statutes Authorizing Asexualization or Sterilization of Criminals or Mental Defectives*, 53 A.L.R. 3d 960, 982–84 (1973).

52 *See* Kevles, *supra* note 49, at 110.

53 274 U.S. 200 (1927).

54 In fact, there were not "three generations of imbeciles." Little is known about Carrie Buck's mother. However, Carrie seems to have had normal intelligence: she went to school for many years and was an avid reader. She became pregnant at 17 – not because she was feeble-minded or immoral but because she was raped. Her illegitimate daughter died young as a result of infectious disease but during her 2 years of schooling performed well and earned a spot on the honor roll. *See* Paul A. Lombardo, *Three Generations, No Imbeciles: New Light on Buck v. Bell*, 60 N.Y.U.L. Rev. 30, 52–54, 61 (1985).

55 *See Buck*, 274 U.S. at 206–07.

56 *See id.* at 208.

57 *Id.* at 207 (citation omitted).

58 *See* Paul, *supra* note 49, at 85.

59 Most state courts that have considered the issue have held that eugenics laws are unconstitutional. However, a handful of courts have upheld the laws as recently as the 1960s or 1970s. *See generally* Annotation, *supra* note 51.

60 316 U.S. 535 (1942).

61 *See id.* at 541–42.
62 *Id.* at 541.
63 *See* NOWAK & ROTUNDA, *supra* note 1, § 14.27, at 797.
64 381 U.S. 479 (1965).
65 410 U.S. 113 (1973).
66 *See* Planned Parenthood v. Casey, 505 U.S. 833 (1992).
67 As of 1995, 22 states had sterilization laws on their books. Their use is restricted by federal regulation. *See* KEVLES, *supra* note 49, at 111.
68 *See* Annotation, *supra* note 51, at 956–66.
69 *See* NOWAK & ROTUNDA, *supra* note 1, § 14.27, at 798; Robertson, *supra* note 16, at 1431.
70 *See* PAUL, *supra* note 49, at 125–29; 135.
71 *See* Mark D. Eibert, *Human Cloning: Myths, Medical Benefits, and Constitutional Rights*, 53 HASTINGS L.J. 1097, 1106–07 (2002).
72 *See* Robertson, *supra* note 16, at 1405. Indeed, most courts have rejected so-called wrongful life tort claims in which a child conceived with birth defects asserts that a doctor negligently permitted him or her to be born in the first place. Courts are reluctant to hold that life itself is a harm to the child. It is very difficult, moreover, to determine compensation when the only alternative to life is nonexistence. *See* DAN B. DOBBS, THE LAW OF TORTS § 291 at 792 (2000); *but see* Lori B. Andrews, *Is There a Right to Clone? Constitutional Challenges to Bans on Human Cloning*, 11 HARV. J.L. & TECH. 643, 667 n.172 (1998) (citing a California case that recognized a claim for wrongful life).
73 The United Kingdom has enacted laws that make human reproductive cloning a crime but permit research cloning. For a good discussion of these laws and other anticloning laws around the world, *see* JOHN CHARLES KUNICH, THE NAKED CLONE 67–69 (on the United Kingdom laws) and Chapter 3 (on anticloning laws around the world) (2003).
74 *See* text accompanying note 10, *supra*.
75 *See* Foley, *supra* note 13, at 725–26.
76 *See* CAL. BUS. & PROF. CODE § 2260.5 (West 2003), §§ 16004, 16105 (West 2004).
77 *See* Eibert, *supra* note 71, at 1111–12.
78 *See* Robertson, *supra* note 16, at 1371.
79 *See* KUNICH, *supra* note 73, at 154.
80 Richard A. Merrill & Bryan J. Rose, *FDA Regulation of Human Cloning: Usurpation or Statesmanship?* 15 HARV. J. L. & TECH. 85, 131 (2001).
81 *See id.*
82 *See id.* at 130–31.

Index